SINAI
Diving Guide

ALBERTO
SILIOTTI

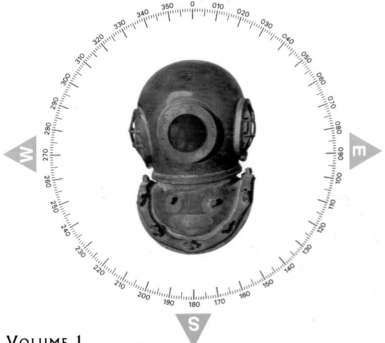

VOLUME 1

TIRAN – SHARM EL-SHEIKH
RAS MOHAMMED – GUBAL – DAHAB

GEODIA

Project Editor Alberto Siliotti

Editorial Coordination Yvonne Marzoni Fecia di Cossato

Texts Alberto Siliotti

Drawings Stefania Cossu, Stefano Trainito (pages 15, 17,18, 20, 21, 29-30)

Aerial and Landscape Photographs Alberto Siliotti/Archivio Geodia, Marcello Bertinetti/Archivio White Star (pages 110 center, 166)

Satellite Photographs Nasa

Underwater Photographs
All the photographs in this book are by Manfred Bortoli except for the following: Franco Banfi (page 149), Claudio Bertasini (cover background, pages 178 center, 242-243), Claudio Cangini (pages 39 below, 197 below), Arnaud Chicurel (pages 30, 40 center, 59 above, 66-67, 74 above, 75, 80 below, 82 below, 83 below, 86 center and below, 87, 105 above, 123 above, 124 above and center, 125, 126 center, 127 above, 129 above, 132 above, 134 center, 135 above, 136-137, 138 center, 139 above, 140, 141, 142 below, 143 above, 148 center, 162 above and center, 168, 169, 221 above, 230 center), Patrick Louisy (page 123 left), Patrick Louisy (page 59 below), Vincenzo Paolillo (pages 190 below, 193 above left, 196 below), Egidio Trainito (pages 40 above, 71 center).

Historiacal Documents Archivio Geodia

Scientific Advice Angelo Mojetta

Technical Advise Mauro Barocci, Heike Bartsch, Diego Cabras, Arnaud Chicurel, Louis Miguel Collavizza, Claudio Di Manao, Gigi Ferrari, Isabella Moreschi, Ahmed Samir

English Translation Heike Bartsch, Kathy Howarth, Richard Pierce

THE AUTHOR

Alberto Siliotti is a science journalist and a scuba diving instructor. He is one of the leading experts on the Red Sea, about which he has directed documentaries and has written many articles and books, including the famous Sharm el-Sheikh Diving Guide (1999), Fishes of the Red Sea (2001), Thistlegorm & Rosalie Moller – The Great Shipwrecks of the Red Sea (2003) and The Red Sea – The Coral Garden (2004).

Copyright © 2005 by Geodia (Verona, Italy)

Printed in Egypt

ISBN 88-87177-65-1   Dar El-Kotub Legal Deposit no. 7047/2005

In the photo: *The main cave at Jackfish Alley (Ras Mohammed)*

CONTENTS

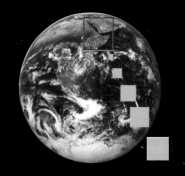

HOW TO USE

Number of the dive site

Photograph of the site to help you locate it

Name of the site

COLOUR TO INDICATE THE DIVE SITE LOCATION

Strait of Tiran

Sharm el-Sheikh Local Dives

Ras Mohammed

Strait of Gubal

Dahab

30 Shark Observatory

27°44.005' N — 34°15.605' E

Second observation terrace

Shark Observatory

Start diving

Cave

N

Aerial view of the promontory of Ras Mohammed with Shark Observatory

GPS bearing

Brief description of the dive

This name indicates not only the first obserbation terrace on the top of the Ras Mohammed promontory, but also the diving site that is on a level with that promontory.
This is a magnificent wall dive, also known as the *Ras Mohammed Wall*; while looking down into the deep blue, you can admire a grandiose environment and at the same time see large pelagic predators and Hawksbill turtles (*Eretmochelys imbricata*). Even a Whale shark (*Rhincodon typus*) has been seen in this area.

A pair of Common lionfish (*Pterois miles*)

The classic dive begins not far from the second observation terrace on the cliff.
After descending to about 15 meters (but not deeper as the route is relatively long and not all scuba divers may have sufficient air) you can explore the wall on your left, which is rich in Alcyonarians, gullies, shelters and caves swarming with life, without losing sight of the blue from which jackfish, barracuda and some sharks might suddenly appear.
On a line with the southern corner of the promontory the wall takes a sharp turn

General topographical map

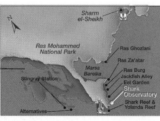

Sharm el-Sheikh

Ras Mohammed National Park

Ras Ghozlani

Ras Za'atar

Marsa Bareika

Ras Burg

Jackfish Alley

Eel Garden

Shark Observatory

Stingray Station

Shark Reef & Yolanda Reef

Alternatives

Access	85'	
Difficulty	◐◐	
Current	from ◐	to ◐◐
Natural scenery	◐◐◐	
Fauna interest	◐◐	
General interest	◐◐◐	

Other characteristics

➡ 📷 ✂ 🐟 🐠 🕐

Brief overall description of the features of the dive

THIS GUIDE

Photographs of characteristic fauna
or typical scenery of the dive site

Number of the
dive site

Name of the site

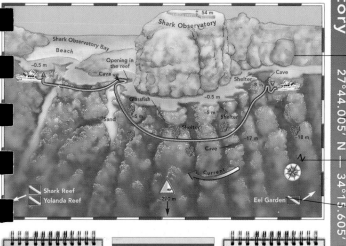

westwards and runs towards
the small beach under the
observatory: here you will see
some large gorgonians
(*Subergorgia hicksoni*) and,
further up, a majestic overhang.
Continue along the wall until
you enter an extremely
beautiful cave that has a large
fissure in its top through which
light filters inside creating
evocative effects.
From this cave you can exit
directly onto the reef.

Whale shark (Rhincodon typus) is the biggest fish on Earth: it has been spotted several times in the summer months along the coast of Sharm el-Sheikh

Brief description
of the dive

3-D plan
of the dive site.
*This plan is shown in large scale in
3-D Atlas of the Dive Sites, at the
end of this book*

GPS bearing

Orientation
of the map

Name and direction
of the nearest diving site

Comments

Check the direction of the
current; it is better to dive
when the tide is ebbing.
Stay at a depth of
15–20 meters and ascend
to 8–5 meters in the last
phase of your dive.
• The afternoon is ideal for
observing the spectacular
effects of the light.

Look out for

Gorgonian   Soft coral   Trevally

Barracuda   Whale
            shark   Lionfish

Turtle

Features

• Superb marine landscape.
• The chance to see large
pelagic predators.

Features and
attractions of the dive

Useful information
and warnings

Typical fish or
organisms
of the dive site

THE RED SEA

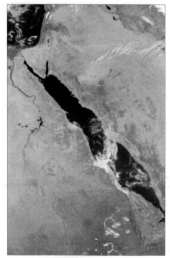

A satellite view of the Red Sea

T he Red Sea is narrow and elongated, bordered by mountains with an average height of 1,000–1,500 meters and with some peaks in the Sinai peninsular such as *Gebel Katherine* and *Gebel Musa* (or Mount Sinai) that are more than 2,500 meters high. It has a deep bottom with a wide, longitudinal, median sea-floor trench which on a level with Suakin (Sudan) is 2,850 meters deep (the Suakin Trench).

The Red Sea is connected to the Indian Ocean by the Strait of *Bab el-Mandeb*, 'the Gate of Tears,' a passage only 29 kilometers wide whose floor rises abruptly to only 134 meters deep, thus limiting the water exchange with the Indian Ocean.

Because of the high air temperature and aridity of the regions around the Red Sea, its evaporation rate – about 200 centimeters per year (approximately 900 billion cubic meters of water) – is a crucial physical factor.

The lack of freshwater from rivers (the Red Sea has no influents) and the limited water exchange with the Indian Ocean, which is just enough to compensate for the loss due to evaporation, causes a significant increase in salinity, which is the highest of all the open seas on Earth: 38‰ (parts per thousand), which becomes 41‰ in the Suez and Aqaba gulfs, as opposed to the average ocean level of 35‰.

Due to the dry air and action of the wind, there is a marked difference between the summer and winter water temperature (10 °C or degrees Celsius), especially in the

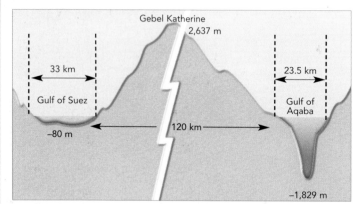

The profile of the Red Sea between the Gulf of Suez and the Gulf of Aqaba, with the Sinai peninsula and Gebel Katherine in the middle

- Red Sea
- Gulfs of Suez and Aqaba
- Average oceanic salinity

41‰

38‰

35‰

Salinity graph

A satellite view of the Red Sea and the Arabian peninsula

Establishing the origin of the name 'Red Sea' with certainty is no easy matter. The great Greek historian Herodotus of Halicarnassus called it the 'Erythraean Sea' already in the 5th century BC, perhaps referring to the mythical king called Erythros, which in ancient Greek means 'red.'
As the Greeks associated the South and the sun with the colour red it is also possible that the adjective 'red' is connected to the southerly position of this sea.
According to another theory the adjective 'red' refers to the colour of the water which, under particular conditions and in very limited areas, takes on a reddish hue because of the proliferation of an alga called Trischodesmium erythraeum.

It is more likely the term 'Red Sea' derives from the fact that its coasts are composed of rocks that often have a reddish colouration because of their high iron oxide content.
It is interesting to note, however, that on old charts and medieval atlases the Red Sea is represented by a red colour and not by the typical blue colour of the seas.

northern part of the Gulf of Aqaba. However, the really distinguishing feature of the Red Sea is that the deeper the basin depth, the higher the water temperature: at 1,000 meters below sea level it is 21 °C, a temperature about 15 degrees higher than that in the rest of the world at that depth. As a matter of fact, the adjacent Indian Ocean registers a water temperature of 6–7 °C at the same depth.

Many parts of the coasts of the Red Sea have rocks with a reddish hue

The cause of this unusual phenomenon is due to the deep median trench on the floor of the Red Sea, a big intercontinental fracture with its origins in Lebanon, crossing the Dead Sea and then stretching out into the African continent.

Along this fracture, the magma rises from the Earth's mantle and comes into contact with the sea water heating it: recent oceanographic surveys have ascertained temperatures of 30–63 °C in the so-called *Atlantis II Trench* situated at a latitude of 21° N with the sea floor reaching a depth of 2,200 meters.

At these depths, the Red Sea is the theatre of intense geothermic

THE RED SEA IN FIGURES

Length: *2,250 km*
Average width: *300 km*
Width at
   Bab el-Mandeb: *29 km*
Area: *438,000 sq.km*
Average depth: *2,000 m*
Maximum depth: *2,850 m*
Depth at
   Bab el-Mandeb: *134 m*
Average salinity: *41‰*
Maximum temperature: *30 °C*
Minimum temperature: *20 °C*
Average temperature: *25 °C*
Average hygrometry: *~70%*
   (in the morning)
Average hygrometry
   at Aqaba: *~45%*
Species of fish: *1,248*
Species of
   endemic fish: *17%*
Species of corals: *~250*
Species of
   endemic corals: *8%*

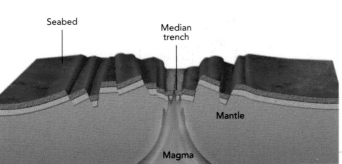

Section of the central area of the seabed of the Red Sea showing the rising of the magma along the median trench

The coasts of the Red Sea are generally uniform with few indentations

activity and there are an incredible amount of minerals which might one day be economically utilised.

The coasts of the Red Sea are often bordered by coral formations and are generally relatively uniform, interrupted by bays and estuaries that in Arabic have different names according to their morphology. The locals distinguish between the *marsa*, an easily accessible bay, open or with a large entry and sandy bottom from where hard coral towers might reach up, and the *sharm*, a deeper bay characterized by a narrow entry and sometimes difficult to identify when viewed from the sea.

Apart from the *marsa* and the *sharm*, in the central and northern Red Sea we also find the *khor*, a narrow bay created by the estuary of a *wadi*, an ancient river valley.

A typical example of a marsa

SMALL DICTIONARY OF GEOGRAPHICAL TERMS

Bahar = *Sea*
Gebel = *Mountain*
Gezira = *Island*
Khor = *Bay at the end of a wadi*
Marsa = *Open bay*
Ras = *Cape; promontory*
Sha'ab = *Extensive coral reef*
Sharm = *Bay with narrow and deep entry*
Wadi = *Valley created by an old river bed*

A typical example of a sharm: Sharm el-Maya in the Sinai

The Red Sea in the History

The ancient Egyptians regularly sailed the waters of the Red Sea to get to the mysterious 'Land of Punt,' a region whose location is still not identified and that was probably located near the Horn of Africa, to stock up on incense, myrrh, ivory, animal skins, ebony and other exotic products. This is documented in the bas-reliefs from the 15th century BC found

Ancient Egyptian sailors cruise the Red Sea on their way to the Land of Punt

in the temple of Deir el-Bahari in West Thebes (Luxor) which illustrate a marine expedition in Punt under the reign of Queen Hatshepsut (1479–1457 BC).

The Red Sea however has only been used as a regular communication route since Ptolemaic times when Ptolomy II (285–246 BC) built the harbour city of *Berenice* situated on the Ras Banas promontory, close to an important caravan route linking the Red Sea with the city of *Coptos* (today Qus) on the Nile.

In this period trade was flourishing in particular with the regions of the Horn of Africa, India and above all with the Arab peninsula that had become the only supplier of incense and myrrh, substances used in abundance for medical purposes, for embalming the dead, and during the religious rites in the temples.

During the Roman period, navigation in the Red Sea received an even stronger boost as trade and commercial exchange with the Orient became more and more important. New ports were built

An emperor angelfish (Pomacanthus imperator) depicted on the walls of the temple of Deir el-Bahari in West Thebes (today Luxor)

Probable location of the Land of Punt, in the southern part of the Red Sea, between today Sudan and Somalia

A Roman ship sails up the Red Sea transporting lions kept in cages and designated for the games in the arenas

Ancient Egyptian sailors carry myrrh trees to load them onto their ships

An Arab ship cruising the Red Sea

*The Swedish scientist Peter Forsskål
(1732–1763)*

*The German naturalist Eduard Rüppell
(1794–1884)*

An original drawing of Rüppell

such as *Ayla*, and *Clysma*, known today as Eilat and Suez. The 'Fleet of the Red Sea' was established in the time of Emperor Trajan (98–117 AD) to protect the Roman commercial ships and to exert control over the trade routes.

From the 7th century AD onwards, the Red Sea fell under the complete control of the Arabs and was regularly crossed by numerous ships mainly transporting coffee cultivated on the Arabian peninsula as well as Muslim pilgrims on their way to Mecca. During the times of the crusaders who built the port of *Ayla* in 1162, European ships also began

*A coffee plant
(Coffea arabica)*

to sail the waters of this sea, and in the following centuries two important ports were established in El-Tor and in El-Quseir. It was, however, not before the second half of the 19th century with the inauguration of the Suez Canal that the Red Sea became a primary route for international trade and communication.

However, the increase of shipping activity was not accompanied by any progress in nautical cartography nor in the construction of lighthouses or beacons to mark the presence of coral reefs which are the biggest danger for commercial traffic in this sea: exactly this absence caused a number of ship wrecks whose remains can still be found on the sea bed in the Strait of Gubal.

Only as recently as the 18th century did this sea begin to be studied from a scientific standpoint. The first naturalist who made a systematic, in-depth study of the fauna in this sea was the Swedish botanist Peter Forsskål, who was a member of the big expedition (1761–1767) led by the German Carsten Niebhur and in 1767 identified 59 species of fish. Forsskål's paper was published only posthumously, in 1775. He was followed by the German naturalists Christian Gottfried Ehrenberg and Friedrich Hemprich (1820–1826), Eduard Rüppell (1826–1828) and Karl Klunzinger (1863–1875). These scientists laid the foundations for our present – day knowledge of this truly extraordinary sea – which Jacques Cousteau called 'the corridor of wonders.'

The scientific study of the fauna of the Red Sea started in the 18th century

Origin and Geology

About 40 million years ago, during the Tertiary period, a series of tectonic movements disrupted the surface of the Earth and led to the formation of the Alps and the Himalayan mountains.

In that period the African and Asian plates began to separate, creating an enormous trench which for the most part was filled in with the waters of the ocean. This was how the Red Sea was born, a body of water with wholly peculiar features, which is considered to be an ocean in the process of formation. In fact, the tectonic movement separating Asia from Africa is continuing to this day, at a rate of about 1.5 centimeter per year. If this velocity remains constant, after another 200 million years the Red Sea will be 3,000 kilometers wide, similar to the present-day Atlantic Ocean.

The Earth during the Cretaceous period, about 100 million years ago

About 5 million years ago, in the Pliocene epoch, which marks the end of the Tertiary period, the sea floor at Bab el-Mandeb rose, thus isolating the Red Sea basin from the Indian Ocean, and because of the effect of high evaporation its waters became more and more salty and warm, hence unsuitable to sustain life including the coral reefs.

The Earth in the Eocene epoch, about 40 million years ago

The current coral reefs of the Red Sea developed in the last 7,000 years

Fortunately this isolation did not last long: the sea floor at Bab el-Mandeb lowered again and the former link with the Indian Ocean was opened again and gave way to the consequent faunistic repopulation of the Red Sea. However, the momentous glacial activity during the Quarternary era gave rise to the formation of huge ice sheets in the two hemispheres, causing a general lowering of the sea level all over the globe. The waters of the Red Sea were at least 100 meters lower than its original level and links with the Indian Ocean were once again interrupted until about 10,000 years ago, when with the end of the last (Würmian) glacial stage the seas rose again, but not reaching previous levels.

The eventful geological history of the Earth had an enormous impact on the development of the fauna in the Red Sea and its splendid and world-famous coral reef, which only after the last rise of the sea level began to become the luxuriant marvel we know today.

The separation of the Asian and African plates is still ongoing today at a rate of 1.5 centimeters per year

The Strait of Bab el-Mandeb marks the boundary of the South of the Red Sea and constitutes a door which opened and closed several times during the geological periods

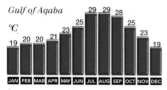

Gulf of Aqaba

°C

Average water temperature

Sharm el-Sheikh

°C

Average monthly air temperatures (min. and max.)

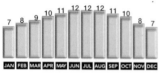

Average hours of sunshine per day in Sharm el-Sheikh

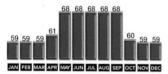

Average values (%) of humidity in the Gulf of Suez

The Climate

In general the Red Sea climate is hot and dry. Because of its latitudinal configuration it has characteristics that vary from area to area, but on the whole the temperature ranges from 22 °C to 30 °C.

As far as the gulfs of Suez and Aqaba are concerned the maximum temperatures are in the June–August period (45 °C) and the minimum (never below 15 °C) are in January and February.

The air humidity level is higher in the summer and decreases in the winter months: the average humidity recorded in this area ranges from a minimum of 59% in winter to a maximum of 68% in summer.

The Winds and Breezes

The seasonal activity of the **winds** is especially evident in the central and southern sections of the Red Sea. Here, northeast winds in the winter and southwest winds in the summer are the influence of monsoons (periodic winds characterized by clear typical seasonal inversions in the tropical zones).

As for the northern area of the sea, the prevailing winds blow all year long from a northerly direction becoming stronger in the winter and tending to calm down in the afternoon and at night. The local seamen call these winds from northern directions *shamal*.

NE monsoon
(November-March)

SW monsoon
(May-September/October)

Beaufort Wind Scale and Effects Observed on the Sea

Force	Definition	Max. Wind Speed m/s	knots	Effects Observed on the Sea	Average Wave Height (m)	Effects Observed on Land
0	Calm	0.2	1	Calm	–	Calm, smoke rises vertically
1	Light air	1.5	3	Almost calm (with small ripples)	0.1	Smoke drift indicates wind direction
2	Light breeze	3.3	6	Wavy	0.1 – 0.5	Wind felt on face
3	Gentle breeze	5.4	10	Choppy	0.5 – 1.25	Leaves constantly moving
4	Moderate breeze	7.9	16	Rough	1.25 – 2.5	Small tree branches move
5	Fresh breeze	10.7	21	Moderately rough	2.5 – 4	Small trees begin to sway
6	Strong breeze	13.8	27	Very rough	4 – 6	Whistling in wires
7	Near gale	17.1	33	Stormy	6 – 9	Whole trees moving
8	Gale	20.7	40	Severe storm	9 – 14	Resistance felt walking against wind
9	Strong gale	24.4	47	Tempestuous	> 14	Slight structural damage
10	Storm	28.4	55			Considerable structural damage
11	Violent storm	32.6	63			Serious damage
12	Hurricane	>32.6	>63			Catastrophic damage

Sometimes this wind can become stronger and can blow for 2–3 days calming down only at night.

In the area of Sharm el-Sheikh and Ras Mohammed the winds are generally moderate; they are stronger in the Strait of Tiran.

To the north, around Dahab and Nuweiba, the northerly winds blow stronger and more often, especially during winter, from December to March.

The same happens in the Strait of Gubal, the southern part of the Gulf of Suez, where you hardly ever find really calm sea. In the months of August and September the dominant northerly winds are less strong and tend to be more variable.

Finally, during the spring months, we have to consider as well the possible occurrence of the *khamsin*, an Arab expression meaning 'fifty' which stands for the amount of days this wind can blow.

The *khamsin* is a very hot and dry wind usually coming from the southwest that can provoke serious sand storms in the Western Desert and hits the northern part of the Red Sea.

Apart from the general winds we also have to take into account the **thermal breezes** caused by the different warming and cooling times between the earth and the sea. During the day the earth heats quicker than the sea and the warm air rises thus generating an area of low pressure over the land that attracts cold air from the sea. This is why it is called a 'sea breeze.'

The situation is opposite at night: the sea water retains warmth better than the land, the warmer air above the sea tends to rise creating an area of low pressure that attracts cold air from the land. This is the so-called 'land breeze.'

The breezes are a local phenomenon and of interest to scuba divers when doing night dives from the boat close to the coast.

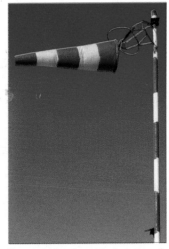

The windsock indicates the intensity and direction of the wind

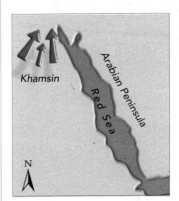

In springtime, a pressure decrease in the Eastern Mediterranean causes the formation of the khamsin

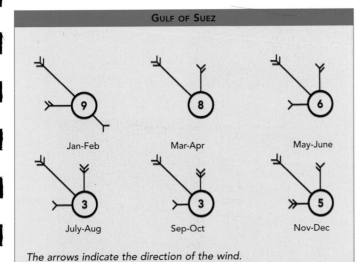

GULF OF SUEZ

9 Jan-Feb

8 Mar-Apr

6 May-June

3 July-Aug

3 Sep-Oct

5 Nov-Dec

The arrows indicate the direction of the wind.
The shaft length is directly proportional to the total number of times the wind has been recorded blowing in this direction.
The number of feathers indicates the average force of the wind on the Beaufort scale. The number in the circle represents the number of days with a calm wind as a percentage.

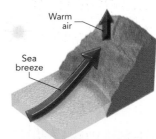

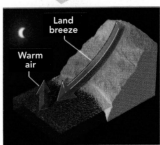

The mechanism of thermal breezes

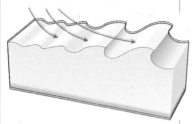

Wind action on the surface of the sea

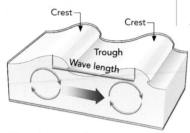

Water dynamics in the waves

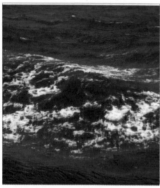

The moderate breeze (strength 4) creates small waves with fairly frequent white horses

With a strong breeze (strength 6), large waves have the characteristic white crests called 'whitecaps' in nautical jargon

Waves

Waves are a phenomenon of motion transfer caused by the wind's effect upon the surface of the water. The height of the wave, that is, the distance between the crest and trough, depends on three factors: the force of the wind, the duration of the wind activity and the amount of open space for the wind to act upon, known as the *fetch*. The wavelength is the distance between two adjacent crests.

The ratio between the length and height of waves is approximately 7:1; in other words, if the wavelength is seven meters, the height will be one meter.

In the open sea, the water in a wave is relatively motionless in that the water particles move in a circular rather than forward direction. By the shore, however, the sudden deceleration of the lowest layers of water in contact with the marine floor creates a 'breaker.' In this case, since the water particles at the crest move faster than those in the mass beneath, they advance and then quickly fall downwards: this is how a wave which crashes on the reef or dry land is created. After the impact with dry land the water must flow back to the sea, creating a contra current known as a backwash. The waves are a phenomenon which only affects the upper layers of the water and therefore are not felt whilst diving, but divers have to pay proper attention to the waves when they come up from a dive or when diving off the shore. Obviously, the diver who goes too close to the coral reef with breaking waves risks being thrown against it with serious consequences: for that reason the moment the diver emerges from a dive he has to swim away from the reef to enable the boat to easily and safely pick him up. In rough sea conditions shore diving can only be done when the entry and exit points from the water are situated in a sheltered area.

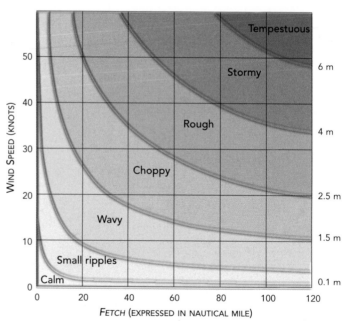

The graphic shows the relation of the wind strength to the effects on the sea

Currents and Tides

There are two types of currents: seasonal currents and tidal streams.

Seasonal currents are influenced by the monsoons and the fact that due to evaporation in the summer months the average level of the waters of the Red Sea descends about 70 centimeters. This mass of lost water is compensated during the winter months by an influx of water from the Indian Ocean.

Such currents therefore move in a N-NW direction in the winter months (November-April) and in the opposite direction in the summer months (May-October). It is estimated that a period of 20 years is needed for a total renewal of the waters of the Red Sea.

In the northern Red Sea these currents are weaker than in the central-southern sector, and here the **tidal streams**, caused by attraction forces from the moon and the sun on the water mass of the oceans, become much more important to scuba divers.

The tide amplitude is directly connected to the phases of the moon. When the moon is full or new, it is on the same axis as the sun: its gravitational attraction is added to that of the sun and consequently the tide amplitude is at its highest (**spring tide**).

When on the other hand the moon is in the first or last quarter its position is perpendicular to that of the sun and their respective gravitational attractions are opposed: in this case the tide amplitude is at the minimum (**neap tides**).

The maximum tide amplitude (or spring tides) of this type of currents is about 180 centimeters in the Gulf of Suez and around 100–120 cm in the southern part of the Gulf of Aqaba, with an average surface and running water speed of about 1.5 knots which, in certain cases, can even attain 5–6 knots, equal to 9–11 km per hour. It is therefore absolutely necessary to be well aware of the tidal streams before diving, especially in those areas in which this type of current becomes strongest, such as in the Strait of Tiran and the Strait of Gubal.

If you want to calculate the force and direction of tidal streams you must check the so-called 'Tide Tables' published annually by hydrographic institutes in several countries.

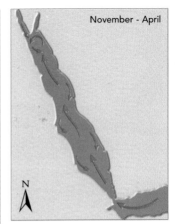
The seasonal currents in the Red Sea during winter

The seasonal currents in the Red Sea during summer

The tide tables for the year 2004 published by the Hydrographic Institute of the Italian Navy

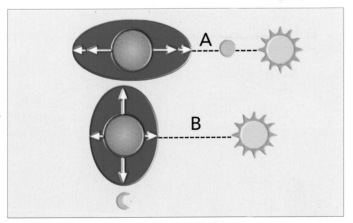
*The position of the moon and sun during spring tides (**A**) and neap tides (**B**)*

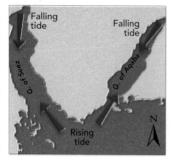

Tidal currents in the Gulf of Suez and in the Gulf of Aqaba have a constant direction: the rising tide moving from south to north, the falling tide from north to south

Time	Increase of Tide
1st hour	+1/12
2nd hour	+2/12
3rd hour	+3/12
4th hour	+3/12
5th hour	+2/12
6th hour	+1/12

Increase of the tidal stream according to the 'Rule of twelfths'

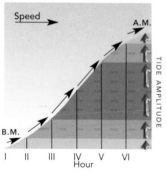

Graphic highlighting the speed of the tidal streams according to the 'Rule of twelfths'
H.T.= high tide
L.T.= low tide

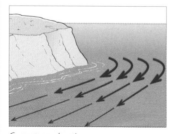

Current acceleration near a promontory

These tables list the times of the tides measured at Suez and, in order to be applied to the Sharm el-Sheikh area in the southern portion of the Gulf of Aqaba, this data must be amended by adding a coefficient that takes into account the time it takes the tidal wave to reach the area in question. In the case of Sharm el-Sheikh this coefficient is equal to –5 hours and 30 minutes (–4h30' in summer during daylight saving time). So to find out the exact time of high tide you must subtract it from the time listed in the tide table. Knowing the exact time of high tide is of the utmost importance in order to be able to swim past the coral reef without any problems when making a shore dive. The speed at which the sea level increases or decreases follows a precise mathematical law and is totally independent from the tide amplitude.

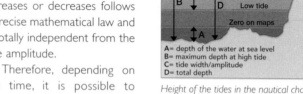

A= depth of the water at sea level
B= maximum depth at high tide
C= tide width/amplitude
D= total depth

Height of the tides in the nautical charts

Therefore, depending on the time, it is possible to determine not only the exact height of the sea level but also the speed of the current by applying the so-called 'Rule of twelfths,' which is represented by a sinusoid correlating the time to the tide.

Currents, furthermore, tend to be stronger in the vicinity of a headland (in Arabic *ras*) and generally in the central points of channels, whereas they decrease in strength in the immediate vicinity of a coastline or reef. Currents present difficulties and potential danger for scuba divers, who should always be aware of them before entering the water.

As a consequence of low spring tides, extensive parts of the coral reef are sometimes exposed

THE CORAL REEF

The coasts of the Red Sea are bordered by an extraordinarily long coral reef composed of hard and soft corals which has been calculated to extend more than 2,000 kilometers.

It should be pointed out that speaking of 'coral' in the Red Sea is slightly inaccurate, because this term should be exclusively used to indicate the Mediterranean Red coral (*Corallium rubrum*) which belongs to the Gorgonacea order.

The mouth of a coral polyp, indicated by the arrow, surrounded by tentacles

Corallium rubrum

Hard corals (madrepores) and soft corals are marine organisms that belong to the Coelenterata and, more specifically, to the important *phylum* Cnidaria. Only since 1726, thanks to the French physician André Peysonnel, have they been recognized as animals.

The basic element is the **coral polyp**, which has different anatomical parts such as the mouth, the gastric cavity and the mobile tentacles with special cells called *nematocysts* which secrete an irritating substance. This characteristic is quite evident in the Hydrozoa, which have smooth calcareous skeletons and polyps with extremely thin tentacles, such as the so-called 'fire corals' belonging to the genus *Millepora*.

The number of tentacles a coral polyp uses to eat with, by directing food towards its mouth, can be 8 or 6 (or a multiple of 6), and this particular anatomic feature is what mostly divides corals into two large subclasses: the *Octocorallia* and the *Hexacorallia*.

Coral polyps are colonial organisms living in symbiosis with special unicellular algae called *zooxanthellae*, which supply the former with carbohydrates and oxygen thanks to their photosynthesis activity.

The Hydrozoa (photograph of a fire coral of the genus Millepora) have extremely thin filaments that secrete an irritating substance

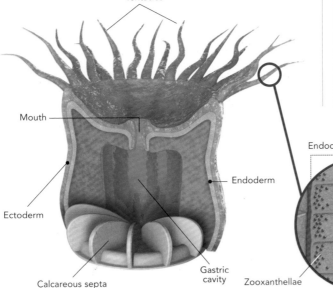

Tentacles

Mouth

Endoderm

Ectoderm

Endoderm Ectoderm

Cnidoblast

Cnidocil

Nematocyst

Calcareous septa

Gastric cavity

Zooxanthellae

mesoglea

The coral polyp

Acropora are the most common hard corals of the reef

A whip coral (genus Juncella) whose skeleton is flexible

Coral polyps live in the intertropical zones from 32° N and 30° S and at a depth of from 50 centimeters to 50 meters.

In order to grow they need light, an average water temperature of 20–30 °C that in any case must never be lower than 18 °C, and salinity ranging from 36 to 41‰.

Madrepores and corals in general show an extraordinary richness of genera and species which develop in very precise chemical and physical conditions. Their growth is in fact influenced by various factors like:

1. light
2. depth
3. temperature
4. salinity
5. currents
6. wave motion

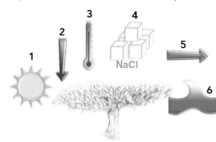

We differentiate between

- **hard corals** or **madrepores**, like the Acropora which secrete a hard calcareous skeleton used by the polyp for both shelter and protection. They can be considered the true reef-forming corals and are thus known as *reef builders* or *hermatypic corals*.
- and **soft corals** which do not have such a hard skeleton. The latter are divisible into two large orders:
  - the **Alcyonacea**
  - the **Gorgonacea**, also known as sea fans, to which 'fan corals' and the so called 'whip corals' belong. Gorgonacea have a more solid structure than the Alcyonacea as they have a flexible skeleton.

Fire corals look like madrepores but actually have a different structure. They belong to the **Hydrozoa** class, along with jellyfish.

THE WORLD OF THE REEF

Coral reefs constitute a fundamental ecosystem that is vital to ocean life.
The importance of conserving its biological balance can only be compared to saving the great tropical rainforests for the earth. Coral reefs extend over a total estimated area of around 280,000 square kilometers in a narrow band between 30° N and 30° S and are the habitat for between 4,000 to 27,000 species of known fish, representing an essential food resource for at least 95 developing countries.

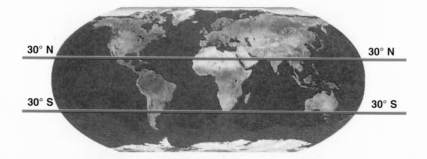

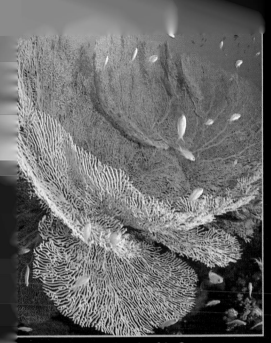

A fan coral belonging to the order of the Gorgonacea (genus Subergorgia)

An individual soft coral belonging to the order of the Alcyonacea (genus Dendronephthya)

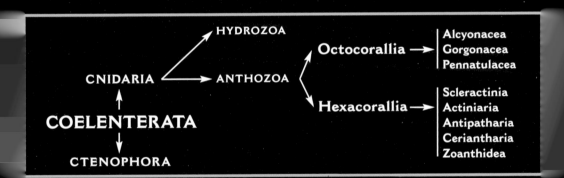

```
                          HYDROZOA                    ┌─ Alcyonacea
                        ↗              Octocorallia → ├─ Gorgonacea
                       ↗                              └─ Pennatulacea
        CNIDARIA ⟶ ANTHOZOA ⟨
          ↑                                            ┌─ Scleractinia
                                      Hexacorallia →  ├─ Actiniaria
    COELENTERATA                                      ├─ Antipatharia
          ↕                                           ├─ Ceriantharia
       CTENOPHORA                                     └─ Zoanthidea
```

...able hard corals of the order of the Scleractinia (genus Acropora)

Massive pore coral
(genus Porites)

Raspberry coral
(Pocillopora verrucosa)

Sinularia, also called Finger coral
(Sinularia sp.)

Pulsing polyp coral
(genus Xenia)

Mushroom coral
(genus Fungia)

Corals are generally anchored to the reef, with the exception of mushroom corals (genus *Fungia*), which are disk shaped and measure from 8 to 28 centimeters: rather than comprising a colony of polyps, they consist of a single polyp and live freely on the sea bed.

There are over 250 species of corals found in the Red Sea, eight percent of which are endemic, meaning they do not live in other seas.

The most common hard corals are Acropora, of which there are over sixty widely different species.

Other common corals are the massive hard corals belonging to the genus *Porites*, which can form extensive banks of huge dimensions especially in zones protected by the currents. Much smaller corals typically found in the shallower parts of the reef are the Finger coral (*Stylophora pistillata*) and the Raspberry coral (*Pocillopora verrucosa*),

Finger coral
(Stylophora pistillata)

A large Salad coral (Turbinaria mesenterina)

both of which have a pinkish colour. Other common inhabitants of the shallows are the reddish Organ-pipe corals (*Tubipora musica*), whose skeleton is made up of small calcareous tubes which look like organ pipes, and brain coral (genus *Platygyra*), which can be recognized by its globular shape and yellowish colour.

Deeper down (usually between 5 and 15 meters) are salad corals, belonging to the genus *Turbinaria*, which are easy to identify due to their pale yellow colour and their large circular shape with a diameter of one to two meters that looks like a large head of lettuce. The awe-inspiring Gorgonians, whose fans can grow to over two meters diameter and wave to the rhythm of the current, are much admired by scuba divers but are difficult for snorkelers to see as their ideal habitat ranges from 10 to 40 meters.

Other more easily viewed Alcyonacea or soft corals are the Broccoli soft coral (*Lythophyton arboreum*), which looks like a broccoli plant; Stalked alcyonarian coral (*Sarcophyton* sp.), of a yellowish-grey colour, shaped like a mushroom but with a leather-like texture; Sinularia (*Sinularia* sp.), which look like small fingers and grow in areas well exposed to the sun; and the pulsing polyp corals (genus *Xenia*), whose continuously moving filaments absorb and filter sea water.

Corals have a wide variety of shapes, sizes and colours, but when they die they all take on a whitish colour.

Among the hermatypic or reef building corals, the *Porites*

Stalked alcyonarian coral (Sarcophyton trocheliophorum)

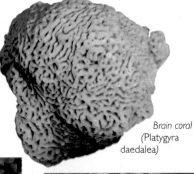

Brain coral (Platygyra daedalea)

Broccoli soft coral (Lithophyton arboreum)

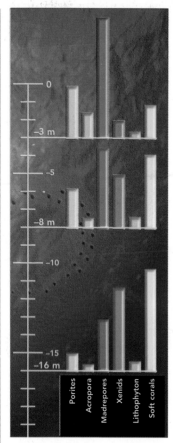

Proliferation of madrepores (hard corals) and soft corals according to depth

and *Acropora* are the most common genera.

Their frequency diminishes with increasing depth whereas the quantity of soft corals, especially those belonging to the family of Xenids, increases significantly.

The hard corals occupy 15–32% of the reef surface at 3 meters: they have the biggest diffusion at this depth whereas their proliferation is reduced to 2–12% at 16 meters. They are represented by above all the genera of *Porites*, *Acropora* and *Pocillopora* whereas the soft corals are largely represented by the Xenids (genus *Heteroxenia*) and with the genera *Lithophyton* and *Sinularia*.

The fire corals (genus *Millepora*) have their maximal proliferation around a depth of 3–5 meters especially in well lit zones with currents. The Alcyonacea represented by the genus *Dendronephthya* appear between 7 to 10 meters and the quantity of soft corals with their maximal proliferation between 8 and 16 meters progressively increases: at this depth the number of Xenids (genus *Heteroxenia*) increases considerably. The Gorgonacea, however, start growing at a depth of 10–12 meters and have their maximum diffusion between 15 and 25 meters. The quantity of dead hard corals is biggest at a depth of 3 meters.

A *Gorgonacea* belonging to the genus *Acabaria* with expanded polyps

CORAL BLEACHING

The general warming of the Earth is due to multiple causes amongst which are the considerable increase in carbon dioxide in the atmosphere and the climatic changes during the last years.

This phenomenon and the stronger influence of periodic warm currents, like the one named El Niño, have increased the water temperature in the oceans entailing massive

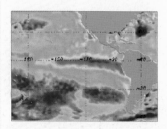

damage and dramatic consequences on the corals in some areas of the earth, such as on the Australian Great Barrier Reef and the Maldives especially in 1998. The zooxanthellae living in symbiosis with the coral polyps are unable to tolerate exposure over a period of time to temperatures 1 or 2 °C higher than their usual range. Yet if this happens these algae

die as the biochemical reactions change modifying thus the process of photosynthesis that converts the sunlight into nutrients for the coral polyp. The polyp dies and the coral assumes a whitish colour: this is called coral bleaching. Fortunately, the Egyptian Red Sea has only been slightly affected so far by such phenomenon.

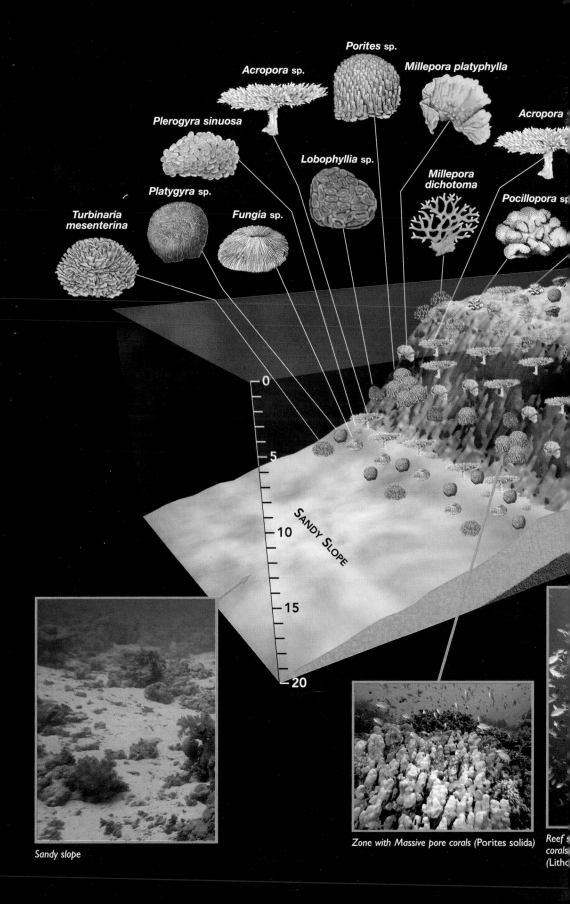

Acropora sp.

Porites sp.

Millepora platyphylla

Plerogyra sinuosa

Acropora

Lobophyllia sp.

Millepora
dichotoma

Platygyra sp.

Turbinaria
mesenterina

Fungia sp.

Pocillopora sp

0

5

SANDY SLOPE

10

15

20

Zone with Massive pore corals (Porites solida)

Sandy slope

Reef
corals
(Litho

Plerogyra sinuosa
Grape coral / Madrepora uva
Blasenkoralle / Corail à bulles
Зеленый пузырчатый коралл

Acropora sp.

Acropora sp.

Acabaria sp.

Tubipora musica
Organ-pipe coral
Corallo a canne d'organo
Orgelkoralle
Corail orgue
Красный органчик

Antipathes sp.
Black coral
Corallo nero
Schwarze Koralle
Corail noir
Черный коралл

Tubastrea sp.

Stylophora pistillata

Pocillopora verrucosa
Raspberry coral
Madrepora lampone
Himbeer-Koralle
Corail framboise
Бородавчатая
поциллопора

Sarcophyton sp.
Stalked alcyonarian
Corallo cuoio
Lederkoralle
Alcyonaire-champignon
Коралл саркофитон

**Lithophyton
arboreum**
Broccoli soft coral
Corallo broccolo
Brokkoli-Koralle
Corail broccoli
Коралл-брокколи

Platygyra sp.
Brain coral
Corallo cervello
Hirnkoralle
Corail-cerveau
Пластинчатая платигира

Dendronephthya sp.

Lobophyllia sp.

Porites solida

Porites lutea

Favia sp.
Groved mosaic coral
Corallo mosaico
Mosaik-Koralle
Favia
Фавитес

Galaxea fascicularis

Turbinaria mesenterina
Salad coral
Corallo lattuga / Salatkoralle
Turbinaire jaune / Турбинария желтоволнистая

Paramuricea sp.
Red gorgonian
Gorgonia rossa
Rot-Gorgonie
Gorgone rouge
Красная
горгония

Fungia sp.
Mushroom coral / Madrepora fungo
Pilzkoralle` / Corail champignon
Грибовидный коралл

Juncella sp.
Whip coral
Corallo a frusta
Peitschenkoralle
Gorgone fouet
Хлыстообразный
коралл

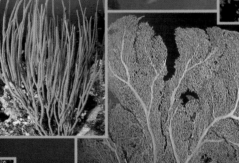

Subergorgia hicksoni
Gorgonian sea-fan
Gorgonia a ventaglio / Hickson's Riesenfächer
Gorgone d'Hickson / Веерный коралл Хиксона

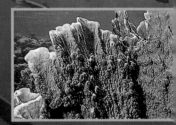

Millepora platyphylla
Fire coral / Corallo di fuoco
Feuerkoralle / Corail de feu en plaques
Уплощенная миллепора

Pachyseris speciosa

Millepora dichotoma
Fire coral / Corallo di fuoco

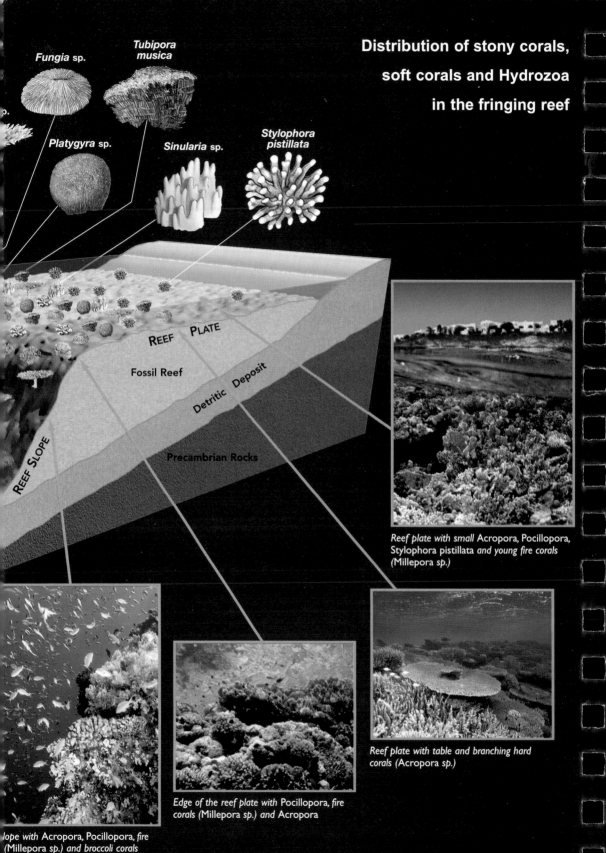

Distribution of stony corals, soft corals and Hydrozoa in the fringing reef

Fungia sp.

Tubipora musica

Platygyra sp.

Sinularia sp.

Stylophora pistillata

REEF PLATE

Fossil Reef

Detritic Deposit

REEF SLOPE

Precambrian Rocks

Reef plate with small Acropora, Pocillopora, Stylophora pistillata *and young fire corals* (Millepora sp.)

Reef plate with table and branching hard corals (Acropora sp.)

Edge of the reef plate with Pocillopora, *fire corals* (Millepora sp.) *and* Acropora

lope with Acropora, Pocillopora, *fire* (Millepora sp.) *and broccoli corals* ohyton sp.)

Architecture of the Coral Reef

Coral reefs have complex and diversified structures which can be classified into three main categories:

1. **fringing reefs**, typical of the Red Sea, these are coral plates, connected to the coastlines: they are in the form of fringes that grow out towards the sea;

Simplified scheme showing the morphology of a fringing reef

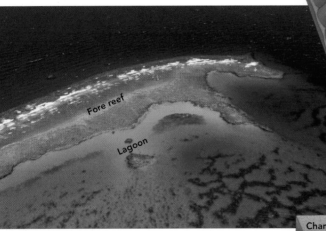

An example of a fringing reef: the reef plate (indicated by the arrow) followed by the seaward facing reef slope

2. **barrier reefs**, considered an evolutionary phase of fringing reefs, these are separated from the coast with a lagoon in between;

Simplified scheme showing the morphology of a barrier reef

An example of a barrier reef: the inner reef followed by a lagoon and the fore reef

3. **atolls** generally lie far from the coast and are characterized by a reef surrounding a lagoon. This type of reef, according to Charles Darwin's theory (proved only in the second half of the 20th century) originally lay around a volcanic cone that later sank, forming a round inner lagoon interrupted by one or more openings that communicate with the open sea. In the Red Sea the only important example of this type of coral formation is in Sanganeb, in Sudan.

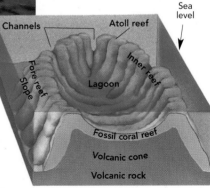

Simplified scheme showing the morphology of an atoll

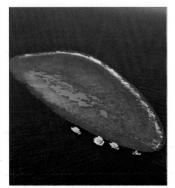

An example of an erg

An example of a gota

An example of a sha'abrur

The madrepores grow at very different speeds depending on the different genus, however, it has been calculated that generally the branching corals (genus Acropora) have the fastest growth with around 150 millimeters per year whereas the massive pore corals (genus Porites) grow more slowly at 10 millimeters per year. A coral reef with its complex structure is estimated to have a general growth rate, influenced by many other factors, of around 9–15 meters per 1,000 year.

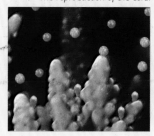

The reproduction of the coral

Morphology of the Coral Reef

The extensive coral formations along the coast are called *sha'ab* in Arabic and have complex and indefinable morphologies.

There are, however, other much smaller structures that take the shape of round or elongated towers rising from the bottom of the seabed up to the surface, which the fishermen and local seamen call differently according to their morphological features:

erg is an isolated round-shaped or oval shaped big tower;
gota is similar to an erg but is much smaller;
sha'abrur, more than just a tower, it is a long narrow reef;
torfa is the final part of a sha'abrur;
habili is a submerged big tower whose upper part can be a few meters below water level (the word means literally 'not born').

The extensive coral reefs or sha'ab can extend to a couple of miles as in the case of Sha'ab Mahmud (shown in the photograph)

THE MARINE FAUNA

An incredible variety of fish species live along the reef; these small and brightly coloured creatures make up the 'reef fauna,' which feed on whatever the reef can offer: plankton, coral polyps, small crustaceans, algae, molluscs and other organisms. The reef's marine fauna also provides a rich feeding ground for large predators: big jacks and barracudas make flash raids on the reef, sure to find an abundance of food. The timid Whitetip reef shark, which is now rare, lives in close proximity to the reef.

Even crevices and caves in the reef can house fish taking advantage of the food available, such as the morays, feeding on small reef fish by night; or the shy but frightening lionfish (genus *Pterois*), the dense schools of the silvery glassfish (Pempheridae family), the Sabre squirrelfish (*Sargocentrum spiniferum*) and the White-edged soldierfish (*Myripristis murdjan*) whose red colour is invisible in the dark.

The most common and numerous reef dwellers are the small and ever-present Anthias, which live in very dense schools just a few centimeters from the corals, as well as fusiliers (Caesionidae family) and sergeant majors (Pomacentridae family), also found in dense schools.

A short distance from the reef, almost at the surface,

Trevallies (genus Caranx) count among the most important predators of the reef

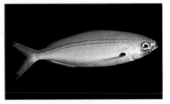
Fusiliers (genus Caesio) live in big schools close to the reef

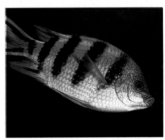
Sergeant majors (genus Abudefduf) are one of the most common reef fish and have gregarious habits

Endemic species to the Indian Ocean — 13%

Endemic species to the Red Sea — 17%

Tropical species of the Indo-Pacific — 70%

Faunistic distribution in the Indo-Pacific area

The big Manta rays (Manta birostris) are found in shallow water, in areas protected from waves and currents and close to the reef where these superb fish easily find the plankton on which they feed

A Red Sea anemonefish (Amphiprion bicinctus) with its anemone

Bluegreen pullers (Chromis viridis)

A Red Sea steepheaded parrotfish (Chlorurus gibbus)

Spotted eagle rays (*Aetobatus narinari*) may be found, and Manta rays (*Manta birostris*) feeding mainly on plankton, as well as Red Sea needlefish (*Tylosurus choram*), which feed on small fish.

Other habitual visitors include Red Sea anemonefish or clownfish (*Amphiprion bicinctus*), which live with sea anemones, damselfish (genus *Dascyllus*) and pullers (genus *Chromis*) which all belong to the big family of Pomacentridae; the brightly coloured butterfly fish (Chaetodontidae family), whose constant presence make them truly characteristic of Red Sea reefs, and angelfish (Pomacanthidae family),

Emperor angelfish
(Pomacanthus imperator)

Half of the fourteen species of butterflyfish in the Red Sea are endemic like these Masked butterflyfish (Chaetodon semilarvatus)

considered to be the most beautiful fish due to their elegant patterns. Typical reef inhabitants are also the multicoloured parrotfish (family Scaridae), which have a sharp beak for chipping away corals in the search for small algae, which they eat, producing an incredible quantity of coral sand (it has been estimated that each fish can produce several hundred kilos per year).

On the reef platform, less than a meter from the surface near the reef, we find several species of surgeonfish (genera *Acanthurus* and *Zebrasoma*) to which Acanthuridae family the unicorn fish (genus *Naso*) also belong.

They all possess sharp blades on the caudal peduncle.

Small schools of Doublebar breams (*Acanthopagrus bifasciatus*) swim close to the reef edge and every so often cross paths with the true king of the reef and one of the larger reef fish, the Napoleonfish (*Cheilinus undulatus*), which can be over two meters long and weigh more than two hundred kilograms.

The Sohal surgeonfish
(Acanthurus sohal)

The Bluespine unicornfish (Naso unicornis)

TYPICAL SPECIES OF THE RED SEA

The exact number of fish species present in the Red Sea is not known as every year new discoveries are made. For the moment being there are 1,248 classified species of which 17% or 212 species are endemic, meaning not found in other seas. Among these, 7 species are represented by the butterfly fish (Chaetodontidae family) out of *a total of 14 known species in the Red Sea.*

Lined butterflyfish
(Chaetodon lineolatus)

The Doublebar seabass
(Acanthopagrus bifasciatus)

The Napoleonfish (Cheilinus undulatus) *is sociable, curious and comes very close*

A potentially dangerous organism is to be named among the starfish: the Acanthaster planci stands for the Crown of Thorns (COT) which feeds on coral polyps and is capable of inflicting massive damage to the reef in the event of uncontrolled proliferation.

In 1998 in the Red Sea, from the Strait of Tiran to the region around Quseir, a real invasion of the Acanthaster took place damaging vast areas of reef in many places. Why this phenomenon occurs is not yet fully understood but might be linked with the reduction of their natural enemies: the Giant triton (Charonia tritonis) which is collected and sold to the tourist as well as the Spangled emperor (Lethrinus nebulosus) or shaour in Arabic, a fish prized by local fishermen and today well appreciated in the tourist restaurants.

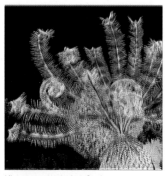

Klunzinger crinoid or featherstar
(Lamprometra klunzingeri)

The Slate pencil sea urchin
(Heterocentrotus mammillatus)

The venomous Pin-cushion sea urchin
(Asthenosoma varium)

Echinoderms

Echinoderms are organisms that vary widely in appearance but which characteristically have a calcareous plate skeleton, radial symmetry, and a water-vascular system. By means of changes of its hydraulic pressure, this system makes hundreds of tiny peduncles (called 'tube feet' or *podia*) straighten and extend, allowing the locomotion of the animal.

The most significant are the **sea urchins**, which belong to the Echinoidea class: in the shallow water of lagoons or on the reef plate, you will almost certainly spot Diadem sea urchins (*Diadema setosum*). The utmost attention must be paid, however, because if they are touched or trodden on, their super fine spines, which grow up to 20 centimeters, can give you a painful sting.

The less common Slate-pencil sea urchin (*Heterocentrotus mammillatus*), earned its name because its spines are large and look like pencils: it is usually found at a greater depth.

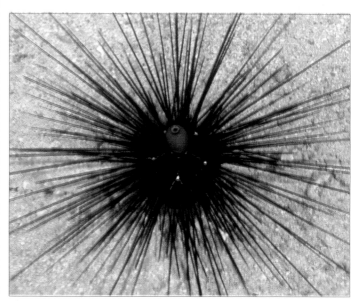

The Diadem sea urchin (Diadema setosum) with long, super-fine black spines

Very common are also the **crinoids** or featherstars characterised by flexible arms which they move to capture their prey. The **starfish**, however, belong to the Asteroidea class and typically have five or more arms. The most beautiful one is undoubtedly the Pearl sea star (*Fromia monilis*) with its unmistakable bright red colour with white dots, whereas the most common is the Reef-crest brittle starfish (*Ophiocoma scolopendrina*), found in just a few centimeters of water on the shoreline. By all means, avoid the Crown of Thorns (*Acanthaster planci*, see box below). Among the echinoderms we also have to point out the **holothurian** or sea cucumber which scuba divers can find.

Fromia monilis

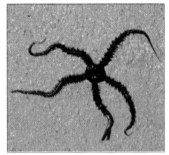

The delicate Reef-crest brittle starfish (Ophiocoma scolopendrina) lives primarily along the shoreline

Molluscs

Molluscs are invertebrates and have a soft body which is distinguished by a mantle on the dorsal side covered generally by a shell and on the ventral side a foot that allows them to move about and feed. Molluscs comprise tens of thousands of species and are subdivided into five large classes, three of which – Bivalvia, Gastropoda and Cephalopoda – are of special interest for anyone who dives in the Red Sea.

Bivalves, as the name indicates, have a body enclosed within a shell consisting of two valves that enclose the visceral masses joined together by a hinge. They are filter feeding creatures and their gills extract oxygen and micro-organisms from the seawater. The biggest bivalve is the Common giant clam (*Tridacna maxima*) which can grow to 40 centimeters long.

Gastropods are characterized by a single shell which can have many shapes: limpets (genus *Patella*) are conical or flattened, cone shells (genus *Conus*) are spiral shaped and can shoot small poisonous darts to catch their prey, or slipper winkles (genus *Nerita*) which are often to be found on the shoreline. The most beautiful gastropod in the Red Sea has now become a rarity: the Giant triton (*Charonia*

The holothurian, also called sea cucumber, has recently been hunted intensively in the Red Sea for food

A Common giant clam (Tridacna maxima) on a Grape coral (Plerogyra sinuosa)

The Giant triton (Charonia tritonis), the biggest archenemy of the Crown of Thorns starfish, is a gastropod which is today threatened by extinction

*The Pyjama slug
(Chromodoris quadricolor)*

Common octopus (genus Octopus)

*The Bigfin reef squid
(Sepioteuthis lessoniana)*

OCTOPUS, CUTTLEFISH AND SQUIDS

*The octopus is an eight-armed Cephalopod and belongs to the order of the Octopods. Octopuses can be found even during the day on the seabed close to the reef in the shallows and near to the crevices in which they can escape at the slightest sign of danger.
The cuttlefish and squids have ten tentacles and belong to the order of the Decapods.*

They are active swimmers frequenting the waters close to the reef barrier especially at night when they are hunting for food. These three Cephalopods share one peculiarity: they are able to change colour very rapidly according to their 'mood,' for camouflage or for communication purposes.

tritons), archenemy of the Crown of Thorns starfish as it feeds on it. There are also particular gastropods without any shell and thus are called Nudibranchs. The most typical and elegant is certainly the *Hexabranchus sanguineus* in the Red Sea, known as the

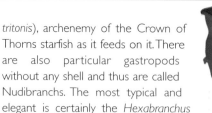

*Spanish dancer
(Hexabranchus sanguineus)*

'Spanish dancer' which can reach a length of 50 centimeters.

The **Cephalopods** are molluscs which in the course of evolution have lost their shell (only the Nautilidae of the genus *Nautilus* have conserved their external shell) acquiring a neutral buoyancy. Cephalopods are distinguished according to the number of tentacles they have (eight or ten) and comprise the octopuses, squids and cuttlefish. In the Red Sea they are represented foremost by the Big red octopus (*Octopus cyaneus*), the Bigfin reef squid (*Sepioteuthis lessoniana*) and by the Common cuttlefish (*Sepia prashadi*).

The Reef cuttlefish (Sepia prashadi)

Crustaceans

The crustaceans belong to a vast and complex group comprising more than 30,000 species in which organisms converge differing enormously in form and size. They are all characterized by two pairs of antennae as well as a rigid, chitinous external skeleton.

Most of the crustaceans found in the Red Sea are very small: in fact they are not longer than a few centimeters and they act as cleaning shrimps for the reef fish, feeding on excrement, mucus and organic residues. We find as well crustaceans of a bigger size like the Coral crab (genus *Carpilius*) becoming up to 10 centimeters and the Red Sea lobster (*Panulirus penicillatus*) which has become very rare and can reach 30 centimeters.

Variable coral crab (Carpilius convexus)

Sponges

The fauna of the Red Sea also comprises a high number of sponges. These organisms belong to the *phylum* Porifera and should not be confused with corals. They are characterised by an extraordinary variety of forms. Sponges filter the sea water which enters their body through a number of pores where special ciliated cellules absorb the nutrients vital to the organism. A sponge of medium size can filter more than a hundred liters of water per day.

Sponges are important elements within the architecture of the reef where they contribute on the one hand to the consolidation of the reef's structure and on the other hand create crevices thanks to the corrosive acids they secrete.

A Siphon sponge belonging to the genus Siphonochanalina

Turtles

The turtles which today risk extinction all over the world, in the Red Sea are presented by 5 species. The most common ones are the Hawksbill turtle (*Eretmochelys imbricata*) which has a pointed beak and does not grow to more than 90 centimeters in length, and the Green sea turtle (*Chelonia mydas*), which has a rounded beak and grows substantially larger: it can exceed 140 centimeters in length and weigh over 300 kilograms. Both species feed on algae, sponges and occasionally on Alcyonacea. They are protected by international laws.

Hawksbill turtle (Eretmochelys imbricata)

Green sea turtle (Chelonia mydas)

Dolphins and Dugongs

Dolphins are among the typical inhabitants of the Red Sea represented by around ten species. The most common are the Tursiops or Bottlenose (*Tursiops truncatus*) and the Stenella or Spinner dolphins (*Stenella longirotris*). The Bottlenose dolphins have a flattened snout, can reach large dimensions and are seen singly or in small pods. The Spinner dolphins are much smaller and live usually in big schools which may number over 200 individuals. They can be often found in the open sea and seen from the boats. The Grampus (*Grampus griseus*) are rare and have a characteristic round head and a body that is frequently streaked with scars. These latter are often incorrectly called 'beluga' by local guides, a name which actually denotes an Arctic genus.

A dugong (Dugong dugon)

The Dugongs (*Dugong dugon*) are herbivores and live in zones with thick underwater vegetation such as sea grass (especially of the genus *Halophila*): some example of these large mammals have been identified in the protected area of Nabq, in the north of Sharm el-Sheikh and in the area of Ras Abu Galum. The larger colonies, however, are found along the western coast of the Red Sea, in the south of El-Quseir.

*A Stenella or Spinner dolphin (*Stenella longirostris*)*

*A Tursiops or Bottlenose dolphin (*Tursiops truncatus*) with baby*

Dangerous Organisms

Contrary to what you may think, sharks are certainly not the most dangerous fish for scuba divers and snorkelers. A much more real threat is posed by the **triggerfish** (Balistidae family) during the nesting season from June to August.

Triggerfish are extremely territorial and aggressive, particularly the Giant triggerfish (*Balistoides viridescens*) ready to attack anyone who strays too near to its nest on the sandy floor. Its mouth is very strong, designed for breaking the hardest corals, and it can grow up to 70 cm in length, so it really can present a danger.

The **lionfish** (genus *Pterois*), on the other hand, are rather more timid and peaceable in nature, but if touched their radial spines, connected to poisonous glands, can inject a very dangerous venom.

Even more perilous is the **Stonefish** (*Synanceia verrucosa*) which lives motionless on hard corals or on sandy or even grassy floors: its dorsal spines inject a toxin lethal even for man.

Also on the sandy floor, and sometimes covered by sand, there are **Bluespotted stingrays** (*Taeniura lymma*) with a poisonous spine on the caudal fin that can inflict a painful sting if inadvertently stepped on. Lastly, take care not to accidentally touch the **surgeonfish** and the **unicorn fish** (Acanthuridae family), which live on the reef plate. Their caudal peduncle has blades as sharp as a scalpel.

The head of the **Giant moray** (*Gymnothorax javanicus*) juts out of the crevices of the reef, they can grow up to 2 meters of length. In spite of their frightening appearance the moray eels are not aggressive, however, they can inflict very painful bites to scuba divers who incautiously come too close to their dens or who try to stroke them. Their sharp teeth are pointed inwards and their wounds tend to infect easily.

Neither do the **Blackfin barracudas** (*Sphyraena qenie*) represent any danger to scuba divers even if they count amongst the most ferocious and voracious of the reef dwellers. Some cases of attacks on divers by Giant barracudas (*Sphyraena barracuda*) are known but

Stonefish (Synanceia verrucosa)

Common lionfish (Pterois miles)

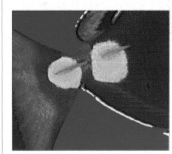
The dangerous caudal blades of a unicornfish (genus Naso)

The frightening Giant triggerfish (Balistoides viridescens) is the most aggressive fish in the Red Sea and does not hesitate to attack scuba divers straying too near

The poisonous spine on the caudal fin of the Bluespotted stingray (Taeniura lymma)

A DANGEROUS MOLLUSC

The Textile Cone shell, Conus textile, is a gastropod characterised by a beautiful white shell decorated with brown diamond markings. This night active mollusc is a common sight on the sandy shallow sea beds and is a voracious predator, it possesses a mechanism similar to a blowpipe with which it can shoot poison darts over a distance of more than ten centimeters. The poison of the Conus textile is used to capture bigger creatures such as crustaceans or other molluscs and is fatal even for man. It is a polypeptide toxin, also called conotoxin which acts on the central nervous system and peripheral receptors and is present in around 400 cone species. The conotoxin produces first a localised and acute pain, then muscle trembling and contractions which extent to the whole body and finally lead to

paralysis: this injury can prove fatal and the patient has to be hospitalized immediately.

Burn caused by a light contact with a fire coral

In the case of a serious burn it turns into a cutaneous sore

they were probably attracted by silvery shining metal elements of the scuba equipment.

The corals, apparently harmless, can sting more or less because they have cells (called *cnidoblasts*) with sacks that secrete an irritating substance. This is particularly prevalent in the Hydrozoa belonging to the Milleporidae family known as **fire corals** which are very common in the Red Sea. They are found in the shallows, generally in areas exposed to currents such as the reef walls.

There are two species of the Milleporidae family, *Millepora dichotoma* and the *Millepora platyphylla*, in the northern Red Sea.

The utmost care must be taken not to touch either as they can cause painful burns which turn into sores that do not heal easily and persist for several days. In case of a burn, the affected area should be washed in very hot, almost boiling water, as the stinging toxin and breaks down when exposed to heat. Apply then an antihistaminic cream.

If touched, the fire coral (in the photo Millepora dichotoma) causes painful burns

DIVING IN THE RED SEA

The dive sites can be reached either by shore or by boat: sometimes you can use both means and thus choose the more suitable option for you.

Shore Dives

Access to dive sites from shore (and with entrance fees) has become rare as the whole coast in the Sharm el-Sheikh area has been developed by hotels.

It is a lot different in Dahab or Nuweiba where the access by shore is not only possible but almost obligatory as diving boats practically do not exist.

In fact, the almost constant presence of a fresh wind from northerly directions generating waves, as well as the existence of easy routes leading directly to the dive sites have discouraged diving centers to purchase boats.

The dive sites are easily accessible by vehicle which does not even have to be a four wheel drive as the road conditions are good. You should, however, always bring along a wide carpet for kitting up to make sure you avoid sand contacting your equipment.

Sometimes the tracks to the dive sites are too narrow for a vehicle to pass, in which case all the equipment (including cylinders!) has to be carried by camel which permits scuba divers to reach their dive site without problems.

The entry to the sea should in any case be done only at the predefined points often identified by 'Easy Entry' signs. This helps to minimise damage to the coral reef.

An off-road vehicle transports scuba divers as well as their equipment, and pulls a trailer with cylinders

Sometimes the camel is the only mode of transport able to reach certain dive sites

The cars park very close to the dive sites and the equipment is put on large carpets

The fixed moorings (in Arabic shamanduras) normally consists of a metal ring fixed to the reef to which is secured a rope or wire together with a buoy: on this one the boats are moored to the attached floating rope. Each shamandura cannot endure more than three boats due to obvious safety and weight reasons.

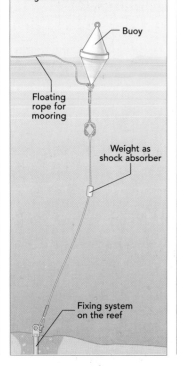

Buoy

Floating rope for mooring

Weight as shock absorber

Fixing system on the reef

Boat Diving

The boat is practically the only means to reach the dive sites in Sharm el-Sheikh, and the local fleet consists of more than 220 boats. At the moment the boats can only depart from the three authorized ports situated in Marina Travco in the south, at Naama Bay in the center and from Shark's Bay in the north.

On board, the boats are divided into two areas: the dry and the wet area.

The dry area comprises the upper deck and the internal saloon which you cannot enter whilst wet and where smoking is usually forbidden. The wet area comprises the dive deck and the bow with no access limitation.

Already on the way to the planned dive site, the *divemaster* assembles the scuba divers usually on the upper deck for the *briefing* and explains in detail how the dive will be carried out and what the divers can expect to observe. Once at the dive site, the boat moors using the so called *shamandura* (fixed moorings, see box) marked by mooring buoys.

The fixed line is often broken so the divemaster jumps with another rope which he secures to the metal ring of the shamandura on the seabed.

The boat must be properly tied up before the mooring dive in a circular pattern can start.

In some cases when the divemaster decides or because the site does not have fixed shamanduras, the dive is done as a *drift dive*: the divers follow the current while the boat is moving.

It is also possible to do a so-called *semi drift dive*, an intermediate solution: the dive starts from the boat on the mooring line and after a period of time agreed

Saloon

Dry area

Dive deck

Wet area

Cylinders

Ladder

In the briefing, the guide or divemaster explains in detail with the help of a map how the dive will be carried out and answers questions from the scuba divers

Nautical charts (which should always be on every boat) are unfortunately seldom used by boat captains who are used to navigate 'by sight.'
The same applies for divemasters.
Nautical charts when properly read, however, can give useful information on depth, position of lighthouses or existing reef banks.
Defining a route in safety,

especially for distant destinations or navigating during night, is only possible with the help of a nautical chart.
The charts are not infallible however: pay the greatest attention when navigating in

The quadrant of a nautical compass

unknown destinations with an accuracy of a few meters.

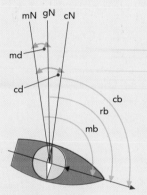

mN = magnetic North
gN = geographic North
cN = compass North
md = magnetic declination
cd = compass deviation
mb = magnetic bow
rb= real bow
cb= compass bow

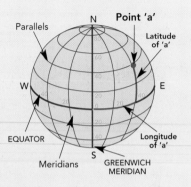

areas with reef banks and avoid the sun in your eyes low on the horizon as possible coral formations close to the surface will not be visible.
The GPS (Global Positioning System) is an indispensable companion to the charts with which you can first of all exactly determine your position on the chart, and allow you to reach

The number indicates the extent of the magnetic declination and its annual variation

Compass rose with indication of the magnetic declination, the difference between the geographic North (the North of the maps) and magnetic North

How to read a nautical chart

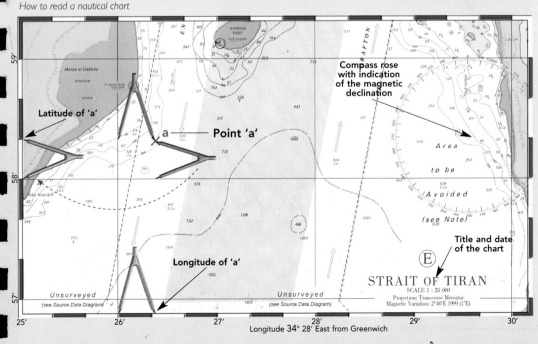

A zodiac is a useful and sometimes indispensable object on a safari boat

beforehand between the boat captain (in Arabic *rais*) and the divemaster the boat leaves the mooring to pick up the scuba divers.

Drift diving offers a wonderful way to explore the reef, however, this technique does require some practice especially with regard to the boat pickup at the end of the dive. In fact, this can be quite difficult in some cases. Every diver should carry a surface marker buoy to signal their position at 5 meters whilst doing a safety stop, or stay very close to the guide who does this.

Once the safety stop is finished the diver ascends to the surface, inflates the BCD and immediately swims away from the reef and waits for the boat. The mask is to be kept on the face, the regulator in the mouth whilst swimming towards the boat. One of the crew members throws a rope to the divers who, then, pull themselves towards the ladder at the stern. If the sea is rough, this is the most

Safari boat towing a zodiac

Travco Marina harbour in Sharm el-Sheikh, always packed in the morning and afternoon, accommodates more than 220 boats

SMALL DICTIONARY OF NAUTICAL TERMS

ITALIAN	ENGLISH	ARABIC	ITALIAN	ENGLISH	ARABIC
Ancora	Anchor	Prosi	Onda	Wave	Mogah
Cima	Rope	Habl	Ormeggio	Mooring	Shamandura
Costa	Coast	Shat, Sahe	Poppa	Stern	Esh
Elica	Propeller	Rafaas	Prua	Bow	Prowa
Equipaggio	Crew	Taqm	Ruota del Timone	Steering Wheel	Doman
Motore	Engine	Makana	Timone	Rudder	Daffah

delicate (and sometimes dangerous) moment of the operation. You need to grasp the ladder firmly whilst holding it away from your body (to avoid it bouncing back onto your head when the stern rises and falls in the waves), put a foot on the lowest rung and come up as quickly as possible.

A zodiac (rubber dinghy) to pick up the scuba divers can prevent a lot of problems in some cases, especially when the sea is rough.

The word **safari** means simply 'journey' and is used for boat trips for two or more days. Safari boats need to have additional equipment to the daily boats, including an electricity generator, compressors to fill the scuba cylinders, an onboard desalination unit as well as a zodiac with outboard motor for mooring the boat or transportation of the scuba divers at the dive site.

The floating filling station to recharge the cylinders in Travco Marina harbour

ON BOARD ITEMS

Every boat must have:
- *a VHF radio*
- *safety devices such as life jackets, fire extinguishers etc.*
- *an oxygen tank with its mask*
- *a Medic First Aid Kit*

ALWAYS ASCERTAIN THESE ITEMS ARE ON BOARD AND IN GOOD CONDITION.

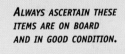

DAN oxigen kit

The small floating jetty situated at the southern end of Naama Bay

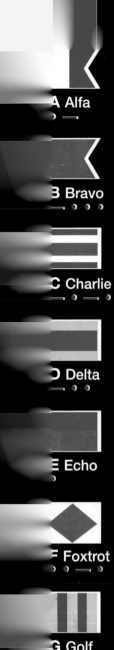

A Alfa ○ ▬

B Bravo

C Charlie

D Delta ▬ ○ ○

E Echo ○

F Foxtrot ○ ○ ▬ ○

G Golf ▬ ▬ ○

H Hotel ○ ○ ○ ○

I India ○ ○

J Juliet ○ ▬ ▬ ▬

K Kilo ▬ ○ ▬

L Lima ○ ▬ ○ ○

M Mike ▬ ▬

N November ▬ ○

O Oscar ▬ ▬ ▬

P Papa ○ ▬ ▬ ○

Q Quebec ▬ ▬ ○ ▬

R Romeo ○ ▬ ○

S Sierra ○ ○ ○

T Tango ▬

U Uniform ○ ○ ▬

V Victor ○ ○ ○ ▬

W Whiskey ○ ▬ ▬

X X-ray ▬ ○ ○ ▬

Y Yankee ▬ ○ ▬ ▬

Z Zulu ▬ ▬ ○ ○

0 Nadazero ▬ ▬ ▬ ▬ ▬

1 Unaone ○ ▬ ▬ ▬ ▬

2 Bissotwo ○ ○ ▬ ▬ ▬

3 Terrathree ○ ○ ○ ▬ ▬

4 Kartefour ○ ○ ○ ○ ▬

5 Pentafive ○ ○ ○ ○ ○

6 Soxisix ▬ ○ ○ ○ ○

7 Setteseven ▬ ▬ ○ ○ ○

8 Oktoeight ▬ ▬ ▬ ○ ○

9 Novenine ▬ ▬ ▬ ▬ ○

Intelligenza
(flown to indicate the
usage of *ISC*)

International Signal Code (ISC) with phonetic alphabet spelling and Morse code alphabet

Communication on Board

Communication between boats and diving centers or between boats and the coast guard or marine police is done through VHF radio (*Very High Frequency*) which is obligatory on every boat. In the last few years, however, mobile phones GSM covering a vast area stretching from the Strait of Tiran to Ras Mohammed have partially substituted the VHF with regards to communication between boats and diving centers. VHF still remains necessary for the 'official' communication and for emergencies.

A VHF radio

The VHF radios can be fixed or mobile and use radio waves with frequencies between 156 and 162 MHz (Megahertz). The Hertz (Hz) expresses the frequency (F) of the electromagnetic waves (also called Hertz waves according to the German physicist Heinrich Hertz who discovered them in 1887) or in other words the number of cycles per second where the cycle represents the distance between two peaks; the prefix Mega (M) stands for one million Hertz (1 MHz = 1,000,000 Hz).

The electromagnetic waves are emitted in direct lines and thus the VHF range is limited apart from the radio power (max. 25 watt) as well as the height of the unit's antennas emitting and receiving: in the most ideal case, the range does not go beyond 50 nautical miles but is usually around 30 nautical miles.

Most of the marine VHF radios have 55 pre-programmed channels which can be either simplex or duplex: with simplex channels the emission frequency is the same as the receiving frequency, thus conversation takes place in only one sense: the one calling and the one receiving cannot talk at the same time. The frequency in duplex channels is different and conversation is similar to that of a normal phone.

Channel 16 corresponds to 156,8 MHz which by international agreement is both the open communication and emergency calling channel. This is different in the area of Sharm el-Sheikh where the open communication channel is **Channel 14** (156,7 MHz). The emergency calling channel remains **Channel 16**.

Procedure for Transmission and Receiving

After having switched the VHF to the desired channel (**16** in case for calling the coast guard or *Search and Rescue* or **14** for calling the diving centers or marine offices) and tuned the switch for background noise reduction (*squelch*) you proceed as follows:

1. Press the button that allows transmission and pronounce the name – not more than three times – of the diving center or boat you wish to contact.

2. You pronounce the name of your radio station (diving center or boat) not more than three times.

3. Release the call button to allow reception.

4. Once communication is established, the channel for further talk is agreed. Both switch to this one thus keeping the calling channels 16 and 14 free.

HERTZ WAVES

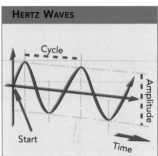

Radio waves expand at the speed of light (300,000 km/sec) in a linear direction, their length unit measured in meters. In order to calculate the length L of a wave (in meters) knowing the frequency F (in kHz or kilohertz or 1,000 Hertz) you need to apply the formula L = 300,000/F, and vice versa you receive the frequency F (cycle per second) knowing the length L when calculating F = 300,000/L.

Knowing that the VHF waves have a frequency between a range of 156 and 162 MHz (1 MHz = 1,000 KHz = = 1,000,000 Hz) and applying the above formula, we calculate that their length is 2 meters, therefore they are also known as metric waves. In order to identify the theoretical range R of a unit on board of a boat and of a coastal unit, and knowing that the VHF waves expand in linear direction, we only have to know the height of the respective antennas (h and H) and apply the formula R = 2,1x($\sqrt{h}$ + $\sqrt{H}$).

SAFETY

The logo of the hyperbaric chamber in Sharm el-Sheikh

EMERGENCY TELEPHONE NUMBERS
Hyperbaric Medical Center Phone from 10:30 to 18:00 069 – 366 09 22/3 24 h   012 – 212 42 92 012 – 333 13 25 hyper_med_center@sinainet.com.eg
International Hospital Phone 069 – 366 08 93/5 24 h   012 – 215 21 96

Safety is the most important part of any dive, and scuba divers would do well to remember that most accidents are caused by dives that are too deep and ascents that are too fast. Another point to bear in mind is that in the Red Sea recreational scuba diving absolutely must not be done at a depth of over 30 meters.

With the financial support of the USAID (*United States Agency for International Development*), the **Hyperbaric Medical Center** was established in 1993 and is directed by Dr. Adel Taher – one of the most well known experts in hyperbaric medicine and Medical Director of DAN EGYPT. The staffs of this specialised institution are on hand to treat the victims of diving accidents from the thousands of scuba divers who dive every month around the waters of Sharm el-Sheikh (it has been calculated that in the high season more than 5,000 dives are done every day).

The Hyperbaric Medical Center, situated around 200 meters from the Travco Marina harbour, and the head office of the organisation

RISK FACTORS AND PRECAUTIONS

*The most common illness among scuba divers in the Red Sea is **DCI** (Decompression Illness). This insidious and serious illness does not hit every scuba diver in the same way.*
It manifests itself with joint pain, torpor and paresthesia, vertigo and nausea and can lead to paralysis.
The onset of DCI is increased by

*different factors such as **1.** dehydration; **2.** stress or fatigue; **3.** obesity; **4.** consumption of alcohol before diving; **5.** excessive repetitive diving.*
If one or more factors apply, divers should increase precautionary measures such as drinking 1 or 2 glasses of water before diving, not

exceeding the maximum depth limit (30 meters), respecting the no-decompression limit of the computer or dive tables, slowing the ascent rate (9 meters/minutes) and always making a safety stop (3 minutes at 5 meters depth).
A second risk comes from the great number of boats around the dive sites, especially by potentially dangerous glass bottom boats for tourists observing the underwater world and which are hovering in shallow water right above scuba divers.
The systematic use of surface marker buoys by scuba divers surfacing in open water is the only solution to prevent serious, even fatal accidents.
Finally, one should always keep in mind an important risk factor caused by possible, even serious traumas (injuries, fractures) when scuba divers come back to their boat: with rough seas, you need to pay special attention when coming up the ladder.

3' SAFETY — 5 m

9 m/1'

30 m

STOP

The limits of recreational diving in the Red Sea

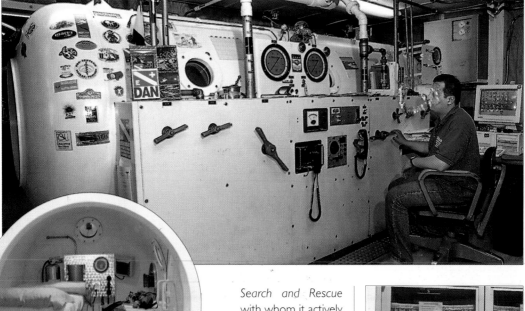

The multiplace, multilock hyperbaric chamber in Sharm el-Sheikh

Search and Rescue with whom it actively collaborates, presides over a hyperbaric chamber fabricated in the United States.

In this center full-time specialist physicians are contacted immediately in case of emergency. More than 800 cases of severe decompression illnesses (DCI) have been treated so far. The quickness of the intervention of the physicians of the center is an extremely important factor for a favourable prognosis and an assisting element for the success of the therapeutic treatment. The Hyperbaric Medical Center organizes so-called *Hyperbaric Tender Courses* on a regular basis for divemasters and instructors who would like to assist injured scuba divers during the different phases of their therapeutic treatment.

Dr. Adel Taher is responsible for the Hyperbaric Chamber in Sharm el-Sheikh

DAN

E + DAN EUROPE

EMERGENCY TELEPHONE NUMBER *24 h hot line: 0039 – 039 60 57 858*

DAN (Divers Alert Network) is a non-profit, international foundation born with the aim to assist divers in difficulties and to make scuba diving safer. In the event of an emergency, DAN offers medical assistance worldwide 24 hours a day, organizes transportation and co-ordinates medical and hyperbaric therapy.
DAN offers a specific insurance cover for scuba diving with no policy excess, and its members are not charged with any follow-up expenses after diving incidents.
Furthermore, DAN conducts scientific research in order to reduce the risks involved in scuba diving and campaigns for safety and danger prevention, as well as courses on Oxygen First Aid and on how to treat injuries caused by aquatic life.
Dr. Adel Taher is currently director of DAN Egypt.

The Search and Rescue (SAR) logo

One of the rescue RIBs of SAR

A SAR dinghy in action assisting a cargo ship run aground on a reef in Dahab

Hamdy Samy, the founder of SAR

The center plans to enlarge its structure in the near future so it can respond to the needs of scuba divers with even higher efficiency. A recompression chamber is also planned for Dahab.

A second hyperbaric chamber has recently been installed in the *International Hospital* in Hay el-Nour.

Safety at sea has improved greatly over the last couple of years thanks to the **Search and Rescue** association (**SAR**). It was established by Hamdy Samy in 2001 and has its headquarters only a few meters away from Travco Marina. SAR offers 24 hour assistance to all boats that find themselves in real danger or whose passengers are in need of emergency medical treatment.

SAR is a member of the ILF (*International Lifeboat Federation*) and collaborates actively with the Ras Mohammed National Park as well as with the coast guard. SAR operates special boats called RIBs (*Rigid Inflatable Boats*) equipped with extremely sophisticated and complete Medic First Aid Kit and with speeds exceeding 40 knots, they can reach all dive sites in Sharm el-Sheikh, Tiran and Ras Mohammed in a few minutes. Since its foundation, SAR has helped in more than 300 cases including diving incidents, heart problems and various traumas.

The organisation is financed thanks to the contributions of its members (currently 160) among which are diving centers, boats, hotels and possible contributions of insurance companies. Branches of SAR have been operating for a long time in Sharm el-Sheikh, Hurghada and Safaga. A new branch is soon to be established in Dahab together with a new hyperbaric chamber to avoid long and dangerous transfers to Sharm el-Sheikh for the injured scuba divers.

EMERGENCY TELEPHONE NUMBERS
Search and Rescue
Phone 24 h   012 – 313 41 58
Fax   069 – 366 41 48
Radio   Channel 16
Email: rescue@sinainet.com.eg

Some of the Search and Rescue (SAR) team members together with their emergency equipment in Sharm el-Sheikh

THE PROTECTION
OF THE MARINE ENVIRONMENT

I n the area of Sharm el-Sheikh alone, we count at least 120,000 divers every month distributed over no more than 30 dive sites. It has been calculated that the 200 boats operating regularly transport between 2,500 to 3,500 divers to the dive sites every day, and those divers do an average of two dives.

Various scientific studies based on statistics have demonstrated that each diver involuntarily destroys an average of 10 grams of coral during each dive: that equals about 14.4 tons of destroyed corals per year. The load of divers is also not evenly distributed around the 30 dives sites, but is dangerously concentrated on the most beautiful and sought-after locations such as Shark and Yolanda Reefs (Ras Mohammed area), and Gordon and Jackson reefs (Tiran area).

In light of these facts, the need to protect the reef has become more than ever a primary concern in order to continue to offer scuba divers sites to a satisfactory level.

This required protection was acknowledged by the Egyptian Government more than 20 years ago in 1983 when law No. 102 was introduced. It prohibited the collection of any living or dead objects and at the same time established the first protected area in the country named *Ras Mohammed National Park*.

The aim was to protect this complex and unique ecosystem which boasts more than 1,000 species of fish and 150 species of hard and soft corals.

The park stretched out initially over a relatively small area of 97 square kilometers but was subsequently enlarged in 1988 to

In peak times, the filling station of Travco Marina harbour fills more than 2,000 cylinders per day which equals only around 50% of the requirement

**NATIONAL PARKS
OF EGYPT**

The logo of the National Parks of Egypt

N

The Ras Mohammed National Park extends over a total territory of 480 sq.km of which 76% comprises the marine environment. It receives more than 200,000 visitors every year

Mediterranean Sea

SUEZ

S I N A I

Ras Sudr

✈

TABA

Gulf of Aqaba

Abu Zenima

Taba
Protected
Area

NUWEIBA ⊙

Abu Rudeis

Gulf of Suez

Abu Galum
Protected Area

Gebel Musa
(Mount Sinai) ▲
_2,285 m_   ▲ _Gebel Katherine_
_2,637 m_

⊙ **DAHAB**

Saint Katherine
Protectorate

EL-TUR

Nabq
Protected
Area

Strait of Gubal

✈

Tiran

Sanafir

NAAMA BAY

SHARM EL-SHEIKH

Ras Mohammed
National Park

N

include the Islands of Tiran and Sanafir (Saudi Arabian territory but governed by Egypt) and some coastal areas around Sharm el-Sheikh adding up to a total surface of 480 square kilometers.

In 1992, with the DPM (*Decree of the Prime Minister*) No. 1511 the Protected Area of Nabq (*Nabq Managed Resource Protected Area*) was established with a surface area of 586.5k sq.km. Nabq is famous for its mangrove forest, the most northerly of the northern hemisphere, and considered to be the biggest and most important one in the whole of the Red Sea.

The same decree also extended by 500 square kilometers the protected zone of Ras Abu Galum (*Abu Galum Managed ResourceProtected Area*) situated around a hundred kilometers north of Sharm el-Sheikh.

A Park Ranger keeps lookout

In 1996, the *Saint Katherine Protectorate* was established covering an area of 4,300 square kilometers which comprises the famous monastery of Saint Katherine as well as the Moses Mountain or Mount Sinai (*Gebel Musa* in Arabic). Finally, in 1998 with DPM No. 316, the *Taba Protected Area* was introduced with a territory of more than 3,590 sq.km.

Visitors to these areas, whether scuba divers or not, are required to observe certain regulations laid down by a committee of experts in order to safeguard both the marine and land environments.

The Rangers control tracks and access points along the shore

These rules of behaviour are logical, and even normal and obvious, for responsible and conscientious divers who respect the environment they use. Naturally, such respect should grow out of conviction and certainly not out of fear of the severe punishment applied to transgressors.

Control of the protected areas and adherence to park regulations are entrusted to the Ras Mohammed Park Rangers, who carefully guard the territory and make sure that all diving boats respect the complementary regulations regarding access

Signposts indicate the routes to follow in the National Park

Around twenty boats transport approx. 200 scuba divers to the wreck of the Thistlegorm every day compromising irreparably both the fauna of the site and the wreck's structure

Scuba divers walking on the reef damage it seriously

Waste is to be put in the provided containers in the Park

to diving sites and the use of fixed moorings. Respecting regulations is not sufficient to protect the fragile but complex equilibrium of the coral reef: we need to do more.

Foremost it is necessary to use the planned shore entry and exit points where indicated with a sign 'Easy Entry.'

In addition, avoid reaching the sea at low tide because this would imply that scuba divers walk on the reef rather than passing over it while swimming.

Walking on the reef is both tiring and dangerous, but above all it destroys the coral polyps and facilitates damage to the corals that live on the reef platform.

Fins have to be used with extreme care as they might not only break corals but can also stir up sand and sediment which suffocates the coral polyps.

Furthermore, it is obvious that nothing should be thrown into the sea, and yet only a few are aware of the timescales involved for our waste to biodegrade. For instance the filter of a cigarette will take around two years to biodegrade and the nicotine that is released from it is extremely toxic for coral polyps and fish. A plastic bag or bottle remains in the water for a period between 100 and

Plastic bags and other non-biodegradable material invade the reefs of the Red Sea

1,000 years. Over the last years, not only a worrying deterioration of many dive sites can be noticed, but also an incredible increase of rubbish thrown into the water by boats carrying tourists or snorkelers (far exceeding the number of scuba divers in the area of Sharm el-Sheikh), and of oil products like petrol and tar essentially linked to the increase of navigation in the gulfs of Suez and Aqaba.

In order to safeguard this extraordinary but fragile marine ecosystem, we urgently need new and more drastic protection measures on behalf of all those who make use of its resources. Only in this way can we minimise the conflict between recreation and conservation.

Many diving centers have designed unconventional but effective posters to promote marine conservation

This part of the coral reef has been worn smooth by too many scuba divers who walk over it to reach the dive site every day: the living coral has practically disappeared giving way to extensive dead areas

Entry to the sea should take place only at the points indicated by the 'Easy Entry' signs

REGULATIONS OF THE PARK

 Do not touch or break any corals or shells.

  Fishing and spearfishing are not allowed in Protected Areas.

 Do not collect or damage any material, either living or dead (corals, shells, fish, plants, fossils, etc.).

 It is prohibited to throw refuse of any kind into the sea.

 It is prohibited to access any closed area and to walk or anchor on any reef area. Please use marked access points.

 Access to diving areas is recommended at designated access points only. This reduces damage to reef areas.

  Fish feeding is prohibited as it upsets the biological balance of the reef.

 Offenders are subject to prosecution according to the terms of Law 102 of 1983.

Take nothing with you – Leave nothing behind

MONITORING THE REEF

The reef represents not only one of the marvels of our planet but also one of its most important economic resources whose conservation is vital for the development of scuba diving and tourism. The coral reefs of the Red Sea together with its fauna – from big predators to the tiny anthias – are currently in good health, yet they are seriously threatened: dangers arise from natural sources but 60% are due to man.

Landsat 7 *satellite takes photographs from an orbital height of 705 kilometers*

NATURAL FACTORS

a. Increase of general water temperature that causes the death of coral polyps.

b. Proliferation of organisms that destroy coral polyps, such as the Crown of Thorns (*Acanthaster planci*).

MAN-INDUCED FACTORS

a. Increased levels in marine waters of nitrogenous residues and other damaging substances due to the use of fertilizers and detergents.

b. Increase in hydrocarbon pollution due to excessive numbers of vessels.

c. Excessive urbanization and population of the coast.

d. Excessive number of scuba divers and snorkelers on dive sites.

e. Excessive fishing for food and a rising demand for aquarium fish.

f. Destructive fishing techniques: 10% of reefs world wide are destroyed by dynamite fishing.

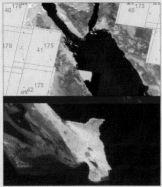

Landsat 7 *has taken 1,490 photographs of the coral reefs in four years*

Monitoring the reef to supervise its health is therefore of paramount importance.

NASA has launched an incentive called *Millennium Coral Reef Project* in collaboration with universities and other scientific institutions that involves mapping the reefs of our planet via satellite: between 1999 and 2003, the satellite *Landsat 7* has taken 1,490 high resolution pictures from a height of 705 kilometers. The whole archive was completed in 2005 and published on the internet under the link: *http://www.seawifs.gsfc.nasa.gov/cgi/landsat.pl*

Despite of the support of technology, observations by scuba divers are still of paramount importance to understand the state of health of the reef. The number of marine biologists responsible for

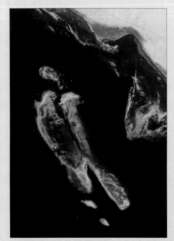

A photograph of Sha'ab Ali taken by Landsat 7

monitoring the coral reefs is far smaller than the number of recreational divers and snorkelers and for this reason their in-water observations may contribute essentially to the work of the scientists.

If every scuba diver or snorkeler learned specific techniques on how to observe the surrounding environment with attention, this data could be gathered without a big effort and, once transmitted to the relevant organisations and researchers, could make an important contribution to protecting and controlling the health of the reef.

A bag of litter deposited in a crevice on the site of The Alternatives

ENVIRONMENT

Observations to record:
1. Water temperature.
2. Number of dead madrepores.
3. Number of broken or damaged madrepores.
4. Number of Alcyonacea (soft corals).
5. Presence of marine plants (seagrass) and/or algae.
6. Presence of rubbish or litter.

FAUNA

As for the fauna, the diver or snorkeler should concentrate on the so called 'indicative' organisms i.e. those that can give information about the health of the reef, in particular butterflyfish (family Chetodontidae): it is important to record existing species and estimating the number of individuals. Also angelfish (family Pomacanthidae), pufferfish and porcupinefish (order Tetraodontiformes) have to be considered as well as some predators like the groupers (family Serranidae). Extremely significant for Invertebrates are Diadem sea urchins (*Diadema setosum*), Crowns of Thorns (*Acanthaster planci*) and Common giant clams (*Tridacna maxima*).

Rangers of the Ras Mohammed National Park collect Crowns of Thorns

A diver records his observations on a slate

REEF INDICATORS*

BUTTERFLYFISH

⊳⊷ 23 cm / ▼ 1-35 m

Chaetodon auriga
Pesce farfalla filamentoso
Threadfin butterflyfish
Fähnchenfalterfisch
Papillon cocher

Feeds on polychaete worms,
coral polyps and algae

⊳⊷ 30 cm / ▼ 2-170 m

Chaetodon lineolatus
Pesce farfalla striato
Lined butterflyfish
Riesenfalterfisch
Papillon linéolé

Omnivorous

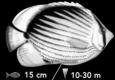

⊳⊷ 15 cm / ▼ 10-30 m

Chaetodon melannotus
Pesce farfalla dal dorso nero
Blackbacked butterflyfish
Schwarzrücken-Falterfisch
Papillon à dos noir

Feeds on small invertebrates

⊳⊷ 13 cm / ▼ 0.5-20 m

Chaetodon austriacus
Pesce farfalla austriaco
Polyp butterflyfish
Polypen-Falterfisch
Papillon cotelé

Feeds on coral polyps
preferably on *Pocillopora*

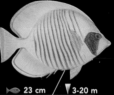

⊳⊷ 23 cm / ▼ 3-20 m

Chaetodon semilarvatus
Pesce farfalla mascherato
Masked butterflyfish
Maskenfalterfisch
Papillon jaune

Feeds on coral polyps
and small invertebrates,
preferably at night

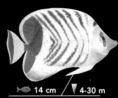

⊳⊷ 14 cm / ▼ 4-30 m

Chaetodon paucifasciatus
Pesce farfalla coronato
Crown butterflyfish
Rotfleckfalterfisch
Papillon orange

Feeds on polyps, worms,
small crustaceans and algae

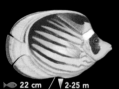

⊳⊷ 22 cm / ▼ 2-25 m

Chaetodon fasciatus
Pesce farfalla fasciato
Striped butterflyfish
Tabak-Falterfisch
Poisson-papillon raton-laveur

Feeds on polychaete worms,
algae and small invertebrates

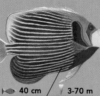

⊳⊷ 18 cm / ▼ 1-210 m

Heniochus diphreutes
Pesce farfalla dal vessillo
Schooling bannerfish
Schwarm-Wimpelfisch
Papillon-cocher grégaire

Feeds on zooplankton

⊳⊷ 20 cm / ▼ 3-50 m

Heniochus intermedius
Pesce farfalla bandiera
Red Sea bannerfish
Rotmeerwimpelfisch
Poissons-cochers de Mer Rouge

Feeds on benthic invertebrates
and plankton, preferably at night

ANGELFISH

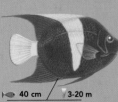

⊳⊷ 40 cm / ▼ 3-20 m

Pomacanthus asfur
Pesce angelo arabo
Arabian angelfish
Halbmond-Kaiserfisch
Poisson-ange demi-lune

Feeds on algae
and small invertebrates

⊳⊷ 40 cm / ▼ 3-70 m

Pomacanthus imperator
Pesce angelo imperatore
Emperor angelfish
Imperatorkaiserfisch
Ange empereur

Feeds on algae
and small invertebrates

⊳⊷ 50 cm / ▼ 4-50 m

Pomacanthus maculosus
Pesce angelo maculato
Arabian angelfish
Arabischer Kaiserfisch
Ange géographe

Feeds on algae
and small invertebrates

⊳⊷ 25 cm / ▼ 1-48 m

Pygoplites diacanthus
Pesce angelo reale
Royal angelfish
Pfauenkaiserfisch
Poisson-ange royal

Feeds on algae
and small invertebrates

* According to Crosby & Reese (1996)

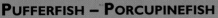

PUFFERFISH – PORCUPINEFISH

>⊂ 120 cm / 5-60 m

Arothron stellatus
Pesce palla stellato
Blackspotted pufferfish
Schwarzfleckkugelfisch
Arothron étoilé

Feeds on small invertebrates,
coral polyps and sponges

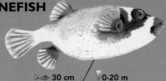

>⊂ 30 cm / 0-20 m

Arothron diadematus
Pesce palla mascherato
Masked pufferfish
Maskenkugelfisch
Arothrons masqués

Feeds on coral polyps,
preferably of Acropora

>⊂ 91 cm / 2-50 m

Diodon hystrix
Pesce istrice
Common porcupinefish
Gewöhnlicher Igelfisch
Grand porc-épic

Feeds on small invertebrates

GROUPERS

>⊂ 40 cm / 1-40 m

Cephalopholis argus
Cernia pavone
Peacock hind
Pfauen-Zackenbarsch
Mérou céleste

Feeds on small fish
and crustaceans

>⊂ 40 cm / 2-150 m

Cephalopholis miniata
Cernia corallina
Coral grouper
Juwelenzackenbarsch
Mérou à points bleus

Feeds on small fish

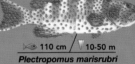

>⊂ 110 cm / 10-50 m

Plectropomus marisrubri
Cernia dei coralli maculata
Red Sea coralcod
Leopardenzackenbarsch
Mérou corallien de Mer Rouge

Feeds on fish and invertebrates

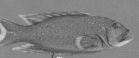

>⊂ 80 cm / 3-250 m

Variola louti
Cernia dalla coda a mezza luna
Moon grouper
Mondflossenzackenbarsch
Mérou à queue en croissant

Feeds on fish and invertebrates

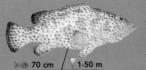

>⊂ 70 cm / 1-50 m

Epinephelus tauvina
Cernia maculata
Arabian grouper
Braunfleckenzackenbarsch
Mérou loutre

Feeds on fish and invertebrates

※ 30 cm / 0.5-70? m

Diadema setosum
Riccio diadema
Diadem sea urchin
Diademseeigel
Oursin-diadème

Feeds on algae and coral polyps

✳ 50 cm / 2-25 m

Acanthaster planci
Stella corona di spine
Crown-of-thorns starfish
Dornenkronenseestern
Étoile couronne d'épines

Feeds on coral polyps

◖◗ 35 cm / 0-15 m

Tridacna maxima
Tridacna
Giant clam
Riesenmuschel
Bénitier

Feeds on plankton

Ok? / Ok.
Ok? / Ok.
Ok? / Ok.
Ok? / Ok.

Mantenere questa quota.
Level off.
In dieser Tiefe bleiben.
Rester a ce niveau.

Quanta aria hai?
How much air have you?
Wieviel Luft hast du?
Combien d'air as tu?

Scendere.
Going down.
Abtauchen.
Descendre.

Problema alle orecchie.
Ears not clearing.
Kein Druck-ausgleich.
Problème d'oreille.

100 bars.
100 bars.
100 bars.
100 bars.

50 bars.
50 bars.
50 bars.
50 bars.

Risalire.
Going up.
Auftauchen.
Remonter.

Guarda.
Look.
Schau.
Regarde.

Poca aria.
Low on air.
Luftreserve erreicht.
Plus beaucoup d'air.

Aria finita.
Out of air.
Keine luft.
Plus d'air.

Qualcosa non va.
Something is wrong.
Irgendetwas stimmt nicht.
Quelque chose ne va pas.

Fine dell'immersione.
End of the dive.
Ende des Tauchgangs.
Fin de palier.

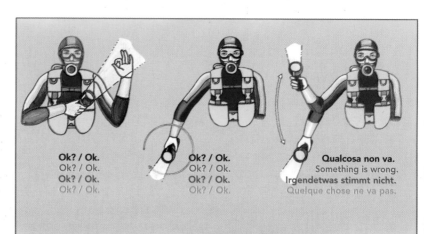

Ok? / Ok.
Ok? / Ok.
Ok? / Ok.
Ok? / Ok.

Ok? / Ok.
Ok? / Ok.
Ok? / Ok.
Ok? / Ok.

Qualcosa non va.
Something is wrong.
Irgendetwas stimmt nicht.
Quelque chose ne va pas.

Aquila di mare
Eagle ray
Gefleckter Adlerrochen
Raie-léopard

Barracuda
Barracuda
Barrakuda
Barracuda

Pesce di vetro
Glassfish
Glasfische
Poisson de verre

Pesce leone
Lionfish
Rotfeuerfisch
Rascasse volante

Manta gigante
Manta ray
Mantarochen
Raie manta

Murena
Moray
Muräne
Murène

Squalo martello
Hammerhead shark
Hammerhai
Requin-marteau

Pesce Napoleone
Napoleonfish
Napoleonlippfisch
Poisson-Napoléon

Nudibranco
Nudibranch
Nacktkiemer
Nudibranche

Squalo
Shark
Hai
Requin

Tartaruga
Turtle
Schildkröte
Tortue

Tonno
Tuna
Thun
Ton

PRESSURE

In the metric system, pressure (F/S, or the force F exerting on a surface S) is measured in *bar* (from Greek *baros* = heaviness): 1 bar is equivalent to the pressure of 1 kilogram on 1 square centimeter and is equivalent to approximately 1 atmosphere (=1 atm).
In the imperial system, however, pressure is measured in *psi* (*pounds per square inch*, or the pressure of 1 pound on 1 square inch).

1 bar = 14.5 psi
1 psi = 0.069 bar

Example:
200 bar = 2,900 psi

DISTANCE

AT SEA
1 km = 0.54 nmi (*nautical miles*)
1 nmi (*nautical mile*) = 1.85 km

ON LAND
1 km = 0.62 mi (*miles*)
1 mi (*mile*) = 1.61 km

NB. The **knot** (*kn*) is a measure of speed, not of distance, and corresponds to one nautical mile per hour.

LENGTH

1 cm = 0.39 in (*inches*)
1 in (*inch*) = 2.54 cm

1 m = 3.28 ft (*feet*)
1 ft (*foot*) = 0.305 m

1 m = 1.09 ya (*yards*)
1 ya (*yard*) = 0.91 m

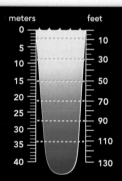

WEIGHT

1 gr = 0.035 oz (*ounces*)
1 oz (*ounce*) = 28.35 gr

1 kg = 2.22 lb (*pounds*)
1 lb (*pound*) = 0.45 kg

TEMPERATURE

0 °C (*degree Celsius or degree centigrade*) = **32 °F** (*degree Fahrenheit*)

from °C to °F   →   multiply by 1.8 and add 32
from °F to °C   →   deduct 32 and divide by 1.8

Example:
100 °C = 212 °F
100 °F = 37,8 °C

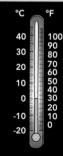

... ... *... ...anual for Monitoring Coral Reefs With Indicator Species. Butterflyfishes as Indicators of Change on Indo Pacific Reefs*, 1996. **Debelius, H.**, *Red Sea Reef Guide*, Frankfurt, 1998. **Harrison, P., Misiewicz, A.**, *Reef Fishes and Corals of the Red Sea*, London, 2000. **Mojetta, A., Ghisotti, A.**, *Pesci e coralli del Mar Rosso*, Milano, 1996. **Randall, J.E.**, *Sharks of Arabia*, London, 1986. **Randall, J.E.**, *Red Sea Reef Fishes*, London, 1983. **Sheppard, C., Price, A., Roberts, C.**, *Marine Ecology of the Arabian Region*, London, 1992. **Siliotti, A.**, *Sharm el-Sheikh Diving Guide*, Verona, 1999. **Siliotti, A.**, *Pesci del Mar Rosso*, Verona, 2002. **Siliotti, A.**, *SS Thistlegorm & Rosalie Moller, I Grandi Relitti del Mar Rosso*, Verona, 2003. **Siliotti, A.**, *Mar Rosso, Giardino di Corallo*, Verona, 2004.

WEB SITES

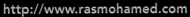

http://www. goredsea.com

A comprehensive site for all indispensable information about the Sinai and the Red Sea.

http://www. diversalertnetwork.org

Official DAN site with all information on safety, the medical aspects of diving and insurance cover.

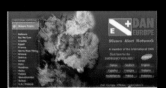

http://www.rasmohamed.com

Official Site of the Ras Mohammed Park with information on different ecosystems, marine biology and some information on diving sites in the protected area.

http://touregypt.net/sinai.htm

Official site giving comprehensive information on main locations and tourist sites of interest in the Sinai.

http://www.eeaa.gov.eg/English/main/Protectorates

Official site of the Ministry of Environment offering interesting information about protected areas and biodiversity in Egypt.

http://sinai4you.com/sinai/links.htm

Complete site about the Sinai giving information and photographs of the desert, Bedouins, sea as well as numerous links to other very interesting sites.

www. wunderground.com/global/stations/62460.com

Complete site on meteorology of the Sinai and the Red Sea. Very accurate weekly weather forecasts.

THE DIVE SITES

STRAIT OF TIRAN

The Strait of Tiran lies at the mouth of the Gulf of Aqaba and is bounded on the west by the coast of Sinai and on the east by the island of Tiran. In the middle of this channel are four coral reefs lying in a northeast-southwest direction that were named after the 19th century English cartographers who drew the first nautical map of this region: **Jackson Reef**, **Woodhouse Reef**, **Thomas Reef** and **Gordon Reef**.

These reefs divide the strait into two canals: to the east is the so-called *Grafton Passage*, which is used exclusively by ships going northwards, while to the west is the *Enterprise Passage* for ships heading south. East of the island of Tiran and the nearby island of Sanafir – both part of Saudi Arabia but granted to Egypt – the configuration of the canal floor makes navigation impossible.

On a level with the Strait of Tiran, the Gulf of Aqaba is reduced from an average width of 10–12 miles to 2.4 miles, while the seabed ranges from a depth of 1,270 meters to 250 meters in Enterprise Passage and a mere 71 meters in Grafton Passage. On the one hand this particular configuration of the strait reduces deep water exchange between the

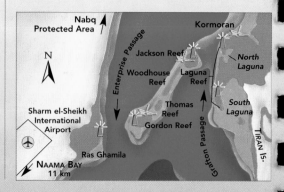

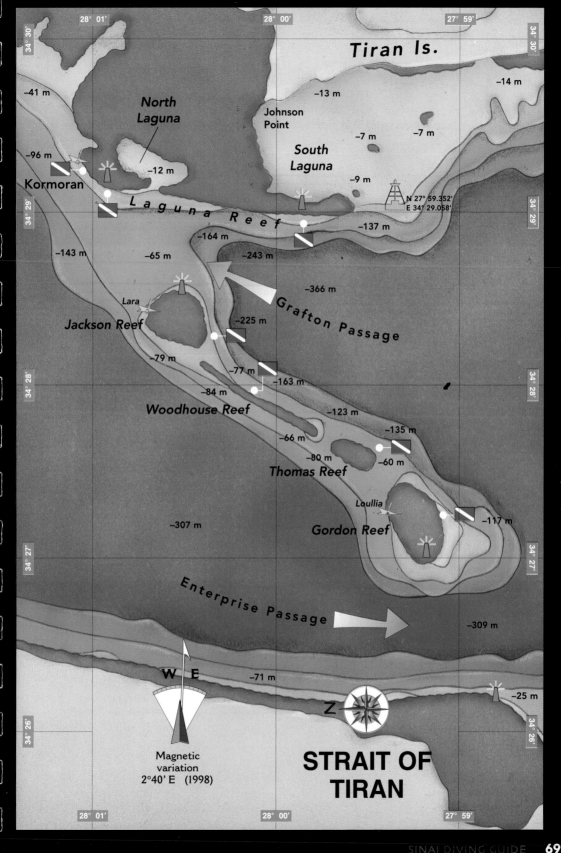

Tiran Is.

−14 m

−41 m

North Laguna

Johnson Point

−13 m

−96 m

Kormoran

−12 m

−7 m

−7 m

South Laguna

−9 m

N 27° 59.352'
E 34° 29.058'

L a g u n a   R e e f

−137 m

−164 m

−143 m

−65 m

−243 m

−366 m

Lara

Grafton Passage

Jackson Reef

−225 m

−79 m

−77 m

−163 m

−84 m

−123 m

Woodhouse Reef

−135 m

−66 m

−80 m

−60 m

Thomas Reef

Loullia

−307 m

Gordon Reef

−117 m

Enterprise Passage

−309 m

W   E

−71 m

−25 m

Z

Magnetic
variation
2°40' E   (1998)

STRAIT OF TIRAN

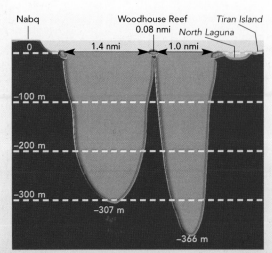

Cross-section of the Strait of Tiran at the level of
Woodhouse Reef (mni=nautical mile)

Gulf of Aqaba and the rest of the Red Sea, causing
an increase of salinity and temperature; on the other
it gives rise also to an increase in the speed of the
tidal currents and the average height of the waves
moved by the wind which, channelled, as it is, by the
tall mountains of Sinai and Saudi Arabia, is in turn
subject to acceleration.

The peculiar topographical arrangement of
these reefs and the presence of prevailing winds
coming from the north, which are stronger in the
morning and calmer in the afternoon, means their
western and northern sides (known as the 'outside')
are much more exposed to the action of the waves
than the eastern and southern ones, which are
'inside' and sheltered.

The strong currents characterizing the Strait of

Strait of Tiran	Snorkeling	Open Water	Advanced Open Water
Jackson Reef	●	●	
Kormoran		●	
Laguna Reef		●	
Woodhouse Reef			●
Thomas Reef			●
Gordon Reef	●	●	

🤿 Snorkeling   Open Water   Advanced Open Water

THE WRECKS OF TIRAN

Apart from the wreck of **Loullia**, **Lara** and **Kormoran**
which will be dealt with in the respective chapters, there
are also other wrecks in the Strait of Tiran. Here is a list:

Maria Schroeder (ex Rolf Jarl) N 28° 11.329'–E 34° 26.523'
Year of construction: 1920
Place of construction: Trondheim (Norway)
Ran aground on the reef in Nabq 11th April 1956

Anghia Vivara (or Aghia Varvara) N 28° 03.700'–E 34° 26.677'
Year of construction: 1950
Length: 76 m
Owned by Gestar Shipping Co. of Famagosta (Cyprus)
Ran aground on the reef in Nabq 27th June 1976

Hey Daroma (ex Lairds Loch) N 28° 03.482'–E 34° 26.398'
Year of construction: 1940
Length: 90.5 m
Displacement: 1,736 t
Owned by Sefinot Ltd of Eilat (Israel)
Ran aground on the reef in Nabq in September 1970

Million Hope (ex Ryusei Maru) N 28° 03.482'–E 34° 26.398'
Year of construction: 1972
Length: 174.6 m
Displacement: 26,000 t
Ran aground south of Nabq on 20th June 1996 exactly
above the wreck of Hey Daroma

Israeli War Ship
Located not far from the Laguna Reef lighthouse.
Yet to be found

Niger Basin
Sank in May 1982 close to Gordon Reef.
Yet to be found

Ralai
Sank in April 1983 close to Gordon Reef.
Yet to be found

Tiran transport great quantities of plankton and
other nutrient material every day, thus supplying
a great deal of food to the corals and hence to the
reef fish, which in turn are eaten by the large pelagic
predators such as barracuda, jackfish, tuna and
above all sharks, which are always present in this
zone. Consequently, scuba divers in the waters of
Tiran are sure to see not only an infinite number of
corals but also rich fauna, both reef and pelagic.
However, they must always be careful of the wind,
tides and currents here, which will condition the
time, place and type of dive.

THE ISLAND OF TIRAN

The Island of Tiran, shaped like an orange segment, is situated at the entrance to the Gulf of Aqaba. Together with the smaller and less well-known island of Sanafir, situated east of Tiran Island, they constitute an integral part of the Ras Mohammed National Park.
Tiran has a territory of 3,100 hectares; its northern part is low and sandy whereas the rest of the island is mountainous with two peaks, Gebel Tiran (525 meters) and the smaller Gebel el-Madhbah (235 meters).
On the western side of Tiran opens a vast bay towards the north called Foul Bay, and to the south we find numerous mangroves (Avicennia sp.) hosting a small population of dugongs (Dugong dugon).
Eight bird species nest in Tiran (Western reef heron or Egretta gularis, Spoonbill or Platalea leucorodia,

Osprey
(Pandion
haliaetus)

White-eyed gull or Larus leucophtalmus, Striated heron or Butorides striatus, White-chekeed tern or Sterna repressa, Lesser crested tern or Sterna bengalensis, Caspian tern or Sterna caspia and Sooty falcon Falco concolor) and the big Osprey (Pandion haliaetus) is a common visitor.
The islands of Tiran and Sanafir belong in reality to Saudi Arabia but they were given as a concession to Egypt for their strategic importance.
In fact, there is an observation post for the MFO (Multinational Force & Observers) on the western side of Tiran Island. It is called Observation Post 3–11 and is situated at a height of 240 meters with a permanent resident team of three military personnel (an officer and two soldiers) who are observing and controlling the navigation of ships in the Strait.
The transportation of these observers, who are substituted every three days, as well as maintaining their supply of food and water, is done by helicopter. On the western side of the island is a huge buoy

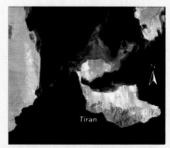

View of Tiran Island taken by Landsat 7

anchored to the seabed at 50 meters. This is a mooring for three ships donated by the Italian Navy and at the disposal of the MFO to control the movements of the ships in the Strait and they are ready to intervene in case of need.
There is also an Egyptian military emplacement at the extreme western side of Tiran close to the coast.
Tiran and Sanafir are considered military zones and going ashore is not allowed. Furthermore you should not forget that apart from sandy beaches, Tiran still has landmines in numerous places.

Foul Bay

Gebel Tiran
▲ 532 m

Gebel el-Madhbah
▲ 235 m

Chisholm Point

North Laguna

South Laguna

Johnson Point

Jackson Reef

N

Aerial view of Jackson Reef

J ackson Reef is the most northerly reef in Tiran and is known for the wreck, partially demolished in 1996, of the Cypriot merchant ship Lara (a cargo boat of 4,752 tonnes), which sank here in December 1981. Diving here usually begins on the southern side, which is sheltered from the waves and wind and where there are some fixed moorings not far from the reef.

The reef on the southern side in the shallows is cut with sandy splits, then descends steeply to the sandy seabed at a depth of 45 meters where we can admire some shy Garden eels (*Gorgasia sillneri*). Going westwards (dive **A**), you will see some gorgonians and a splendid red anemone at a depth of 28 meters. This is followed by a plateau that connects to Woodhouse Reef by a saddle. The southwest corner of Jackson Reef, where numerous fire corals (*Millepora dichotoma*) can be seen, is subject to currents which can be extremely violent. If conditions are right (especially when the tide is ebbing), it is possible to make a drift dive on the eastern part of the reef (dive **B**). Here, about 15 meters down, is a sandy ledge that sinks into the blue to the north. It is quite easy to spot turtles (*Eretmochelys* sp.)

Scalloped hammerhead shark (Sphyrna lewini)

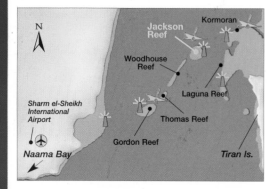

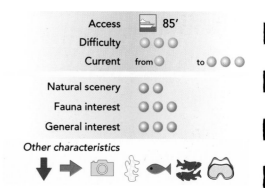

Access	🛥️ 85′
Difficulty	○ ○ ○
Current	from ○ to ○ ○ ○

Natural scenery	○ ○
Fauna interest	○ ○ ○
General interest	○ ○ ○

Other characteristics

⬇️ ➡️ 📷 🪸 🐟 🐠 ⛑️

The remains of the Lara *after some partial demolitions that made the wreck unrecognizable: the propeller is situated at a depth of 56 meters*

and large pelagic fish in this zone: Whitetip reef sharks (*Triaenodon obesus*), Grey reef sharks (*Carcharhinus amblyrhynchos*) and Scalloped hammerhead (*Sphyrna lewini*), are especially common at this point from July to September, as well as regular sightings of them on the northern side of the reef, out in the blue from the wreck of the Lara at a depth between 10 to 30 meters.

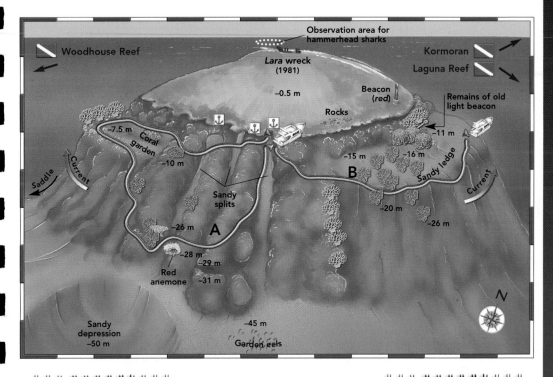

Comments

• *Diving difficulty varies according to sea conditions.*
• *Currents may become very strong.*
• *This site is often crowded.*

Look out for

Gorgonian   Fire coral   Turbinaria

Anemonefish   Turtle   Whitetip reef shark

Grey reef shark   Hammerhead shark   Garden eel

Features

• *An abundance of pelagic and predatory fish.*
• *Turtles and sharks can be observed.*
• *You can make different types of dive.*
• *Suitable for snorkeling and mooring for lunch.*

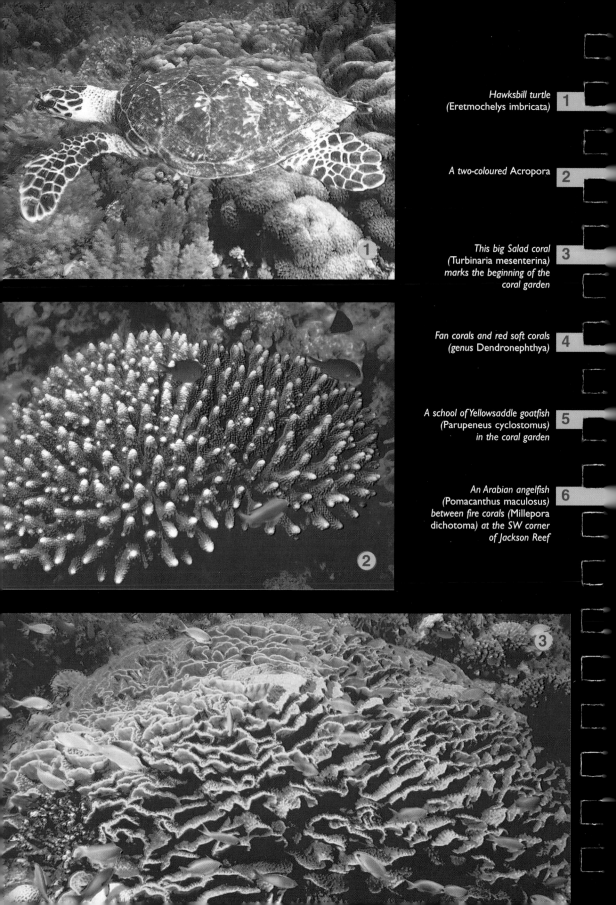

Hawksbill turtle
(Eretmochelys imbricata) **1**

A two-coloured Acropora **2**

This big Salad coral
(Turbinaria mesenterina) **3**
marks the beginning of the
coral garden

Fan corals and red soft corals
(genus Dendronephthya) **4**

A school of Yellowsaddle goatfish
(Parupeneus cyclostomus) **5**
in the coral garden

An Arabian angelfish
(Pomacanthus maculosus) **6**
between fire corals (Millepora
dichotoma) at the SW corner
of Jackson Reef

28°01.063' N — 34°29.242' E

The big winch visible on the deck of the wreck is still perfectly conserved

In August 1984 the ship *Kormoran*, built in 1963 in the Rostock shipyards (Germany) was coming from Aqaba with a cargo of phosphate when an error in navigation caused it to hit the northern side of the reef bordering the island of Tiran, known by divers as *Laguna Reef*. The impact was tremendous and the vessel, which in 1980 had been renamed *Zingara*, lost almost all of its bow, two large cracks opened on its left side and the superstructure was irreparably damaged.

Now scuba divers at Sharm el-Sheikh can enjoy the interesting experience of going to see this wreck, which is still relatively unknown.
A few minutes from the North Laguna beacon, lying in the shallows less than 12 meters, the *Kormoran*, which is about 80 meters long, is easy to find because its stern is partly above the surface.

There is no difficulty in diving here, but it must be done when the sea is calm to ensure good visibility. The best conditions for a dive are usually in the afternoon, when the tide changes and the current is at its slowest.
The stern, propeller, 6-cylinder engine that once enabled the ship to achieve a

KORMORAN

Type of ship: merchant
Year of construction: 1963
Length: 82.4 m
Width: 12.7 m
Tonnage: 2.733 t
Date of shipwreck:
    22nd August 1984
Depth: 0–12 m

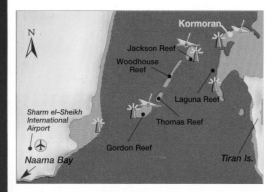

Kormoran
Jackson Reef
Woodhouse Reef
Laguna Reef
Sharm el–Sheikh International Airport
Thomas Reef
Gordon Reef
Naama Bay
Tiran Is.
N

Access   105'
Difficulty   ○
Current   from ○   to ○ ○ ○

Natural scenery   ○ ○
Fauna interest   ○
General interest   ○ ○

Other characteristics

Bow and propeller of the wreck

speed of 12 knots, rudder and winch on the deck are all well preserved. The name of the ship 'KORMORAN' is still clearly visible on the port side on the left.

The metal structures are colonized by small table corals, pocillopore and surrounded by numerous Sohal surgeonfish (*Acanthurus sohal*) and schools of Yellowfin goatfish (*Mulloidichthys vanicolensis*).

Features

- *The only dive onto a wreck suitable for OW divers.*
- *The wreck is easy to reach and spot.*
- *Some parts of the ship are really well preserved.*
- *Interesting views for photography buffs.*

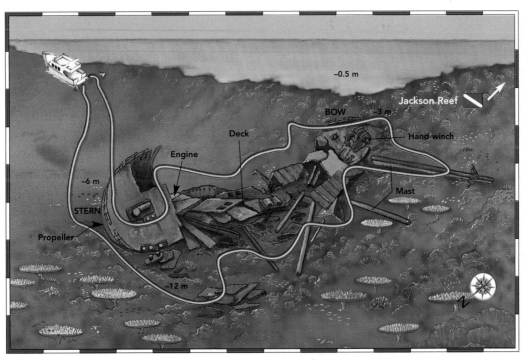

Comments

- *Dives must be made in a calm sea, preferably in the afternoon.*
- *Strong currents possible*
- *Visibility is sometimes poor.*

Look out for

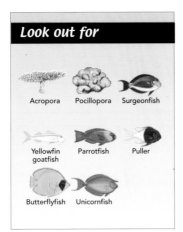

Acropora   Pocillopora   Surgeonfish

Yellowfin goatfish   Parrotfish   Puller

Butterflyfish   Unicornfish

Perfectly conserved anchor winch

Laguna Reef

Aerial view of Laguna Reef

Sanafir Is.

Gebel Tiran
(532 m)

Foul Bay

South Laguna

North Laguna

Kormoran

T he western side of Tiran Island is bordered by a madreporic formation standing over a splendid coral lagoon with an average depth of 10 to 12 meters, and known by scuba divers as *Laguna Reef*. A transverse hard coral wall divides the lagoon in two parts – *North* and *South Laguna* – both of which are marked by a beacon.

South Laguna, the larger of the two and known amongst local fishermen as *Marsa Shabir*, is the best mooring point in the region and offers safe shelter

The green and white beacon of North Laguna

The green beacon of South Laguna

from any unfavourable sea conditions. Its marvellous turquoise waters are a truly unforgettable sight. You can access South Laguna by going round its beacon.

The outer side of Laguna Reef is an interesting dive site in the rea between the North Laguna beacon (which is green and white) and the South Laguna one (green).

This area is strongly influenced by tidal currents which will determine the southerly or northerly direction of your dives, which should be made preferably in the afternoon.

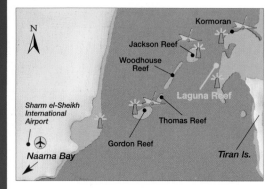

N

Kormoran

Jackson Reef

Woodhouse
Reef

Laguna Reef

Sharm el-Sheikh
International
Airport

Thomas Reef

Gordon Reef

Tiran Is.

Naama Bay

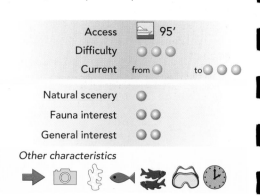

Access	🚤 95'
Difficulty	⬤ ⬤ ⬤
Current	from ⬤ to ⬤ ⬤ ⬤

Natural scenery	⬤
Fauna interest	⬤ ⬤
General interest	⬤ ⬤

Other characteristics

➡ 📷 🪸 🐟 🐠 ⬗ 🕐

A big table coral (Acropora sp.)

South of the South Laguna beacon, at a depth of 15–25 meters, is a wide plateau with large table corals (*Acropora* sp.) that narrows gradually in a northward direction, becoming a steep wall rich in reef fauna that swims among numerous species of hard and soft corals and some gorgonians. Near North Laguna there is another plateau with many colonies of table corals and fire corals.

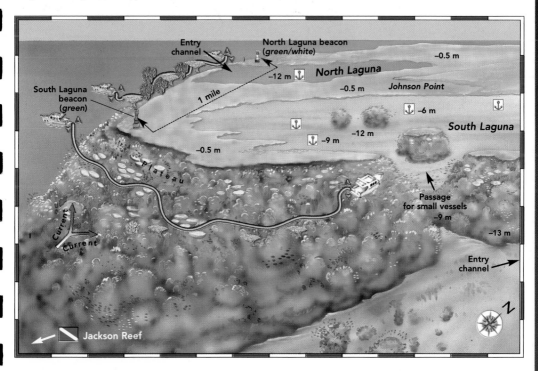

Comments

• *Dives should be made only in suitable weather conditions.*
• *Carefully note the direction of the current before diving.*

Look out for

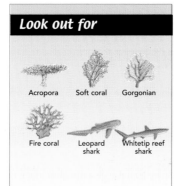

Acropora   Soft coral   Gorgonian

Fire coral   Leopard shark   Whitetip reef shark

Features

• *Rich in coral and reef fauna.*
• *Possibility to observe Leopard sharks (*Stegostoma fasciatum*) and Whitetip reef sharks (*Triaenodon obesus*), especially on the plateau in front of the South Laguna beacon.*
• *A good alternative when the other sites in the strait are too crowded.*

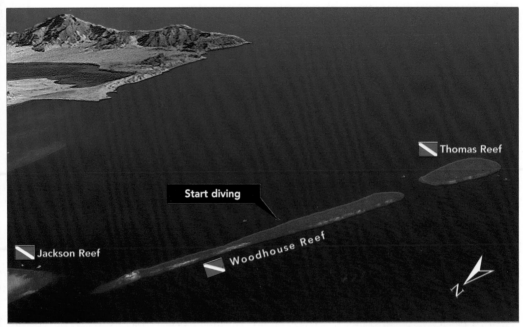

Aerial view of Woodhouse Reef

L ocated between Thomas Reef and Jackson Reef, Woodhouse Reef is narrow and long and thus offers no shelter at all to boats and has no fixed moorings. Consequently scuba divers in this spot must make a drift dive – and this must be done only in good weather conditions. The best time is usually the morning because of the direct sunlight.

The most interesting part of the reef, which is around 0.8 miles long, is the northern half of the eastern side, with a canyon that opens out at a depth of about 30 meters and runs parallel to the main axis of the reef until it reaches a sandy ledge. At the exit of the canyon on its right side you can find a red anemone. The sandy ledge then widens northwards to a depth of 14 meters, leading to the saddle that connects Woodhouse and Jackson reefs. For the entire route the water is remarkably clear and it is quite easy to see jackfish, sea turtles, sharks and a great many corals, both hard and soft, including some colonies of black coral

The canyon of Woodhouse

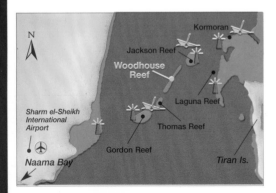

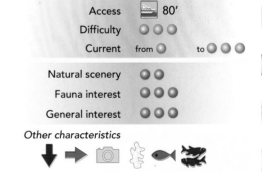

Access	80'
Difficulty	○ ○ ○
Current	from ○ to ○ ○ ○

Natural scenery	○ ○
Fauna interest	○ ○ ○
General interest	○ ○ ○

Other characteristics

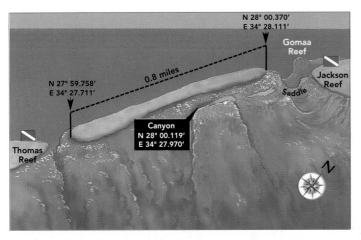

(*Antipathes* sp.) that are at a depth of about 22–26 meters. It is advisable to end your dive before the saddle, especially when the sea is choppy because water turbulence with vortices may be created and you may come upon a dangerous, powerful eddy nicknamed 'the washing machine' by local scuba divers, which can be crossed only in the best weather conditions.

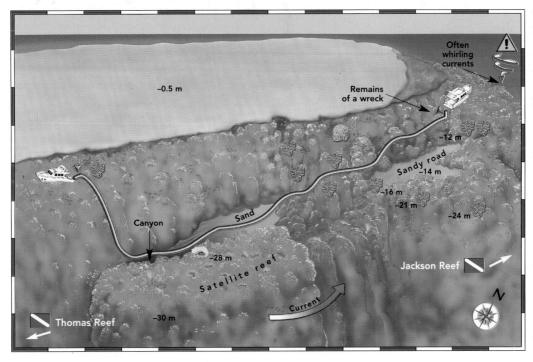

Comments

• Begin the dive after having passed the mid-way point of the reef.
• Avoid venturing far into the canyon.
• Be careful of the current, which tends to get stronger towards the northern end of the reef.

Look out for

Black coral — Gorgonian — Anemonefish

Turtle — Grey reef shark — Whitetip reef shark

Leopard shark — Hammerhead shark — Eagle ray

Features

• One of the best sites for observing sharks (Whitetip reef shark, Grey reef shark, Leopard shark and Hammerhead shark), Spotted eagle rays (Aetobatus narinari) and sea turtles (Eretmochelys sp.).
• An abundance of corals.
• The marine environment is beautiful, especially around the canyon.

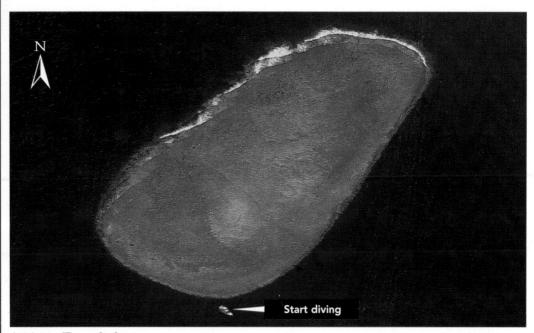

Aerial view of Thomas Reef

This reef is one of the most spectacular diving sites in the northern Red Sea. The lack of mooring points makes drift diving necessary: the southern corner of the reef is the classic starting point for your underwater itinerary, which continues along the eastern side where the wall, rich in multicoloured coral, descends to a sandy plateau that begins at a depth of about 25 meters and has a slight incline. Here on the wall you can see large Alcyonarians (*Dendronephthya* sp.), impressive gorgonians and whip corals, colonies of black coral (genus *Antipathes*) and other Antipatharians (genus *Cirrhipathes*) with their characteristic spiral shape. After passing a double line of gorgonians, at 35 meters a splendid and extremely deep canyon opens out, running

The deep canyon of Thomas Reef

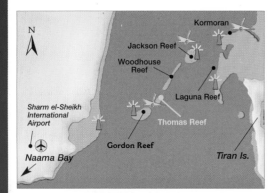

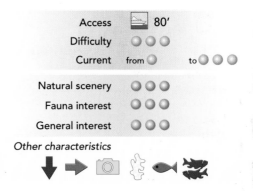

Access	80'			
Difficulty	○ ○ ○			
Current	from ○		to ○ ○ ○	
Natural scenery	○ ○ ○			
Fauna interest	○ ○ ○			
General interest	○ ○ ○			

Other characteristics

parallel to the reef and crossed by three impressive arches. At the eastern corner of the reef you may come upon a very strong counter-current. If you can get past this point and conditions are favourable, you can go around the entire reef. This will allow you to explore the northern wall, which has some nice shelters and splits, and the western one, where you will see many crevices and caves, and a wealth of fauna

consisting of sea turtles, reef fish and pelagics.

Whip corals (Juncella sp.)

Features
• *An extraordinary, grandiose marine environment.*
• *You may come upon an exceptional array of fauna, with large pelagic fish, especially the Whitetip reef shark* (Triaenodon obesus).

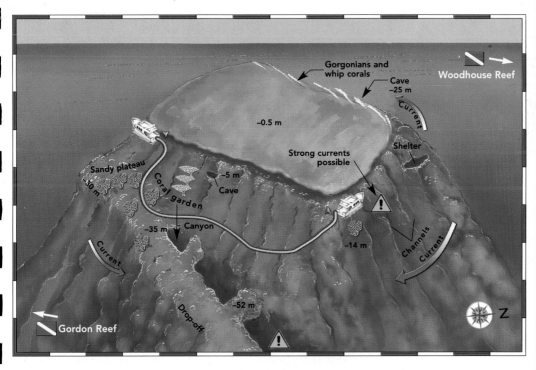

Comments
• *Diving here is only for experienced divers because of the possibility of strong currents.*
• *In general the morning is the best time for diving.*
• *Avoid venturing far into the canyon.*

Look out for
Soft coral Gorgonian Black coral
Turtle Angelfish Grouper
Surgeonfish Barracuda Whitetip reef shark

A Common lionfish (Pterois miles) on some soft corals

5 Thomas Reef
27°59.437' N — 34°27.644' E

SINAI DIVING GUIDE **83**

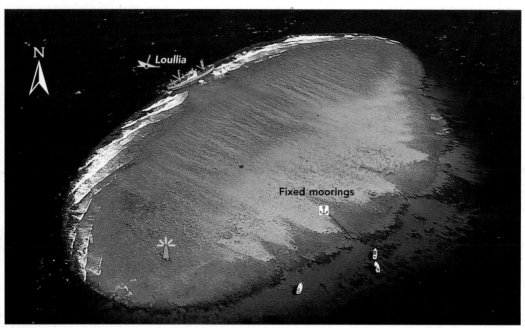

Aerial view of Gordon Reef

Loullia

Fixed moorings

Gordon Reef is known and easily identified by the wreck of the Panamanian cargo ship *Loullia* (3,461 tonnes), which ran aground on the northern end in September 1981. The fact that there is a fixed mooring on the southern side and a wide and rather shallow (10–24 meters) plateau that fans out in a south-westerly direction, makes this dive site safer than the preceding ones. A red and white beacon lies on the south-western corner. The first dive (**A**) starts off from the mooring point and winds in an easterly direction and then northwards along the eastern side of the reef. Halfway along this side you can see many metal drums scattered at a depth of 10 to 20 meters. From here you can either double back to the starting point or make a drift dive and proceed north (dive **B**); in this case you will come across a rather small sandy plateau on which some Garden eels (*Gorgasia sillneri*) live. On the third dive (**C**) you

The wreck of the Loullia, run aground in 1981, looks like this today: the bow has been separated due to the collision with another vessel in 2000

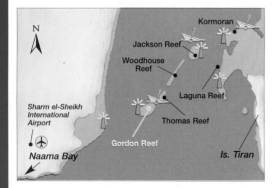

Kormoran

Jackson Reef

Woodhouse Reef

Laguna Reef

Sharm el-Sheikh International Airport

Thomas Reef

Gordon Reef

Naama Bay

Is. Tiran

Access	🚢 75'	
Difficulty	from ◐◐	to ◐◐◐
Current	from ◐	to ◐◐◐

Natural scenery	◐◐
Fauna interest	◐◐◐
General interest	◐◐◐

Other characteristics

➡️ 📷 🪸 🐟 🐠

can explore the vast plateau that extends in a southerly direction. After reaching the sand-filled depression with a vaguely circular shape (known as the 'Amphitheater' or 'Shark Pool') you will pass by a mass of cables and metal bars. From here you can go back to the starting point either by heading towards the reef or, after crossing a zone filled with fire corals (*Millepora dichotoma*), by drift diving along the western side.

The beacon of Gordon Reef and, to the left, the rest of the metallic structure of the old one

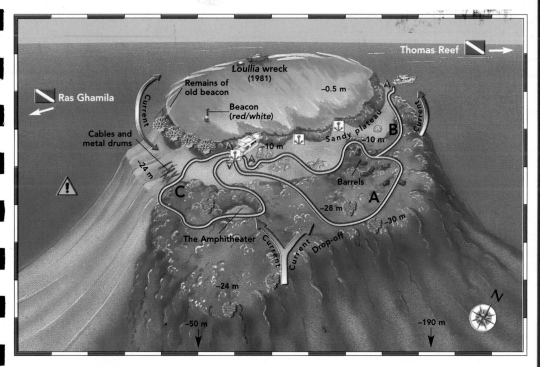

Comments

- *Beware of the current at the south-western corner of the reef, near the beacon, as it could make it hard to return to your boat or even prevent you from doing so.*

Look out for

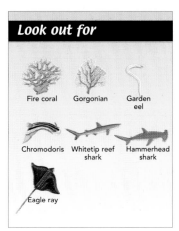

Fire coral — Gorgonian — Garden eel

Chromodoris — Whitetip reef shark — Hammerhead shark

Eagle ray

Features

- *The opportunity to observe various species of coral, small nudibranchs hidden in the crevices of the madrepores and, with a bit of luck, Whitetip reef sharks, Hammerhead sharks and Spotted eagle rays.*
- *This site is suitable for snorkeling.*
- *Safe mooring sheltered from the wind.*

2005

1995

1

2

The wreck of the Loullia in 1995 and ten years later **1**

A couple of Scribbled filefish (Aluterus scriptus) and a small Striped butterflyfish (Chaetodon fasciatus) swim above Porites corals **2**

Numerous metal drums are visible on the south-eastern side of the reef **3**

Emperor angelfish (Pomacanthus imperator) between white soft corals **4**

Tar and bitumen flows out of one of the metal drums **5**

Scalefin anthias (Pseudanthias squamipinnis) over a coral bank **6**

3

SHARM EL-SHEIKH LOCAL DIVES

The generic name 'Local Dives' (due to their closeness to Sharm) covers all the shore diving sites north and south of Naama Bay between the Strait of Tiran and the little town of Sharm el-Sheikh.

Naama Bay, still a desert at the end of the eighties, is now a famous international tourist resort. This splendid bay was originally called *Marsa el-Aat*, situated at the outlet of *Wadi el-Aat*.

Naama Bay has one of two jetties that diving boats in the area usually embark from: the other, Travco Marina, is situated to the southwest in the bay of Sharm el-Sheikh, known locally as *Sharm el-Maya*, or the 'bay of the harbour' due to the large tourist port which is also present.

You reach the different local dive sites from Naama Bay following a boat ride that may take anywhere from 10 to 70 minutes. North of Naama Bay there are nine diving spots on a 7.5 mile stretch of coast. **Ras Ghamila**, the furthest away, lies almost directly opposite Gordon Reef; **Ras Nasrani** is on a level to the international airport; the others, within a short distance of each other are **Ras Bob**, **White Knight**, **Shark's Bay**, **Far Garden**, **Fiddle Garden**, **Middle Garden** and **Near Garden** (corresponding to the northerly tip of Naama Bay).

South of Naama Bay are a further nine diving sites: **Sodfa**, **Tower**, **Pinky Wall**, **Amphoras**, **Turtle Bay**, **Paradise**, **Ras Umm Sid**, **Temple** and **Ras Katy**. The last-mentioned site corresponds to the northerly tip of the Sharm el-Maya Bay.

Generally speaking, besides their vicinity to Naama Bay, these diving sites have other features in common due to their position, sheltered from waves and strong currents, and to the configuration of the fringing reef, which has found an ideal

N

Shark's Bay

Far Garden

Fiddle Garden

Middle Garden

Near Garden

Naama Bay

Jetty

SHARM EL-SHEIKH
LOCAL DIVES

Hotels and Resorts along the coast

1. Solymar Belvedere
2. Conrad Sharm el-Sheikh Resort
3. Baron Sharm el-Sheikh Resort
4. Melia Sinai Paradise
5. Hilton Sharks Bay
6. Concord El-Salam
7. Maxim Plaza White Knight Res.
8. Savoy Sharm el-Sheikh
9. Four Season Resort
10. Tropicana Grand Oasis Resort
11. Royal Rojana Resort
12. Shark's Bay Oasis Resort
13. Pyramisa Resort
14. Holiday Inn Resort
15. Coral beach Tiran
16. Mövenpick Jolie Ville Golf Res.
17. Sinai Groove
18. Sinai Grand
19. Maxi Grand
20. Domina Coral Bay Resort
21. Sheraton Al Pacha Resort
22. Crowne Plaza Resort
23. Intercontinental Garden Reef Resort
24. Hyatt Regency Resort
25. Sofitel Beach Resort
26. Sonesta Beach Resort
27. Oonas Hotel
28. Days Inn Gafy Resort
29. Al Bostan Hotel
30. Marriot Beach Resort
31. Novotel Sharm el-Sheikh
32. Hilton Fayrouz Resort
33. Ghazala Hotel
34. Mövenpick Jolie Ville
35. Helnan Marina Sharm
36. Lido Sharm Iberotel
37. Halomy Sharm Hotel
38. Sharm Club
39. Tower Club & Resort
40. Dreams Vacation
41. Dreams Beach Resort
42. Haloha Club Resort
43. Amphoras Holiday Inn Resort
44. The Ritz-Carlton Hotel
45. Iberotel Grand Sharm
46. Queen Sharm
47. Kirosez Three Corners Beach Club
48. Royal Paradise Resort
49. Hilton Waterfalls Resort
50. Renaissance Golden View Beach Resort Sharm el-Sheikh Marriott
51. Iberotel Club Fanara
52. Reef Oasis Hotel
53. El-Farana King Snefru Hotel
54. Beach Albatros Resort
55. Sethi Sharm Hotel
56. Iberotel Palace Sharm el-Sheikh
57. Turquoise Beach Resort

Magnetic variation:
2°40′ E (1998)

Marina TRAVCO
Hyperbaric chamber
Search & Rescue

SHARM EL-SHEIKH

Sharm el-Mina
Sharm el-Maya
−91 m
Ras Katy
Temple
Ras Umm Sid
Paradise
Turtle Bay
Amphoras
Pinky Wall
Tower
Sodfa
−930 m

NAAMA BAY
Marsa el-Aat

Near Garden
Middle Garden
Fiddle Garden
Far Garden

Coral Bay
Marsa Umm Mureika
−1,370 m

Shark's Bay

White Knight
−1,090 m

Ras Bob
Ras Nasrani

Ras Ghamila
−221 m

Sharm el-Sheikh International Airport

Sharm el-Sheikh Local Dives	Snorkeling	Open Water	Advanced Open Water
Ras Ghamila	●	●	
Ras Nasrani	●	●	
Ras Bob	●	●	
White Knight	●		●
Shark's Bay	●	●	
Far Garden	●		●
Fiddle Garden	●	●	
Middle Garden	●	●	
Near Garden	●	●	
Sodfa	●	●	
Tower	●		●
Pinky Wall			●
Amphoras	●	●	
Turtle Bay	●	●	
Paradise	●	●	
Ras Umm Sid	●		●
Temple		●	
Ras Katy	●	●	

Legend: Snorkeling · Open Water · Advanced Open Water

ecosystem for its growth along this stretch of coast. Diving here can be enjoyed by divers at all levels and, in good conditions, you can observe many genera of madrepores (hard corals), innumerable varieties of Alcyonarians (soft corals) and an almost complete range of reef fish, from the small anthias to the large Napoleonfish (*Cheilinus undulatus*), multi-coloured butterflyfish and angelfish to parrotfish, triggerfish to surgeonfish.

A Masked butterflyfish (Chaetodon semilarvatus)

Aerial view of Travco Marina in Sharm el-Sheikh bay

Satellite view of the coast from Ras Umm Sid to Shark's Bay

Navigation times (from Naama Bay)	
Ras Ghamila	70'
Ras Nasrani	60'
Ras Bob	58'
White Knight	55'
Shark's Bay	30'
Far Garden	20'
Fiddle Garden	18'
Middle Garden	15'
Near Garden	10'
Sodfa	15'
Tower	20'
Pinky Wall	22'
Amphoras	23'
Turtle Bay	35'
Paradise	36'
Ras Umm Sid	38'
Temple	43'
Ras Katy	45'

Aerial view of the southern part of Naama Bay showing the jetty

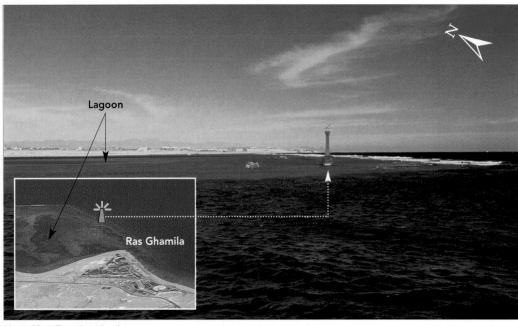

View of Ras Ghamila and its beacon

The name 'Ras Ghamila', ('Delightful Cape' in Arabic) is not on official maps, but is used by divers to indicate the tongue of reef that juts out eastwards and supports the green beacon marking the western end of the Strait of Tiran. All the ships that come down from the ports of Aqaba and Eilat must pass between this beacon and the red and white one on Gordon Reef. The coral reef of Ras Ghamila separates a vast and rather shallow sandy lagoon from the sea.
Ras Ghamila is an interesting place for a fine drift dive that is not too difficult. The classic dive, which must be followed in any case when the tide is swelling, begins immediately after you have passed the hotel structures of the Conrad Resort; from this point you dive onto a vast sandy plateau with a slight incline, staying at a depth of about 15 meters, and then continue in a sort of gliding motion northwards, parallel to the edge of the reef at a level with the beacon. On the gentle slope of the reef, which descends to an average depth of about 8 meters, there are many large colonies of Porites coral and some Giant triggerfish (Balistoides viridescens) often pass by, while on the plateau there are large Acropora corals (table corals), around which schools of pelagic fish swim.

Coral grouper (Cephalopholis miniata)

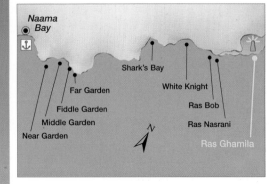

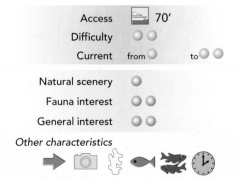

Access		70'	
Difficulty	○ ○		
Current	from ○	to	○ ○

Natural scenery	○
Fauna interest	○ ○
General interest	○ ○

Other characteristics

Table corals (Acropora sp.)

Features

- The dives here are usually easy and pleasant and allow you to observe many coral colonies and mixed fauna, both reef and pelagic.
- The site is usually not crowded.

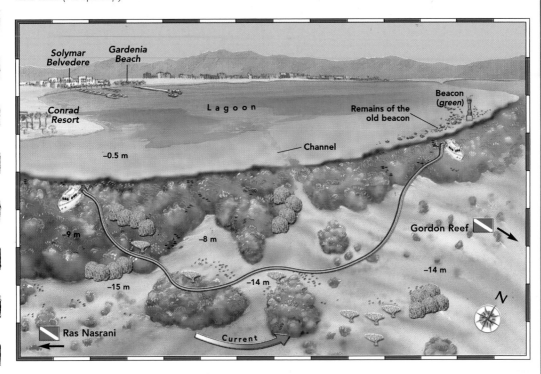

Solymar Belvedere
Gardenia Beach
Conrad Resort
L a g o o n
−0.5 m
Channel
Remains of the old beacon
Beacon (green)
−9 m
−8 m
−15 m
−14 m
Gordon Reef
−14 m
Ras Nasrani
Current
N

Comments

- You need not venture far from the slope of the reef to observe coral formations and the reef and pelagic species that move around the plateau.
- When you are close to the beacon, go straight to the open sea to facilitate your return to the boat.
The current may be strong.

Look out for

Porites   Acropora   Parrotfish

Butterflyfish   Angelfish   Grouper

Triggerfish   Trevally   Barracuda

Ras Ghamila beacon

Ras Nasrani with its distinctive "lighthouse" building

Melia Sinai Resort

The name of this locality means 'Christian Cape' in Arabic. It lies 11 kilometers north of Naama Bay and immediately south of Ras Ghamila. Ras Nasrani can also be reached by land: take the road leading to the *Baron* and *Conrad* resorts.
However, the classic dive is usually made from boats, either as a drift or mooring dive. Start the dive from the floating pontoon close to the big hard coral ridge above a shelter that opens at a depth of 30 meters and then come up slowly towards a submersed sandy

bay. At a depth of 12.5 meters on the northern side of the bay you can see a lovely example of a red anemone. Beyond this

The red anemone of Ras Nasrani

point the sand gives way to the corals. You then head northwards, keeping the reef to your left and taking advantage of the current, which ranges from weak to moderate and tends to get faster near the headland. After you have passed some large gorgonians located at about 20 meters, you will come upon large colonies of massive hard corals of the genus *Porites* that form extensive banks; these become even more numerous beyond the headland. The dive goes through the zone between the reef slope, which has many small crevices studded with

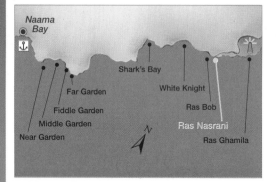

Naama Bay

Shark's Bay

Far Garden

White Knight

Fiddle Garden

Ras Bob

Middle Garden

Near Garden

Ras Nasrani

Ras Ghamila

N

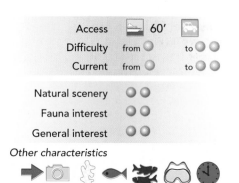

Access   60'

Difficulty   from ○   to ○ ○

Current   from ○   to ○ ○

Natural scenery   ○ ○

Fauna interest   ○ ○

General interest   ○ ○

Other characteristics

A specimen of a Tridacna sp.

multicoloured Alcyonarians, and the drop-off situated about 30 meters away. Ras Nasrani is the ideal spot to observe the giant clam, or bivalve mollusc *Tridacna* sp., as this area has the highest population density of this creature in the entire Red Sea. Sometimes the giant clams, whose mantle take on a blue or greenish colour given by their zooxanthellae, are sandwiched into hard corals of the genus *Porites*.

Features

• *Easy diving which will allow you to observe pelagic and reef fauna.*
• *A good spot for night diving, during which you can see many nudibranchs such as the Spanish dancer (Hexabranchus sanguineus).*
• *You can find numerous crustaceans when looking carefully between the hard corals.*

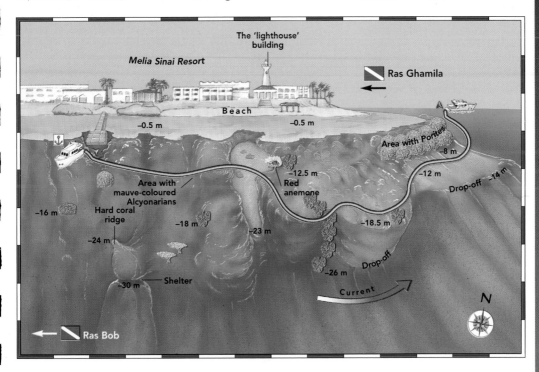

Comments

• *The current may become very strong around the headland.*

Look out for

Gorgonian · Porites · Soft coral

Anemonefish · Giant clam · Spanish dancer

Crustaceans · Trevally · Barracuda

An extensive bank of the massive hard corals (Porites sp.) characteristic to this site

Overview of Ras Bob

Do not bother looking for this name on nautical maps, since not even the locals are familiar with it. It was coined some years ago by some diving instructors at Sharm el-Sheikh to indicate the southernmost part of Ras Nasrani as a tribute to the underwater cameraman Bob Johnson, who worked for years in this area. Ras Bob is sheltered from the waves and wind and usually has weak currents. The classic dive is made from your boat, moored at the shamandura on the floor, at a depth of 20 meters.

The dive runs northeast at a depth of from 15 to 20 meters until you reach the pre-

Lined butterflyfish (Chaetodon lineolatus)

established point of return, following the small reef ledge back. There are many small bays with light-coloured sandy floors in which you will see numerous small caves and gullies in the shallow water (3–6 meters' depth). Crocodilefish (*Papilloculiceps longiceps*) and Bluespotted stingrays (*Taeniura lymma*) often rest on the sand of the inlets.

Snorkelers can skirt the reef both east and west of the fixed mooring to explore the marvellous configuration and admire the many corals, both hard and soft.

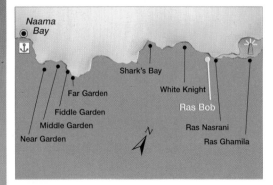

Access	58′
Difficulty	○
Current	○
Natural scenery	○○
Fauna interest	○○
General interest	○○

Other characteristics

Crocodilefish (Papilloculiceps longiceps)

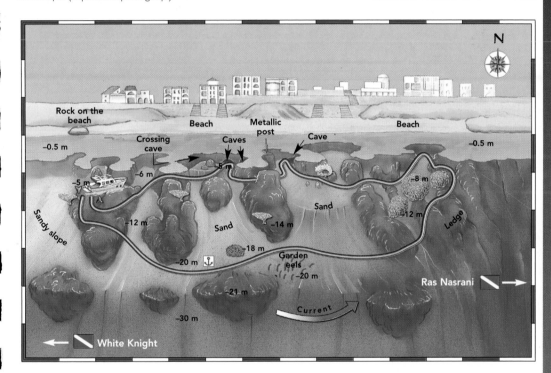

N

Rock on the beach

Beach

Metallic post

Caves

Crossing cave

Cave

Beach

−0.5 m

−0.5 m

−5 m

−6 m

−5 m

−8 m

Sand

Sandy slope

−12 m

Sand

−14 m

−12 m

Ledge

−18 m

Garden eels

−20 m

−20 m

Ras Nasrani

−21 m

−30 m

Current

White Knight

Comments

• The most interesting part of this site is at a depth of 4–12 meters.
• When conditions are suitable, it is possible to make an interesting drift dive reaching the shamandura of Ras Nasrani.

Look out for

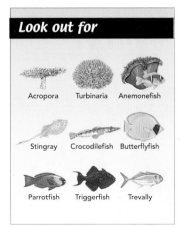

Acropora   Turbinaria   Anemonefish

Stingray   Crocodilefish   Butterflyfish

Parrotfish   Triggerfish   Trevally

Orangestriped triggerfish
(Balistapus undulatus)

The bay of White Knight with the entry from the beach marked by a deep fraction in the reef

White Knight is a small bay bordered by a rather well developed reef with a large crevice that opens onto a sandy plateau from 6 to 18 meters deep. Here there is a mooring point near a colony of Garden eels (*Gorgasia sillneri*). On the southwestern side of the bay, at a depth of 8 meters, is a beautiful canyon with a sandy floor that descends to a depth of 38 meters. The eastern side of this canyon is composed of two hard coral buttresses on which you will see a large Acropora formation

Sabre squirrelfish
(Sargocentron spiniferum)

and a Salad coral (*Turbinaria mesenterina*). Next to the entrance of the canyon is a tunnel that begins at a depth of 10 meters and opens into the canyon at 13 meters. If you descend to 19 meters you will see a metal drum that marks the opening of a cave, whilst at 21 meters on the opposite side there is another cave. Lastly, at 27 meters there is a small ledge over a precipice with a veritable sand flow that inspired the name given to this site a few years ago – 'Wichita Falls'. On the left-hand side of this ledge is the entrance to a third

Naama Bay

Shark's Bay

Far Garden

White Knight

Fiddle Garden

Ras Bob

Middle Garden

Near Garden

Ras Nasrani

Ras Ghamila

Access	🚤	55'
Difficulty	from ○	to ○ ○
Current	○	

Natural scenery	○ ○ ○
Fauna interest	○ ○
General interest	○ ○

Other characteristics

The wreckage of Noose One: *the hull is no longer visible*

cave which, surprisingly, runs steeply upwards.

From the overhang you can either go northwards, doubling back to the starting point, or to the southwest to see the wreck of *Noose One*, a diving boat that sank in 1994 after a fire and that in the summer of 2004 drifted into the blue. Today there are only a few metal pieces left over, cylinders and parts of the engine with little interest.

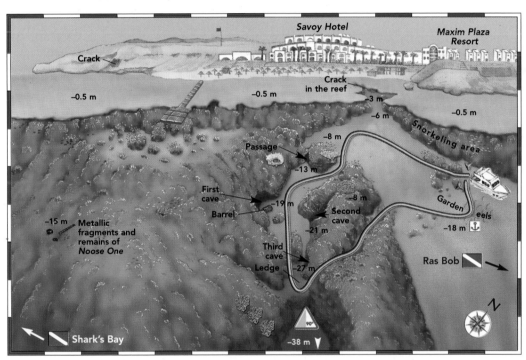

Comments

• *Avoid going below the maximum depth allowed in the canyon (30 meters).*
• *The current is usually weak or non-existent*

Look out for

Acropora   Turbinaria   Anemonefish

Garden eel   Crocodilefish   Manta ray

Features

• *A grandiose, spectacular marine environment.*
• *You can observe interesting corals.*
• *The site is usually well sheltered from the wind and waves.*
• *Manta rays (Manta birostris) may be seen, especially on summer afternoons.*

Jump-About-Gib

Shark's Bay Resort

Royal Rojana Resort

Tropicana Grand Oasis Resort

N

Jetty

Canyon

Overall view of Shark's Bay with its jetty and, on the beach, the boat Jump-About-Gib

C ontrary to what you might expect, Shark's Bay is not frequented by sharks but only by crowds of tourists attracted to the lovely sand beach that borders the entire bay. It seems that the name 'Shark's Bay' derives from the fact that local fishermen once came here to unload the sharks they had caught. At the northern part of the bay is the *Shark's Bay Resort*, which offers accommodation as well as a diving center, supermarket and fish restaurants. At the southern part of the bay, we

A Stonefish (Synanceia verrucosa)

find the beach of the *Pyramisa Resort*, open only to hotel guests. On that beach is an old sailing ship, *Jump-About-Gib*, which hit the reef many years ago and was sequestrated by the Egyptian authorities.
The beach of the *Shark's Bay Resort* (access with entrance fees) allows shore diving, whereas for those diving by boat there is the possibility to moor on one of the fixed shamanduras in the bay.
A small jetty allows the use of Shark's Bay as a starting point for the boats.
The classic dive runs through

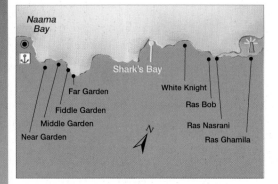

Naama Bay

Shark's Bay

Far Garden

Fiddle Garden

Middle Garden

Near Garden

White Knight

Ras Bob

Ras Nasrani

Ras Ghamila

N

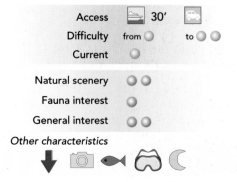

Access	30'
Difficulty	from ○	to ○ ○
Current	○

Natural scenery	○ ○
Fauna interest	○
General interest	○ ○

Other characteristics

A Common lionfish (Pterois miles) between the red soft corals (genus Dendronephthya)

some large coral formations that rise from the sandy floor, sadly disfigured today by numerous waste objects. Here you turn into the entrance of the deep sandy canyon on the south-western side of the bay. After following the canyon for a depth of 30 meters, come slowly up to 18 meters to explore a sandy plateau and the reef ledge, which has a remarkable variety of hard and soft corals (Alcyonarians).

Features

• *A perfect place for beginners or inexperienced divers, and for check dives.*
• *You may see manta rays, especially during the summer.*
• *Very good night diving where you may see many gastropods, echinoderms, lionfish and squids.*

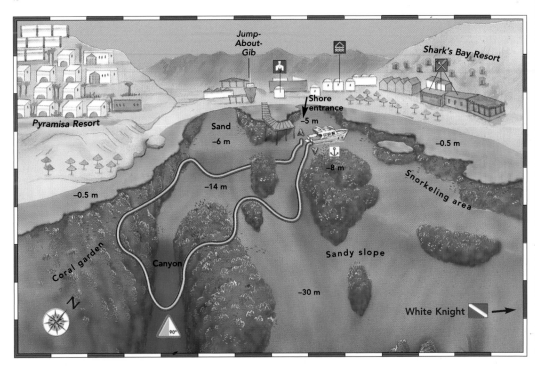

Comments

• *The bay can be very crowded.*
• *Because of widespread plankton the water is sometimes murky (especially in summer).*
• *The sandy floor is not very clean at several points and is covered by waste.*
• *During your night dives you can observe the rare Conus textile, the cone shell.*

Look out for

Soft coral — Cone shell — Sea urchin
Squid — Lionfish — Crocodilefish
Stonefish — Parrotfish — Butterflyfish

The fearsome Textile cone shell (Conus textile)

Crowne Plaza Resort

Floating pontoon

Cave with glassfish

Overview of Far Garden with the hotel structure of the Crowne Plaza Resort

Far Garden is situated in the northernmost part of a splendid bay just north of Naama Bay. Because of the many coral formations and their configuration, Far Garden is considered a veritable underwater garden.

It differs from the other localities in the bay, since there is a series of large coral pinnacles located between the ledge along the reef and the drop-off, which becomes gradually steeper in an eastward direction. Here you can make either a mooring dive (dive **A**) or a drift dive (**B**).

The first dive (**A**) allows you to explore the pinnacles, which are about thirty meters from one another and feature an extraordinary selection of both

Massive hard coral (Porites lutea)

hard and soft corals. They are frequented by a great number of reef fish, small Scalefin anthias, common lionfish (genus *Pterois*), Suez fusiliers (genus *Caesio*) and Sergeant fish (genus *Abudefduf*). Continue to the east until you reach a cave – the entrance of which is crowned by a colony of *Porites lutea* coral – that opens out at 5 meters' depth and houses a large school of glassfish (Pigmy sweepers, *Parapriacanthus ransonneti*).

An alternative, if weather conditions are favourable, is to make a drift dive (**B**) from this

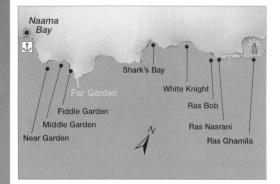

Naama Bay

Shark's Bay

White Knight

Far Garden

Ras Bob

Fiddle Garden

Middle Garden

Ras Nasrani

Near Garden

Ras Ghamila

N

Access	🚤	20'
Difficulty	⚪⚪	
Current	from ⚪	to ⚪⚪
Natural scenery	⚪⚪	
Fauna interest	⚪⚪	
General interest	⚪⚪	

Other characteristics

The numerous glassfish populating the small cave at Far Garden

cave, descending diagonally to 30 meters' depth, where you will see, from above, the top of a majestic and vast overhang known as 'The Cathedral' that opens out at a depth of about 32 meters and penetrates the reef for a dozen meters. From this point you can start your ascent keeping the reef to your left and you may reach a large private steel and cement jetty that marks the end of the dive.

Features

- *This site is usually sheltered from waves and wind.*
- *A wealth of corals and reef fish.*
- *Many scorpionfish (Scorpaenopsis sp.) and nudibranchs, which can usually be seen at night.*
- *A suitable site for snorkeling.*

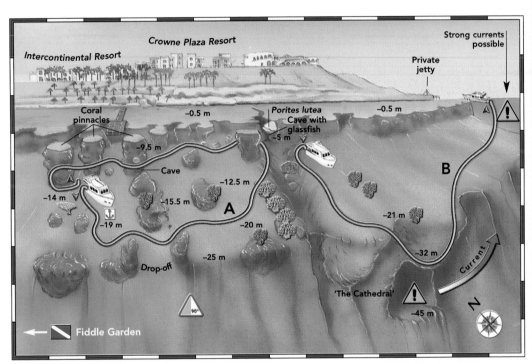

Crowne Plaza Resort

Intercontinental Resort

Private jetty

Strong currents possible

Coral pinnacles

−0.5 m

Porites lutea Cave with glassfish
−5 m

−0.5 m

−9.5 m

Cave

−12.5 m

−14 m

−15.5 m

A

−19 m

−20 m

B

−21 m

−25 m

−32 m

Drop-off

'The Cathedral'

−45 m

Current

N

90°

Fiddle Garden

Comments

- *The current, which generally runs eastwards, tends to get stronger closer to the headland.*
- *Do not dive too deeply, especially in the vicinity of 'The Cathedral'.*

Look out for

Gorgonian   Porites   Chromodoris

Anthias   Lionfish   Fusilier

Glassfish   Sergeantfish   Scorpionfish

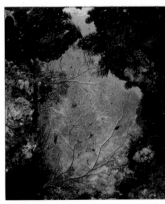

A gorgonian between the corals

Fiddle Garden

Overall view of Fiddle Garden and the dive site of Far Garden in the background

The dive site has been baptized 'Fiddle Garden' by local diving instructors as it is situated practically half way between Far Garden and Middle Garden. The two fixed moorings, one in the north and the other around 200 meters to the south and its sheltered position are elements that continually attract boats and scuba divers. The dive is very easy and it is possible to do either a mooring dive with the boat secured or one of the shamanduras, or a drift dive towards Far Garden a few hundreds meter away.

The seabed is sandy, flat and shallow (the average depth is around 10 meters) with coral structures contouring sandy 'streets' from where some massive pore corals (genus *Porites*) rise up. The most characteristic element of this site constitutes two coral pinnacles (**A** and **B**) which rise from the seabed at 17 meters up to 9.3 meters. Around the second pinnacle (**B**), which is dominated by fire corals, we can admire a big bright red Fire sponge (genus *Latrunculia*) highly toxic for fish and only a

An arborescent Fire sponge (genus Latrunculia)

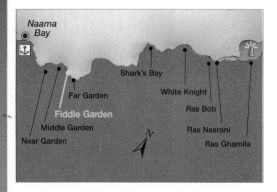

Access	18'
Difficulty	○
Current	○
Natural scenery	○
Fauna interest	○
General interest	○

Other characteristics

The neck and the handles of an amphora probably from Roman times

few nudibranchs can feed on it. Nearby at a depth of 6.5–7 meters lies the relatively well preserved residual of an antique big amphora originating probably from Roman times.

Other remains of amphoras, but clearly not as interesting, are visible between the reef ledge and the shamandura. The drop-off starts between 20 and 14 meters but its exploration is of little interest.

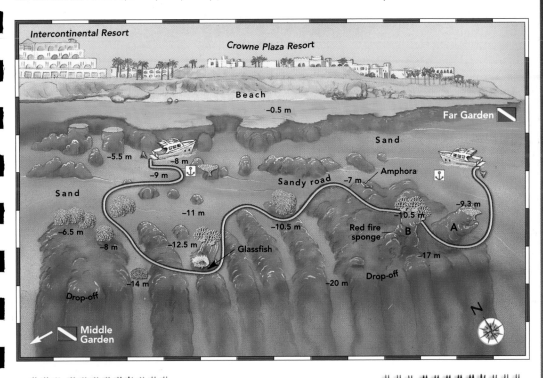

Comments

• *Easy dive without currents, suitable for divers with little experience or for check dives.*
• *Possible to use the fixed moorings.*

Look out for

Porites Acropora Turbinaria

Fire coral Sponge Anemonefish

Features

• *Very good alternative to Far Garden when this site is overcrowded.*
• *Ideal spot to take a break between two dives.*
• *Some archaeological remains.*

General view of Middle Garden showing the Hyatt Regency Resort and its floating pontoon

A s its name implies, this site lies in the central part of the bay between Far Garden and Near Garden, more or less on a line with the impressive *Hyatt Regency Resort*.

Totally sheltered from wind, waves and currents, you start the dive in line with the height of the central body of the hotel where there is also a floating pontoon. A vast sandy plateau stretches out onto the reef ledge ending at a depth of 5 to 6 meters and the drop-off is situated between 12 and 14 meters. After having gone a few dozen meters, the sandy plateau narrows, giving rise to a beautiful road of white sand: it is bordered by hard corals, most of which belong to the genus *Acropora*, some massive pore corals (genus *Porites*) that rise up from the sand like small islands, and other coral pinnacles.

Some table corals (genus *Acropora*) are scattered all around often creating small sandy avenues which recall garden paths: these gave rise to the name of this site. Experienced divers who have a good reserve of air can go as far as the coral pinnacles situated at Fiddle Garden. An alternative is a drift dive

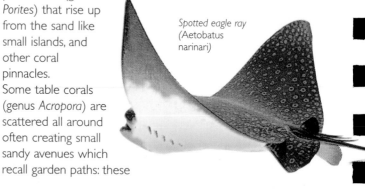

Spotted eagle ray (Aetobatus narinari)

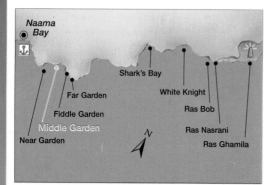

Naama Bay

Shark's Bay

Far Garden

White Knight

Fiddle Garden

Ras Bob

Middle Garden

Near Garden

Ras Nasrani

Ras Ghamila

Access	15'
Difficulty	○
Current	○
Natural scenery	○
Fauna interest	○ ○
General interest	○

Other characteristics

heading southwest towards Near Garden; naturally, this can be done when the tide is ebbing and the current is favourable.

Schools of fusiliers (genus *Caesio*), pufferfish, triggerfish, dominos (genus *Dascyllus*), pullers (genus *Chromis*), Bluespotted stingrays (*Taeniura lymma*) and also some Spotted eagle rays (*Aetobatus narinari*) constitute the typical fauna of this site.

*Bluespotted stingray (*Taeniura lymma*)*

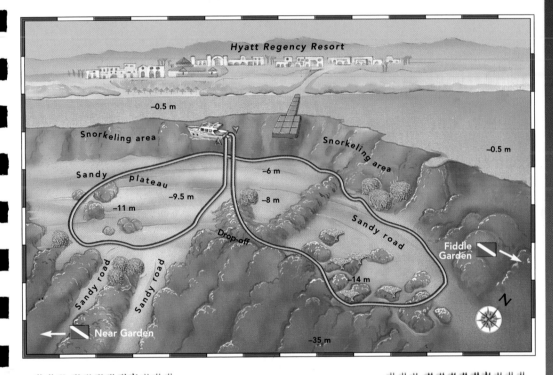

Comments

• *Since this site is fine for a lunch break, the shamandura is often crowded with many boats, especially in the late morning.*

Look out for

Acropora   Porites   Eagle ray

Manta ray   Stingray   Fusilier

Triggerfish   Damselfish   Puller

Features

• *Easy diving suitable for beginners and for check dives.*
• *An ideal spot when the sea conditions are not optimal elsewhere.*
• *Here you may see Spotted eagle rays (*Aetobatus narinari*) and Manta rays (*Manta birostris*) during the summer.*

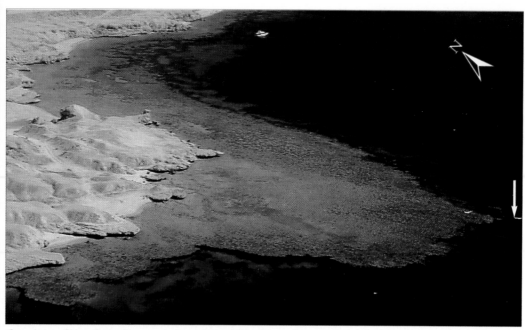

General view of Near Garden. The arrow indicates the beginning of the underwater ridge which characterises this site

This is the dive site closest to Naama Bay and the most southerly of the 'Gardens'. Unfortunately, because of the excessive number of divers and the debris deposited on the corals during the construction of the neighbouring hotel complexes, this locality has lost parts of its original allure. At the south-west sector of the site there is a vast whitish area with a great number of dead corals, often called the 'dead area'.
Yet Near Garden still remains today an interesting dive site and, thanks to its location, a

good alternative for afternoon and night dives.
Diving begins while descending

Red sponge (Latrunculia sp.)

onto a sandy plateau at about 15–20 meters which is bordered on the edge of the drop-off by a series of hard coral heads, and then proceed along numerous gorgonians up to a ridge with four pinnacles running in a northwest-southeast direction that become deeper and deeper.
After passing this underwater ridge, go northwards to explore the numerous gullies in the reef by crossing a narrow passageway between two coral formations inhabited by a colony of Cave sweepers

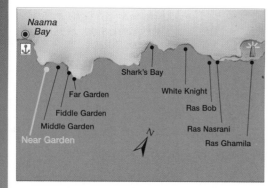

Naama
Bay

Shark's Bay

Far Garden
White Knight
Fiddle Garden
Ras Bob
Middle Garden
Ras Nasrani
Near Garden
Ras Ghamila

N

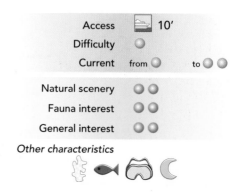

Access		10'
Difficulty	○	
Current	from ○	to ○ ○

Natural scenery	○ ○
Fauna interest	○ ○
General interest	○ ○

Other characteristics

Whitetip reef shark (Triaenodon obesus)

(*Pempheris vanicolensis*). If conditions permit you might turn to the north to reach the site of Middle Garden. During your dive you will come upon many Bluespotted stingrays (*Taeniura lymma*), Napoleonfish (*Cheilinus undulatus*) and triggerfish (*Balistapus undulates, Odonus niger*). Some small Whitetip reef shark (*Triaenodon obesus*) has chosen this site as its home.

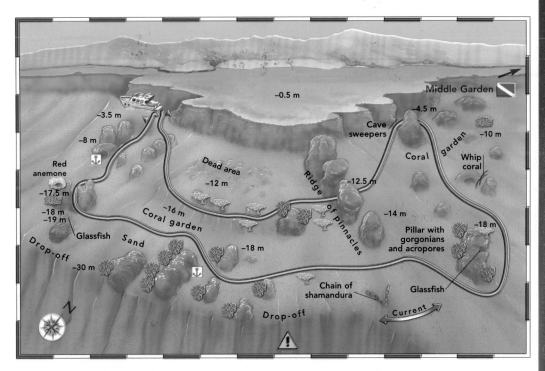

Comments

•*Beware of the many glass-bottom boats that pass near the reef without any regard whatsoever for divers.*
•*Strong currents possible at the ridge of the pinnacles*
•*Sometimes poor visibility.*

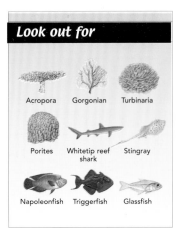

Look out for

Acropora Gorgonian Turbinaria

Porites Whitetip reef shark Stingray

Napoleonfish Triggerfish Glassfish

Features

• *Easy diving that allows you to observe many species of multicoloured soft corals, sponges and a fairly wide variety of corals.*
• *A suitable site for night dives and snorkeling.*

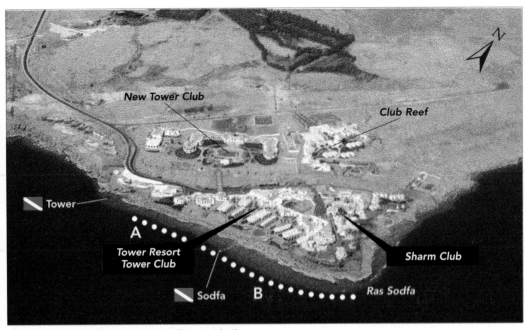

New Tower Club

Club Reef

Tower

A

Tower Resort
Tower Club

Sharm Club

Sodfa   B

Ras Sodfa

Aerial view of Ras Sodfa with the dive sites Tower and Sodfa

This site is immediately northeast of the much better-known and more popular Tower, on a level with a small promontory jutting into the sea, on which four large tourist villages have been built: the *Tower Resort* and *Club*, *Sharm Club* and, behind these two, the *New Tower Club* and *Club Reef*. The dive begins at the height of the floating jetty of the *Tower Club*, which is, however, only for the hotel's guests. This is the reason why dives are usually made from a boat and are therefore of the drift variety. Two types of dives are possible at Sodfa: the first route (**A**) towards the west in direction to the dive site Tower and the second (**B**) towards the East in direction of Ras Sodfa, described in the three dimensional map beside. Both dives lead along a sandy slope at an average depth of about 12 meters, between the reef

Ras Sodfa

*View of the dive **B***

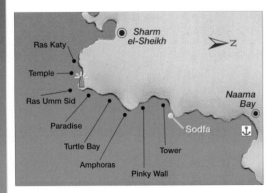

Sharm el-Sheikh

Ras Katy

Temple

Ras Umm Sid

Paradise

Turtle Bay

Amphoras

Naama Bay

Sodfa

Tower

Pinky Wall

Access		15'	
Difficulty	from ◌		to ◌ ◌
Current	◌		

Natural scenery	◌
Fauna interest	◌ ◌
General interest	◌

Other characteristics

*Yellowtail tang
(Zebrasoma xanthurum)*

ledge and the drop-off between 18 and 22 meters.

On the sandy slope some coral pinnacles rise up whereas at the near the drop-off you will see some large gorgonians at a depth of 20–22 meters. Even if both dives share a lot of features, the route **B** offers a more various panorama with a higher richness in corals and fauna represented by fusiliers (genus *Caesio*), surgeonfish (genus *Acanthurus* and *Zebra-* soma), triggerfish (genus *Odonus* and *Balistapus*), anthias, dominos (genus *Dascyllus*), parrotfish (genus *Scarus*, *Chlorurus* and *Cetoscarus*), glassfish (Pigmy sweepers, *Parapriacanthus ransonneti*), Red Sea bannerfish (*Heniochus intermedius*) and Common lionfish (*Pterois miles*). Massive pore corals (genus *Porites*), big table corals, gorgonians and yellow soft corals are common elements on this site.

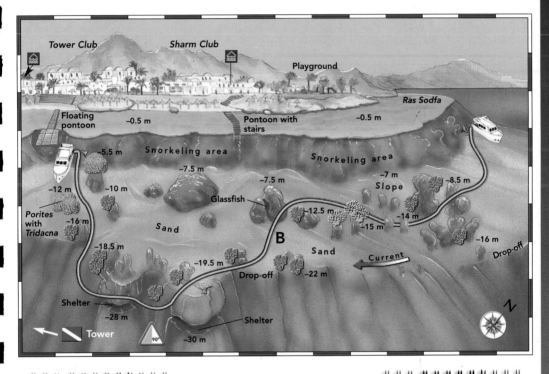

Comments

• *Before making your dive, check the direction of the current: if it is going northwards (flood tide), change the direction of your dive.*

Look out for

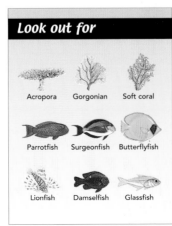

Acropora   Gorgonian   Soft coral

Parrotfish   Surgeonfish   Butterflyfish

Lionfish   Damselfish   Glassfish

Features

• *An easy dive that allows you to observe many species of coral, both soft and hard, and a wide range of reef fauna.*
• *This site is less frequented than Tower.*

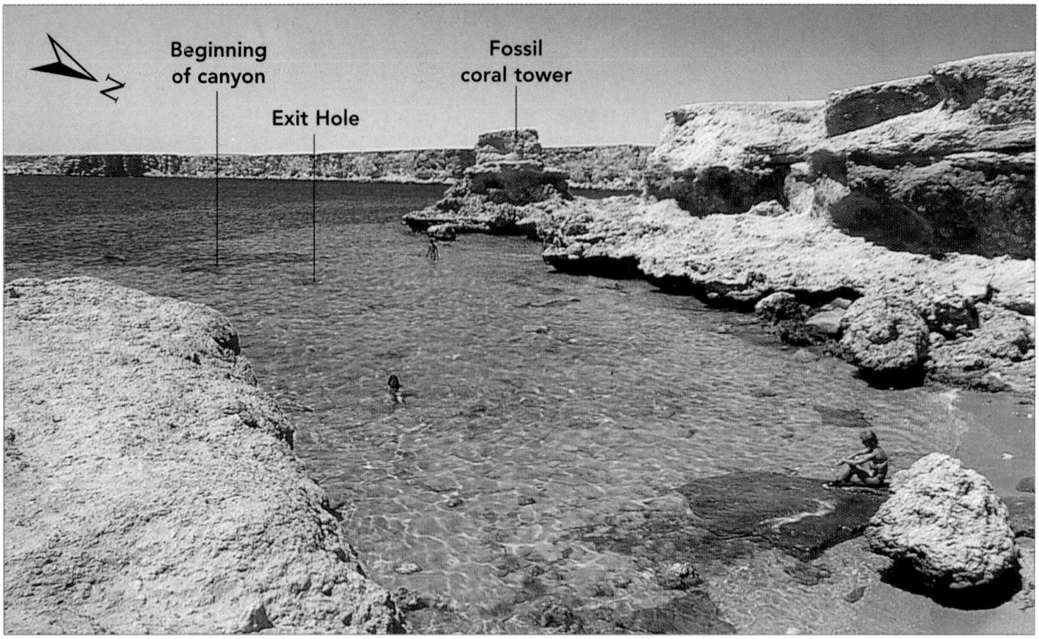

The access from the shore to the site Tower from the beach of the tourist village Tower Club

Tower is a spectacular dive site characterized by a deep canyon whose walls descend vertically for over 120 meters. It is also accessible from the land (with entrance fees) from the tourist hotel *Tower Resort* and Tower *Club*. The dive is more spectacular when entering the water off the small beach in the bay by the large fossil coral tower the site was named after. If you dive from the shore, after having swum past the reef ledge that borders the bay and extends for a few dozen meters, you will find yourself over the deep canyon with its crystal-clear waters. By keeping the reef to your left and descending for 15 meters, you will soon reach the edge of a large, slightly inclined sandy plateau that runs at a depth of 12–25 meters and that has some coral pinnacles. You return by doubling back on the same dive, but this time swimming upwards at 12–5 meters to explore the crevices and caves, one of which has a school of glassfish (Pigmy sweepers, *Parapriacanthus ransonneti*). Before resurfacing, you should explore the two interesting large caves at the beginning of the canyon towards the beach, at about 5 meters' depth: apart from the common glassfish, they are populated by Common lionfish

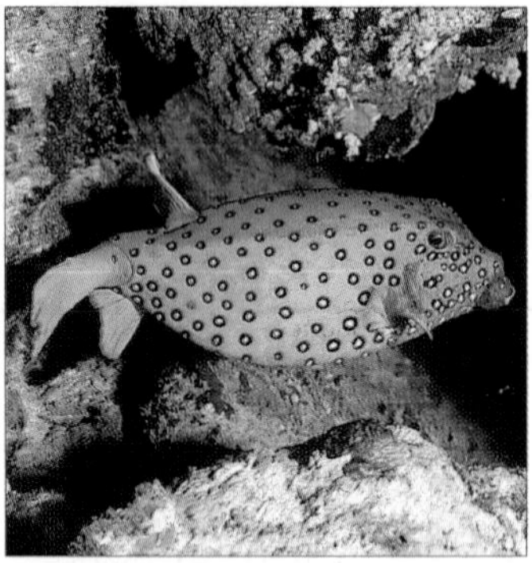

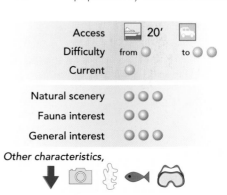

Cube boxfish (Ostracion cubicus)

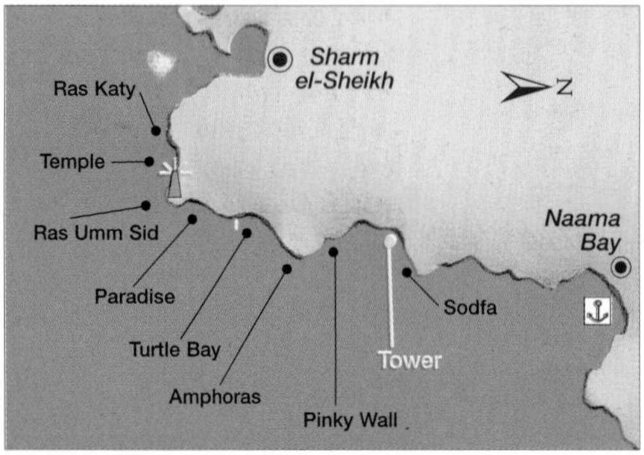

Access	20'	
Difficulty	from ●	to ● ●
Current	●	
Natural scenery	● ● ●	
Fauna interest	● ●	
General interest	● ● ●	

Other characteristics,

(*Pterois miles*), Sabre sqirrelfish (*Sargocentron spiniferum*) and Common bigeyes (*Priacanthus hamrur*). Other elements of the local fauna are represented by parrotfish, Cube boxfish (*Ostracion cubicus*), and species of butterflyfish whereas in the blue there are schools of fusiliers and pelagic fish (trevalleys, barracudas). If diving from a boat you also have the opportunity to make a drift dive towards Sodfa keeping the reef to your left.

A male Red Sea steep-headed parrotfish (Chlorurus gibbus)

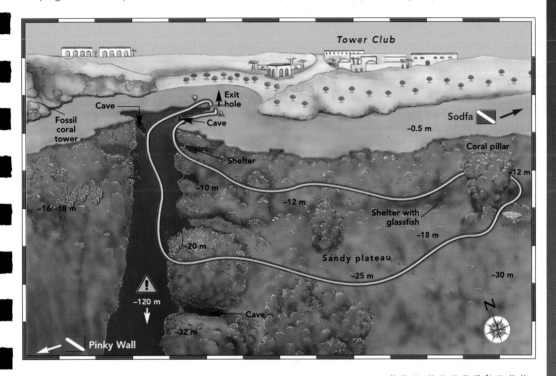

Comments

• *If you dive from the land make sure the tide is not low, because you may damage the reef.*
• *Be careful of your depth in the canyon.*
• *A depth of 5–20 meters is the most interesting for observing the fauna of the site.*

Look out for

Glassfish	Lionfish	Squirrelfish
Parrotfish	Boxfish	Butterflyfish
Fusilier	Trevally	Barracuda

Features

• *A strikingly beautiful underwater landscape.*
• *Rich in reef fauna, with many Parrotfish (Scarus sp., Clorurus sp. and Cetoscarus bicolor).*
• *Various pelagic predator species.*
• *A suitable site for snorkeling and night diving.*

The underwater part of Pinky Wall: the wall descends vertically to more than a depth of 180 meters

Pinky Wall (this seems to be the correct name even if this site is also written diversely as 'Pinky's Wall' or 'Pinkies Wall') is the first of a long series of diving sites between Tower and Ras Umm Sid. Strangely enough, despite the sheer beauty of this wall dive site, which was named after the multitude of pink Alcyonarian corals, there are very few guides who know Pinky Wall and take divers there.
The dive site is also accessible from land. If you arrive by boat you will have to make a drift dive, since there is no mooring. The configuration of the reef is quite different here from the other sites because the coral platform that generally follows the shoreline is very narrow and the steep wall, which is mostly studded with soft corals (*Dendronephthya* sp.), immediately plunges precipitously for a depth of more than 180 meters.
Dive by keeping the reef to your left and at an average depth of about 15 meters, because this is where you will see the largest concentration of soft corals.

Moving northeast you will note some majestic gullies in the steep vertical wall that follow one another in sequence, giving the impression of organ pipes. Along the route there are different types of Scaridae or parrotfish (genus *Scarus, Chlorurus* and *Cetoscarus*), splendour wrasses (genus *Cheilinus*) and some groupers (for instance the Moon grouper or *Variola louti*). If current conditions are favourable you can double back with a drift dive in the opposite direction and go as far as the Amphoras site.

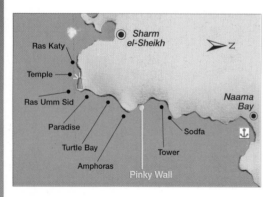

Access	🚤 22' 🚙
Difficulty	⚪⚪
Current	⚪
Natural scenery	⚪⚪
Fauna interest	⚪⚪
General interest	⚪⚪

Other characteristics

➡️ 🪸 🐟 ⬭

Alcyonarians or soft corals (Dendronephthya sp.)

Features

• *An impressive marine landscape that is unusual for the Sharm el-Sheikh diving sites.*
• *Extraordinarily rich in multicoloured soft corals.*
• *The site is usually not crowded.*

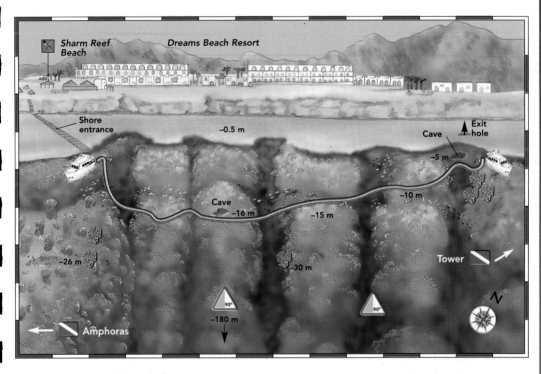

Sharm Reef Beach

Dreams Beach Resort

Shore entrance

−0.5 m

Cave −16 m

−15 m

−26 m

−30 m

90° −180 m

90°

Cave

Exit hole

−5 m

−10 m

Tower

N

Amphoras

Comments

• *Dive only when the sea is calm.*
• *Be careful of your depth.*
• *This dive is rarely proposed.*

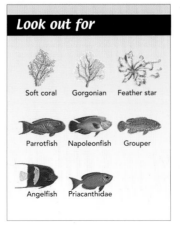

Look out for

Soft coral   Gorgonian   Feather star

Parrotfish   Napoleonfish   Grouper

Angelfish   Priacanthidae

Crinoid on a soft coral

The Ritz-Carlton Hotel

General view of the site Amphoras with The Ritz-Carlton Hotel

The name of this site derives from 17th-century shipwreck of a Turkish vessel with a cargo of amphoras containing mercury. Amphoras lies southwest of Tower, on a line with the northern tip of *The Ritz-Carlton Hotel* and is also accessible by land. The topography is quite simple: there is a sandy slope that begins at a depth of about a dozen meters and has some coral pinnacles of various shapes with a crust of a huge number of multicoloured Alcyonarians belonging to *Dendronephthya*

Fragment of an amphora which belonged to the cargo of the Turkish vessel (17th century)

genus, that create a sort of magnificent garden.
The dive starts of a half-submerged concrete jetty situated at about a dozen meters to the north of the more visible floating pontoon. Descending to a depth of 22 meters you immediately find a big, long chain leading to a huge modern anchor situated behind a coral pinnacle at about a depth of 25 meters. Continue to the north keeping the reef to your left and you come along some coral towers, one of them is surrounded by a school of anthias and accommodates numerous glassfish (Pigmy sweepers, *Parapriacanthus*

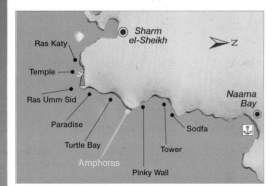

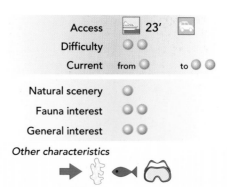

Access	23'	
Difficulty	◐ ◐	
Current	from ◐	to ◐ ◐ ◐

Natural scenery ◐
Fauna interest ◐ ◐
General interest ◐ ◐

Other characteristics

The huge modern anchor

ransonneti) in one of its splits. You reach a huge table coral before some coral pinnacles behind which, at a depth of 23.5 meters and firmly stuck into the reef, you can still see the stock of the original anchor of the ship with inscriptions as well as fragments of the amphoras: these were part of the ship's cargo wrecked in the 17th century whose structure has virtually disappeared today.

Features

• *Although there are not many, the remains of the Turkish vessel cargo are always fascinating.*
• *The multicoloured Alcyonarians are beautiful.*
• *The most interesting part lies between 18 and 25 meters of depth.*
• *Site suitable for snorkeling.*

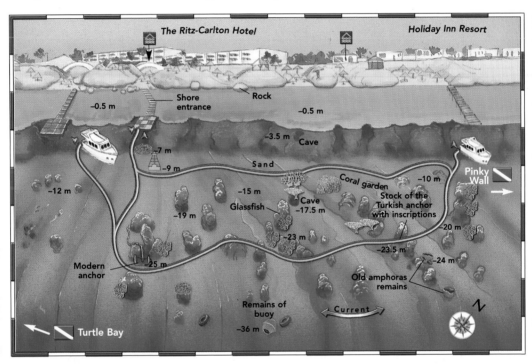

The Ritz-Carlton Hotel · Holiday Inn Resort · Shore entrance · Rock · −0.5 m · −0.5 m · −3.5 m · Cave · −7 m · Sand · −9 m · Coral garden · −10 m · Pinky Wall · −12 m · −15 m · Cave −17.5 m · Glassfish · −19 m · Stock of the Turkish anchor with inscriptions · −20 m · −23 m · −23.5 m · −24 m · Modern anchor · −25 m · Old amphoras remains · Turtle Bay · Remains of buoy · −36 m · Current · N

Comments

• *Sometimes the local current can be strong and visibility may be limited.*
• *Finding the fragments of amphoras is not easy, so you must look around carefully.*

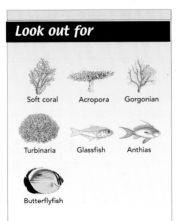

Look out for

Soft coral · Acropora · Gorgonian

Turbinaria · Glassfish · Anthias

Butterflyfish

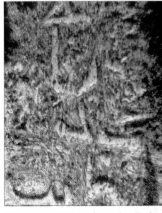

Turkish inscriptions on the ancient anchor

Iberotel Grand Sharm

General view of the site Turtle Bay with the hotel Iberotel Grand Sharm

This site lies immediately south of Amphoras and its topographical configuration is quite similar: a slope with an average incline of 30° that runs at a depth of 10–26 meters and on which some coral pinnacles stand. The classic dive is a drift, either northwards or southwards depending on the direction of the current – even though the latter is more frequent.

After a descent towards the drop-off, situated at a depth of about 26 meters (at the beginning of a vertical wall that goes down about 110 meters), you explore the reef slope, circling the coral towers, among which there are some gorgonians at a depth of 15–23 meters.

In the northernmost part of the dive you cross an area rich in madrepores and Alcyonarians that form a sort of 'coral garden' on the edge of which are large Salad coral (*Turbinaria mesenterina*) and some large mushroom-shaped coral heads made up of colonies of *Porites* sp.

Snorkelers will be able to observe beautiful and varied reef fauna on the ledge that descends to about 10 meters and is a continuation of

Starfish (Fromia sp.)

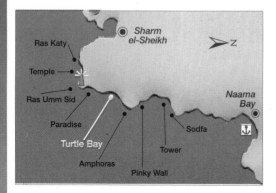

Ras Katy
Temple
Ras Umm Sid
Paradise
Turtle Bay
Amphoras
Pinky Wall
Tower
Sodfa
Sharm el-Sheikh
Naama Bay

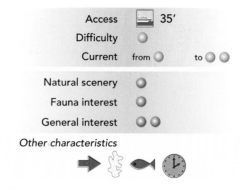

Access		🛥	35'
Difficulty		○	
Current	from ○		to ○ ○
Natural scenery	○		
Fauna interest	○		
General interest	○ ○		

Other characteristics

A Royal angelfish (Pygoplites diacanthus)

the reef outcrop that borders the beach. Apart from numerous butterflyfish (genus *Chaetodon*), anthias, Sergeant majors (*Abudefduf vaigensis*) and some Royal angelfish (*Pygoplites diacanthus*), you can also observe Common lizardfish (*Synodus variegatus*) and Forster's hawkfish (*Paracirrhites forsteri*).
When conditions allow, it is possible to reach the nearby dive site of Amphoras.

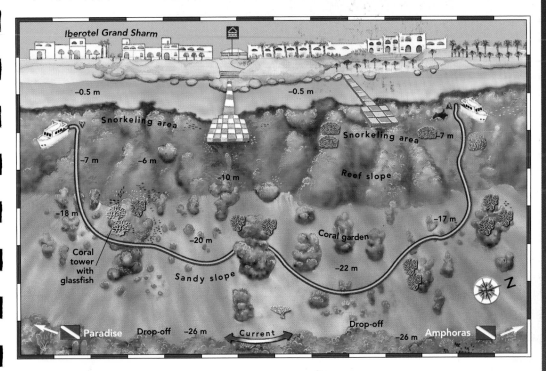

Comments

• *Dive only when the sea is calm.*
• *You may come across a local current.*

Look out for

Acropora Gorgonian Soft coral

Turbinaria Porites Butterflyfish

Angelfish Anthias Sergeantfish

Features

• *A quiet, uncrowded site, ideal for the high season.*
• *A wealth of soft and hard corals.*

Hilton Waterfalls Resort

Royal Paradise Resort

Kiroseiz Three Corners Beach Club

General sea view of the site Paradise with the Royal Paradise Resort *and* Hilton Waterfalls

Although its conformation is similar to Amphoras and Turtle Bay and, indeed, is common to this entire stretch of coast, Paradise differs in the taller coral pinnacles that rise on the slope between the reef ledge and the drop-off. Here these towers look like pieces of sculpture with a variety of hues due to the growth of red, pinkish and yellow Alcyonarians (genus *Dendronephthya*). The overall effect is a magnificent environment that is unique in its kind. This site extends between the two small beaches on a line with the *Royal Paradise Resort*. Access can be gained from the shore by asking permission from the diving center there. However, the classic dive is a drift to the south from a boat if the current is favourable keeping the reef on your right. After descending for 24–28 meters, near the drop-off area and keeping the reef to your left, you can glide through the pinkish pinnacles that are sometimes crowned with *Acropora* sp. Other larger table corals grow on the bottom, from which some gorgonians also break loose.

Arabian angelfish (Pomacanthus maculosus) in search of food

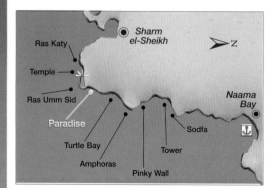

Sharm el-Sheikh

Ras Katy

Temple

Ras Umm Sid

Paradise

Turtle Bay

Amphoras

Pinky Wall

Tower

Sodfa

Naama Bay

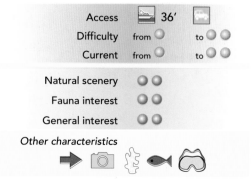

Access	36'	
Difficulty	from ○	to ○ ○
Current	from ○	to ○ ○

Natural scenery ○ ○

Fauna interest ○ ○

General interest ○ ○

Other characteristics

Soft coral (Dendronephthya sp.)

By going through this superb marine landscape you will be able to admire a host of reef fauna, from parrotfish to the large Napoleonfish (*Cheilinus undulatus*), swarms of butterflyfish and the ever-present Anthias (*Pseudanthias squamipinnis*), not to mention some beautiful Giant morays (*Gymnothorax javanicus*) that dwell in the crevices of the pinnacles, especially in the southern-most part of the dive.

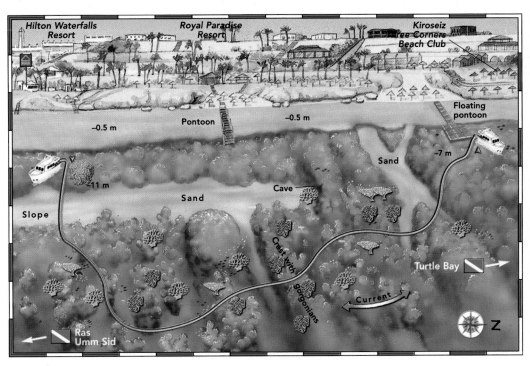

Comments

• Check the direction of the current.
• The best time for your dive is at ebb tide when the current, which runs south, is fastest.

Look out for

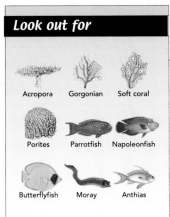

Acropora Gorgonian Soft coral

Porites Parrotfish Napoleonfish

Butterflyfish Moray Anthias

Features

• Easy diving without any problem.
• A varied and colourful landscape.
• Large areas of soft coral growth.
• A wealth of reef fauna.
• Suitable for night diving.

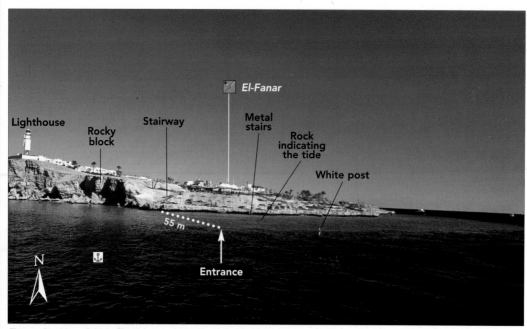

Lighthouse
Rocky block
Stairway
El-Fanar
Metal stairs
Rock indicating the tide
White post
55 m
N
Entrance

The site Ras Umm Sid seen from the sea during the high tide (the rock between the metal stairs and the white post is submerged)

Ras Umm Sid is the name of the promontory with a high lighthouse that marks the beginning of the Strait of Tiran on the western coast. The dive site, easily accessible by land, is immediately east of the lighthouse, opposite the famous Italian restaurant *El-Fanar*. It is renowned for the extraordinary proliferation of gorgonians (*Subergorgia hicksoni*) that create a veritable forest here, the most beautiful in all the northern Red Sea. Access from the beach, which is facilitated by a stairway, is possible only when the tide is

high enough to allow you to swim past the reef platform, which is quite extensive here. A shamandura is fixed on the seabed at the height of a huge

Ras Umm Sid lighthouse

rocky block visible from the coast. The classic dive – whether you choose to dive from the shore or from a boat – starts from a big massive pore coral (genus *Porites*) inhabited by a colony of anthias and descends to 25 meters, where you pass through the famous gorgonian forest, and then an ascent to the plateau at 14 meters' depth. Here, among numerous coral pinnacles covered with Alcyonarians, there are hundreds of reef fish, Common lionfish (*Pterois miles*) and parrotfish and huge Napoleonfish (*Cheilinus undulatus*). From this point, if you

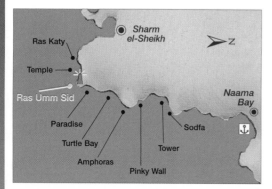

Sharm el-Sheikh
N
Ras Katy
Temple
Ras Umm Sid
Naama Bay
Paradise
Sodfa
Turtle Bay
Tower
Amphoras
Pinky Wall

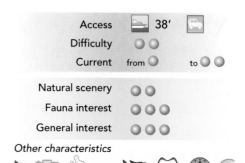

Access		38'	
Difficulty	○ ○		
Current	from ○		to ○ ○

Natural scenery	○ ○	
Fauna interest	○ ○ ○	
General interest	○ ○ ○	

Other characteristics

The massive pore coral (genus Porites) *indicating the start of the dive*

have dived from the shore you can return shallow, keeping the reef to your right at a depth of 5-6 meters to explore the gorges, in particular some small caves with a colony of glassfish or Pigmy sweepers (*Parapria-canthus ransonneti*) and Cave sweepers (*Pempheris vanicolensis*). If you have a boat you can continue in the direction of Paradise while crossing the extensive platform known as *Fiasco Plateau*.

Features

• *A splendid gorgonian forest.*
• *Rich in reef and pelagic fauna (jackfish, barracuda, tuna).*
• *An interesting night dive during which you can observe parrotfish sleeping in their lair.*
• *Excellent for snorkeling.*

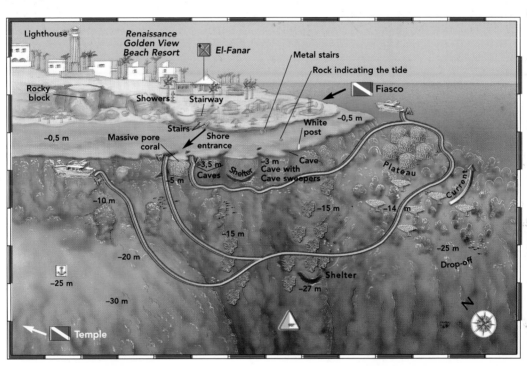

Comments

• *There may be strong currents, especially near the cape.*
• *It is high tide when the rocky bluff on the reef is almost completely covered by the water.*

Look out for

Gorgonian   Porites   Soft coral

Parrotfish   Napoleonfish   Lionfish

Glassfish   Trevally   Barracuda

*A Common lionfish (*Pterois miles)

A Spanish dancer (Hexabranchus sanguineus) on the coral surrounded by schools of Xenidi (genus Xenia)

A Red Sea steep-headed parrotfish (Chlorurus gibbus) sleeps on a Red sponge (Cliona vastifica)

One of the big gorgonians (Subergorgia hicksoni) which occur between 12 and 30 meters on the wall of Ras Umm Sid

One of the caves on the wall of Ras Umm Sid at a depth of 5 meters with a red soft coral (genus Dendronephthya) next to the entry

4

27°51.000' N — 34°18.600' E

Main coral pillar

General view of Temple dive site as seen from the coast

This site lies in the middle of a large bay between Ras Umm Sid and Ras Katy that is bordered by a tall cliff of fossil coral on which two large tourist villages have been built – *Farana King Snefro* and *Reef Oasis*.
On a vast sandy plateau at a depth of 6–30 meters there are three coral pillars that resemble the columns of an ancient temple, hence the name given to this site by the first divers in the early 1970s. A few moorings situated around the largest coral pillar, which touches the surface and

The coral pillar with a colony of massive pore corals tilted during the earthquake in 1995

which has a black post fixed on it, make it easy to tie up your boat, made even easier by the total lack of wind and waves in this sheltered bay.
Temple is one of the most popular sites in this area because it guarantees easy diving without any technical problems in any weather condition.
Although it has certainly suffered from overcrowding, the site is still rather interesting and is particularly suitable for night dives. Furthermore, the presence of many species of butterflyfish, parrotfish, lionfish,

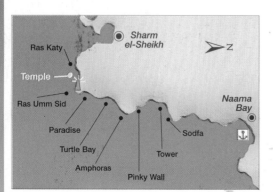

Access		43'
Difficulty	○	
Current	○	
Natural scenery	○ ○	
Fauna interest	○	
General interest	○ ○	

Other characteristics

A madrepore colony belonging to the genus Pavona

Batfish (*Platax orbicularis*) and some Napoleonfish (*Cheilinus ondulatus*) is virtually guaranteed.

Since Temple is rather small, you can explore the site choosing your own diving route, however, it should include a visit to the beautiful gorgonian with glassfish (Pigmy sweepers, *Parapriacanthus ransonneti*) situated at a depth of around 30 meters on the edge of the drop-off.

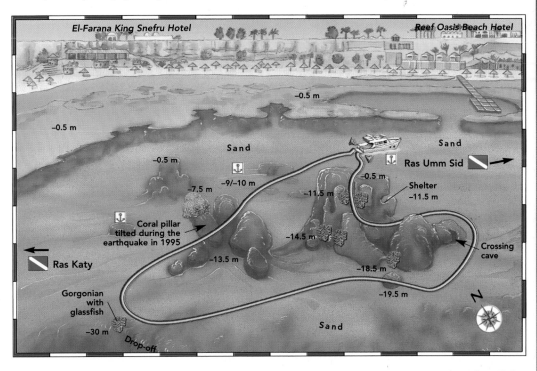

El-Farana King Snefru Hotel

Reef Oasis Beach Hotel

−0.5 m

−0.5 m

Sand

Sand

Ras Umm Sid

−0.5 m

−0.5 m

−7.5 m

−9/−10 m

−11.5 m

Shelter −11.5 m

Coral pillar tilted during the earthquake in 1995

−14.5 m

Crossing cave

Ras Katy

−13.5 m

−18.5 m

N

Gorgonian with glassfish

−19.5 m

Sand

−30 m

Drop-off

27°51.000' N — 34°18.600' E

Comments

• During night dives you should have a compass to get back easily to your boat.
• Do not get too close to the triggerfish, especially during the nesting period, as they may attack you.

Look out for

Porites   Gorgonian   Butterflyfish

Parrotfish   Lionfish   Angelfish

Napoleonfish   Triggerfish   Anthias

Features

• Easy dive: a site suitable for check dives and relatively inexperienced divers.
• An interesting underwater landscape rich in hard and soft corals.
• Excellent for night dives and snorkeling.

27°50.838' N — 34°18.107' E

Aerial view of the Ras Katy site

Marina TRAVCO
Sharm el-Mina
SHARM EL-SHEIKH
Beach

Ras Katy is a few hundred meters west of Temple and in some respects has a similar configuration. Boats usually moor from the bow at the shamandura, which is located near a large outcropping coral pillar. Since this site is well sheltered from prevailing winds you can moor there without any problem. Dives are made at the coral pinnacle colonized by small table corals and Raspberry corals (*Pocillopora verrucosa*) which rises almost up to the surface. The sandy seabed is slightly inclined starting from an initial

The frightening Giant triggerfish (Balistoides viridescens)

depth of about 5 meters to 18–20 meters at a point on line with the drop-off, where there are some gorgonians. While exploring the plateau you will see two more coral pinnacles a few dozen meters from one another that are covered by Alcyonarians with numerous specimens of Broccoli soft coral (*Lithophyton arboretum*) frequented by anthias and butterflyfish (the genera *Chaetodon* and *Heniochus*), Dominos (*Dascyllus trimaculatus*) and fusiliers (genus *Caesio*). In the crevices along the walls of the pinnacles you

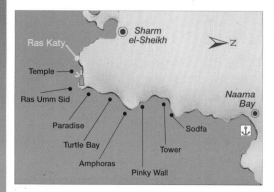

Access		45'
Difficulty	○	
Current	○	
Natural scenery	○ ○	
Fauna interest	○	
General interest	○ ○	

Other characteristics

A feather worm on a Raspberry coral (Pocillopora sp.)

will see glassfish, lionfish and bigeyes, while along the sandy bottom there are Crocodilefish (*Papilloculiceps longiceps*), Bluespotted stingrays (*Taeniura lymma*) and some scorpionfish (*Scorpaenopsis sp.*). Sometimes, when the tide is rising, you may come upon a rather strong local current that will allow you to make a drift dive to Temple (about 400 meters away), going over numerous coral formations and large table corals.

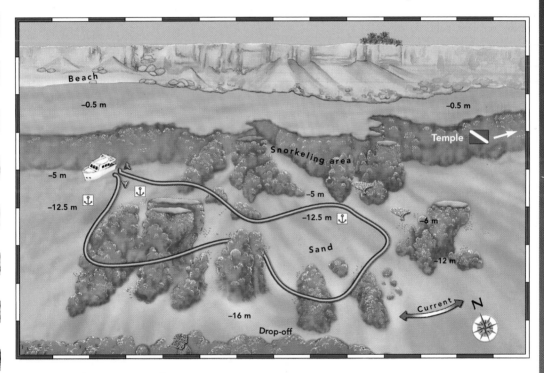

Comments

• *Diving is best in the afternoon.*
• *Beware of the triggerfish during the nesting period.*

Look out for

Acropora	Gorgonian	Soft coral
Anthias	Butterflyfish	Glassfish
Crocodilefish	Scorpionfish	Triggerfish

Features

• *Easy dives suitable for beginners and check dives.*
• *Rather rich reef fauna in an interesting underwater environment.*
• *This site is recommended for night dives and snorkeling.*

RAS MOHAMMED

South of Sharm el-Sheikh the coast is totally deserted, with no shelter, for more than a mile, up to the small bay named *Marsa Ghozlani*, where the **Ras Mohammed National Park** begins.

This is followed by another bay, *Marsa Bareika*, which is much larger and deeper. It penetrates the land for 2.8 miles, forming the *Ras Mohammed* peninsula, which extends south-eastwards into the Red Sea for almost 5 miles and separates the Gulf of Aqaba from the Gulf of Suez.

The eastern coast of the Ras Mohammed peninsula is composed of a tall fossil coral reef that is interrupted for a few dozen meters by the only accessible beach in the area, *Aqaba Beach*, and ends at the Ras Mohammed headland – 'Mohammed's Cape' in Arabic, because its profile is like the bearded one of the Prophet. The rocky spur is about 60 meters high; on top of it is the *Shark Observatory* balcony.

On the southern side of the peninsula there are three beaches – *Shark Observatory Beach*, *Main Beach* and *Yolanda Beach* – the sandy, shallow *Hidden Bay*, the mouth of which is almost completely blocked by a long coral reef that divides the peninsula of Ras Mohammed into two rocky land spits.

A shallow channel forms a small island called *Mangrove Island* on the western side with a small beacon. On the sides of the channel grow numerous mangroves (*Avicennia marina*), which represent an important ecosystem. Mangroves are special plants, quite rare in the Sinai, and thanks to their incredible root system they are able to filter nutrients from the seawater, expelling salt crystals through their leaves.

The western side of the peninsula is low and sandy, and its primary attraction is the only mooring, which is well sheltered, in the area on a level with the half-submerged remains of an old jetty known as *The Quay*. Because of its geographic

Marsa Bareika · Salt Lake · The Quay · Mangrove Channel · Hidden Bay · Mangrove Island · Yolanda Beach · Main Beach · Ras Mohammed · Ras Za'atar · Ras Burg · Jackfish Alley · Eel Garden · Shark Observatory · Yolanda Reef · Shark Reef · Anemone City

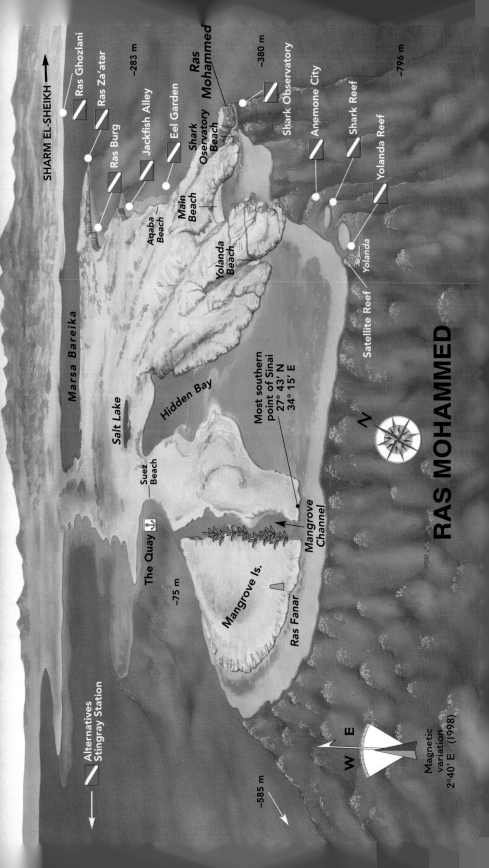

RAS MOHAMMED

SHARM EL-SHEIKH →

Ras Ghozlani

Ras Za'atar

−283 m

Ras Burg

Jackfish Alley

Eel Garden

Shark Oseratory Beach

Ras Mohammed

−380 m

Shark Observatory

Anemone City

Shark Reef

Yolanda Reef

−796 m

Aqaba Beach

Main Beach

Yolanda Beach

Yolanda

Satellite Reef

Marsa Bareika

Salt Lake

Hidden Bay

Most southern point of Sinai
27° 43′ N
34° 15′ E

N

Suez Beach

The Quay

−75 m

Mangrove Channel

Mangrove Is.

Ras Fanar

W   E

Alternatives
Stingray Station

−585 m

Magnetic variation
2°40′ E (1998)

RAS MOHAMMED

A cave next to the promontory of Ras Mohammed

Navigation times (from Naama Bay)	
Ras Ghozlani	35'
Ras Za'atar	65'
Ras Burg	60'
Jackfish Alley	70'
Eel Garden	75'
Shark Observatory	85'
Shark & Yolanda Reef	90'

position the Ras Mohammed peninsula is a privileged area distinguished for the strong, massive currents that transport large quantities of plankton and other food that give rise to an extraordinary growth of hard and soft corals and attract large schools of both reef and pelagic marine fauna. With the great abundance of food, barracuda, jackfish, tuna and sharks swarm in these waters, especially between June to August, offering divers the chance to make extremely interesting and exciting dives. The classic diving sites begin at the northern and southern-most tip of Marsa Bareika, respectively known as **Ras Ghozlani** and **Ras Za'atar**, and continue along the eastern coast with **Ras Burg**, **Jackfish Alley**, **Eel Garden** and **Shark Observatory** (also known as *Ras Mohammed Wall*), and at the southern end of the peninsula with Anemone City, Shark Reef and Yolanda Reef.

Ras Mohammed	Snorkeling	Open Water	Advanced Open Water
Ras Ghozlani		●	
Ras Za'atar		●	●
Ras Burg		●	
Jackfish Alley		●	●
Eel Garden	●	●	
Shark Observatory	●		●
Shark & Yolanda Reef			●

Snorkeling | Open Water | Advanced Open Water

Aerial view of the channel and the Mangrove Island

THE NATIONAL PARK OF RAS MOHAMMED

Ras Mohammed constitutes the southern-most promontory of the Sinai separating the Gulf of Aqaba and the Gulf of Suez. The impressive rock masses are made from fossil corals, of which the most ancient go back to the Pleistocene era (from 1.8 million to 10,000 years ago). They are testimony to an important variation of the sea level.

Due to its particular position, its geo-morphological features with huge desert planes, dune zones, wadis and mountainous terrain as well as a series of other factors such as the presence of a coral bank extraordinary rich in fauna and a mangrove zone, the whole area proves to have an extraordinary ecological and faunistic richness comprising 218 coral species

*A White stork
(Ciconia ciconia)*

(hard and soft), more than 1,000 fish species, 80 plant species, 220 bird species, and 14 mammal species. There are thousands of migrating birds during the autumn in Ras Mohammed, in particular the White Storks (Ciconia ciconia) who stop for a pause during their journey from Europe to southern Africa where they live. In order to protect and conserve the entire area of Ras Mohammed, the Egyptian Government established its **first national park** in 1983 which initially covered a territory of 97 square kilometers. It was extended in 1988 with the annexation of the northern coast of Sharm el-Sheikh and the Islands of Tiran and Sanafir to give a total territory of 480 square kilometers.

The marine part of the protected area is predominant, as it comprises 76% of its territory with a total of 365 square kilometers

The central area of the Ras Mohammed National Park viewed by the satellite Landsat

compared to 115 square kilometers of land. Around 150,000 tourists are drawn to this area every year (only 10% of the territory is open to the public, the rest is closed for conservation purposes) and at least 100,000 tourists arrive by sea.

27°47.527' N — 34°15.752' E

Aerial view of Ras Ghozlani

Red and green post

Marsa Ghozlani

Marsa Bareika

Ras Za'atar

N

The deep bay of Marsa Bareika has the dive site of Ras Ghozlani on its northern tip and Ras Za'atar to the south. The bay was opened to scuba divers only a few years ago, and access is still restricted and allowed on its outer sides only. A small stake with two banners, red and green, set into the sandy coast indicate the area not to be entered. There used to be two fixed moorings situated on the accessible coastal part which then were removed, so today the dive at Ras Ghozlani has to be done as a drift. The route winds along an

One of the huge branching table corals of Ras Ghozlani

Sharm el-Sheikh

Ras Mohammed National Park

Ras Ghozlani

Ras Za'atar

Marsa Bareika

Ras Burg
Jackfish Alley
Eel Garden

Stingray Station

Shark Observatory

Shark Reef & Yolanda Reef

Alternatives

Access		35'	
Difficulty	from ○		to ○ ○
Current	○		

Natural scenery ○ ○ ○

Fauna interest ○ ○

General interest ○ ○ ○

Other characteristics

extensive sandy slope starting at a depth of 6 meters which descends to the drop-off

An enormous Blackspotted pufferfish (Arothron stellatus) resting on the sand

situated at around 25 to 30 meters. A series of coral pinnacles, often covered with red and pink soft corals and populated by dense schools of anthias, together with huge Acropora table and branching corals rise up from the sand, especially by the drop-off. This formation creates fantastic and fascinating landscapes that take over the aspect of a real coral forest, especially close to the entrance to the bay.

The table corals offer shelter to batfish (*Platax* sp.), glassfish or Pigmy sweepers (*Parapria-canthus ransonneti*) and groupers, whereas on the sandy slope there are Bluespotted stingrays (*Taeniura lymma*), pufferfish (genera *Arothron* and *Diodon*) and triggerfish (genera *Odonus* and *Pseudobalistes*). Unfortunately, the beauty of this site attracts numerous scuba divers who are slowly beginning to overcrowd this site.

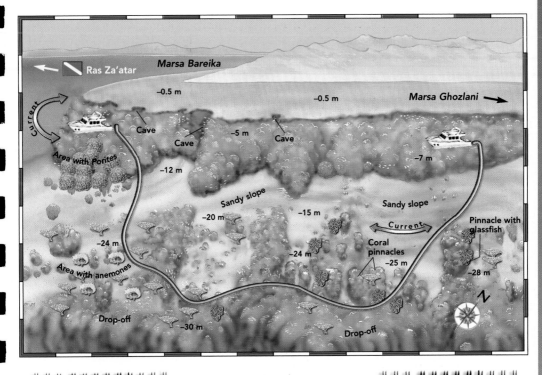

Comments

- *Morning and afternoon dives can vary greatly, with the sunlight in the afternoon primarily illuminating the coral pinnacles and large hard coral formations (genus* Acropora) *close to the drop-off.*
- *Sometimes there can be too many scuba divers.*
- *Current is never strong, often from north to south.*

Look out for

Acropora   Gorgonian   Porites

Soft coral   Anemonefish   Stingray

Pufferfish   Glassfish   Grouper

Features

- *It is one of the most beautiful dives in the Ras Mohammed area.*
- *Possible to admire extraordinary table corals, still intact, as the dive site was opened to tourism only a few years ago.*
- *Fantastic and surrealistic landscape.*

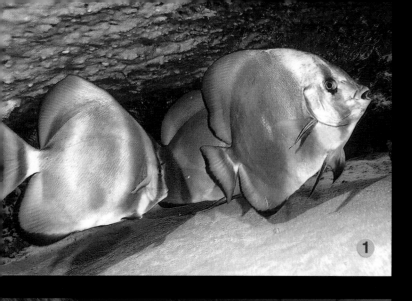

1

A group of Circular batfish
(Platax orbicularis)
resting under the umbrella of
a table coral

1

Pink and red soft corals
(genus Dendronephthya)
close to a gorgonian

2

A dense school of glassfish (Pigmy
sweepers, Parapriacanthus
ransonneti) finds shelter under
the umbrella of a huge table
coral (Acropora sp.), which also
protects a red soft coral

3

Sometimes the table corals
(Acropora) provide shelter for
the Serranids, like this Arabian
grouper (Epinephelus tauvina)

4

2

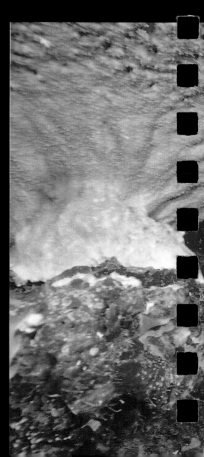

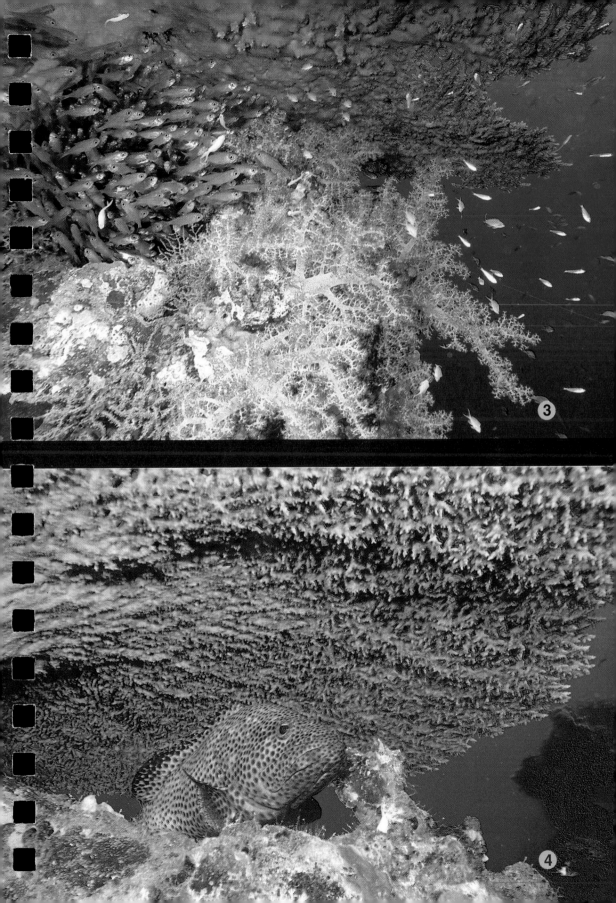

3

4

Aerial view of Ras Za'atar

The splendid wall of Ras Za'atar decorated by red soft corals

R as Za'atar is the rocky promontory which delimits the deep bay of Marsa Bareika to the south. The lack of a mooring (shamandura) means you have to make a drift dive that skirts the headland. This may be done in either direction, depending on the current; the most frequent moves northeast with the reef on your left. Since the most interesting part of the dive is around the headland, it is important to start your dive past the large crevice that can be seen on the coastline. The dive starts at a coral pinnacle

with a table coral situated at a depth of 21 meters and winds along the gorgeous wall which descends vertically. The wall is decorated by colourful Alcyonarians and lovely gorgonians with a peculiar horizontal disposition as well as colonies of Black coral (Antipathes dichotoma). It is a good idea to come up to a depth of 10 to 15 meters in order not to miss the spectacular chimneys which begin at this depth and narrow towards the surface where they open into the reef platform: from these crevices the rays of the sun

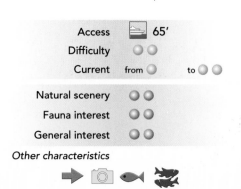

Access		65'
Difficulty	◐ ◐	
Current	from ◐	to ◐ ◐
Natural scenery	◐ ◐	
Fauna interest	◐ ◐	
General interest	◐ ◐	

Other characteristics

Gorgonians and multicoloured Alcyonarians adorn the wall of Ras Za'atar

penetrate the recesses creating spectacular effects. In these chimneys the typical inhabitants of crevices live: Lionfish, Pigmy sweepers (*Parapriacanthus ransonneti*) and some big groupers (genus *Epinephelus*). Once past the tip of the wall, turn into Marsa Bareika bay over a sandy slope with many coral pinnacles that create a true coral garden. Jackfish, barracuda and some tuna cruise the blue in search of prey.

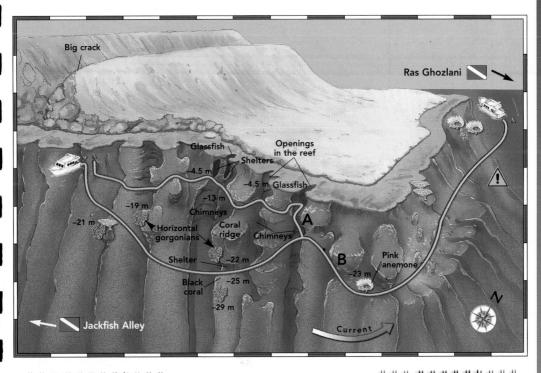

Comments
• *Keep at a depth of 10 to 15 meters if you want to visit the chimneys, the most scenic point of the dive*
• *The current may get stronger around the headland.*

Look out for

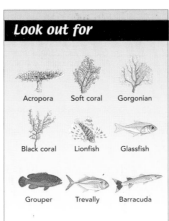

Acropora   Soft coral   Gorgonian

Black coral   Lionfish   Glassfish

Grouper   Trevally   Barracuda

Features
• *A splendid wall covered with multicoloured Alcyonarians.*
• *On a level with the chimney further north there is a spectacular landscape.*
• *Spectacular landscape at the northernmost chimney.*

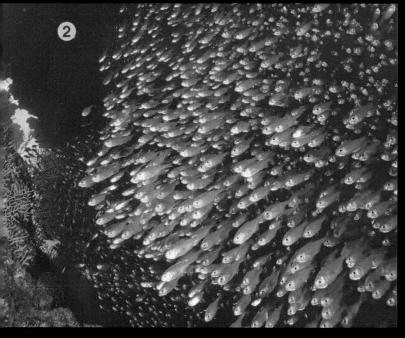

A Coral grouper
(Cephalopholis miniata)
ready to eat its prey

1

A dense school of
glassfish (Pigmy sweepers,
Parapriacanthus ransonneti)
inside the first chimney

2

A Sabre squirrelfish
(Sargocentrum spiniferum)
escapes into the deeper part
of the chimneys

3

Sunlight penetrates through
big crevices in the reef plate
around the chimneys creating
impressive scenes

4

4

Marsa Bareika

← Jackfish Alley

Ras Za'atar ↗

Aerial view of the site of Ras Burg

It is useless to look for information about this dive site which is about 500 meters south of Ras Za'atar: it is a dive site illustrated and suggested for the first time in this guide. The site is certainly less spectacular than the one at Ras Za'atar, but its wall has a similar configuration, and it offers the double advantage of not yet being crowded and is practically intact. The dive starts at a fossil coral pinnacle jutting out of the water for a couple of meters like a tower which gave this site its name (*Ras Burg* is Arabic for 'Tower Cape'). Descend along the wall where some Bluespine unicornfish (*Naso unicornis*) and schools of fusiliers (genus *Caesio*) cruise up to a depth of 20 meters, keeping the wall to your right. After some dozens of meters you reach a wide chimney with an open summit, recalling the one of Ras Za'atar. In the inside you can admire a vast number of gorgonians of a sparkling yellow colour, Red sponges (*Cliona vastifica*), siphon sponges, butterflyfish (genus *Chaetodon*) and anthias in its upper part which forms an arch

A Hawksbill turtle (Eretmochelys imbricata) between the Alcyonarians and fire corals

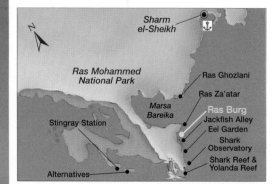

Sharm el-Sheikh

Ras Mohammed National Park

Ras Ghozlani
Ras Za'atar
Ras Burg
Marsa Bareika
Jackfish Alley
Eel Garden
Shark Observatory
Stingray Station
Shark Reef & Yolanda Reef
Alternatives

Access	🚤 60'	
Difficulty	from ○	to ○ ○
Current	○	
Natural scenery	○ ○	
Fauna interest	○ ○	
General interest	○ ○	

Other characteristics

➡ 📷 🪸 🐟

with its roof ascending to 3.5 meters. After having visited the chimney, proceed along the wall from which numerous pinnacles with diverse forms jut out. You reach a second chimney, definitely less impressive than the previous one, whilst ascending gradually to the end of the dive. Hawks-bill turtles (*Eretmochelys imbricata*), jackfish (genus *Caranx*) and fusiliers (genus *Caesio*) are common visitors to this site.

The inside of the chimney of Ras Burg is covered with encrusted sponges and soft corals

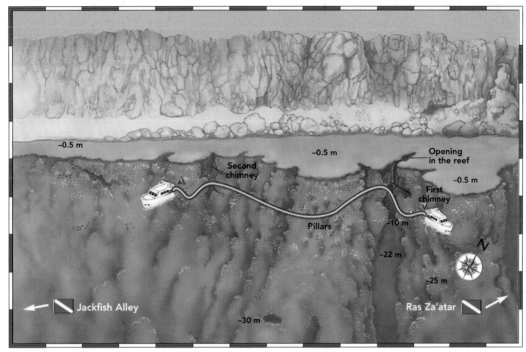

Comments

• *Dive site suitable for small groups of scuba divers.*
• *The first chimney, the main point of attraction, is relatively narrow and should not be visited by more than 3 to 4 scuba divers at a time, so as to avoid damage to the walls.*
• *Excellent site for photographers, especially at midday when the sun is in the zenith.*

Look out for

Soft coral   Sponges   Turtle

Trevally   Fusilier   Grouper

Unicornfish   Butterflyfish   Anthias

Features

• *Site is little frequented with madrepores and Alcyonarians (soft corals) still intact.*
• *Nice wall with an interesting chimney rich in fauna and colours.*
• *Generally sheltered by wind and waves.*

27°46.000' N — 34°15.400' E

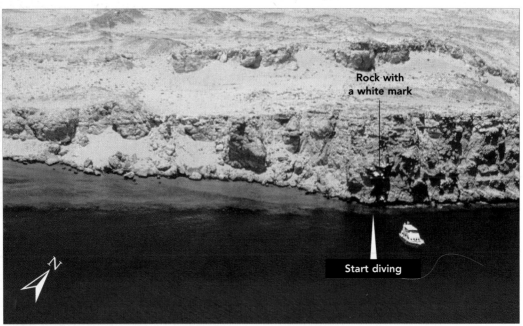

Rock with
a white mark

Start diving

Aerial view of Jackfish Alley dive site

The name of this site derives from the wide sandy 'road' between the coral ledge bordering the coast and a parallel satellite reef that is often frequented by jackfish and other predators. Jackfish Alley, which was originally known as *Fisherman's Bank* or also *Ras Kusba*, is south of Ras Za'atar. The beginning of the drift dive is easy to spot owing to the white mark on the cliff. After descending to 6 meters you will immediately see the large entrance to the first cave, which penetrates the reef for about 40 meters and from

The crossing cave **A** at Jackfish Alley

which you exit, keeping to your left at a depth of 9 meters. Proceeding to the southwest, with the reef on your right, you will come to a large coral outcrop beyond which, at 14 meters, there is another cave that runs upwards and has a wide exit hole at 6 meters. This is the home of a myriad of glassfish (Pigmy sweepers, *Parapriacanthus ransonneti*). A little further south there is a sandy bay that must be crossed in a southwest direction in order to see, at a depth of 11 meters, another coral outcrop swarming with life and

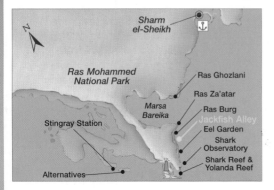

Sharm el-Sheikh
Ras Mohammed National Park
Ras Ghozlani
Ras Za'atar
Marsa Bareika
Ras Burg
Jackfish Alley
Stingray Station
Eel Garden
Shark Observatory
Shark Reef & Yolanda Reef
Alternatives

Access 70'
Difficulty
Current from to
Natural scenery
Fauna interest
General interest
Other characteristics

A group of Bigeye jackfish (Caranx sexfasciatus)

populated by another colony of glassfish. From here continue to proceed southwest and, once past a zone rich in madrepores, at a depth of 18–20 meters you will be at the sandy 'alley' this site is named after. Whitetip reef sharks (*Triaenodon obesus*) and Manta rays (*Manta birostris*) as well as jackfish (genus *Caranx*), Blue triggerfish (*Pseudobalistes fuscus*) and Bluespotted stingrays (*Taeniura lymma*) have often been spotted in this area.

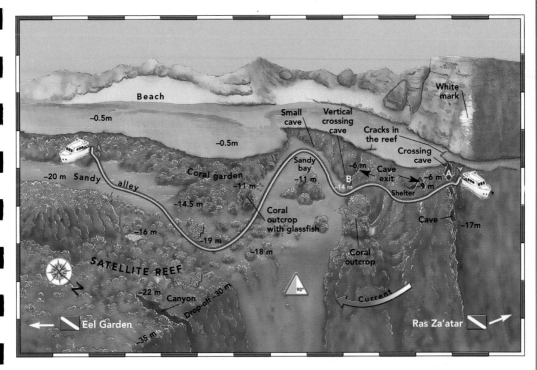

Comments

• At the start of the dive do not descend more than 5–6 meters or you will miss the entrance to the first cave.
• Only small groups of expert divers are allowed to explore the caves.
• Carry a torch with you.
• Do not explore the caves for too long a time.

Look out for

Acropora   Gorgonian   Trevally

Glassfish   Triggerfish   Stingray

Whitetip reef shark   Manta ray

Features

• An extraordinary marine landscape.
• Caves with spectacular light effects.
• Quite varied reef fauna.
• The possibility to see pelagic predators.

General view of the Eel Garden site, with access by land

Eel Garden, situated in front of a small beach south of Jackfish Alley and immediately before Shark Observatory, is accessible by land. Here, the impressive fossil coral cliff which stretches from Ras Mohammed to Ras Za'atar diminishes in height and gives way to a passage.

Eel Garden is well sheltered from the currents, but since it is exposed to prevailing winds and waves, you must pay attention to the condition of the sea, especially if you are diving from the shore.

Very few scuba divers visit this

Garden eels (Gorgasia sillneri)

place which is nonetheless very interesting from the biological point of view. The dive is extremely easy and the route winds through the sandy plateau slightly inclined to the east opposite the beach. On the central part of the sandy ledge there is a small cave out of which appears to flow an impressive V-shaped stream of sand.

The middle section of the plateau is populated by a lovely colony of Garden eels (*Gorgasia sillneri*) belonging to the Congridae family. This species is endemic and

Sharm el-Sheikh

Ras Mohammed National Park

Ras Ghozlani

Ras Za'atar

Marsa Bareika

Ras Burg
Jackfish Alley
Eel Garden
Shark Observatory
Shark Reef & Yolanda Reef

Stingray Station

Alternatives

Access	75'
Difficulty	○
Current	○
Natural scenery	○ ○
Fauna interest	○ ○
General interest	○ ○

Other characteristics

can exceed 80 centimeters in length. The eels emerge from the sand for about two-thirds of their length, swaying in the current in search for their favourite food, plankton.

A *Bluespotted stingray* (Taeniura lymma)

Their lairs, which they never abandon, are cylindrical holes dug out of the sand, the grains of which are held together by a special secretion from a gland near the eels' tail.

These creatures must be approached with extreme caution, since they are very timid and will slip quickly back into their lairs at the first sign of danger.

Features

• *The best place to observe Garden eels.*
• *A good site for snorkeling.*

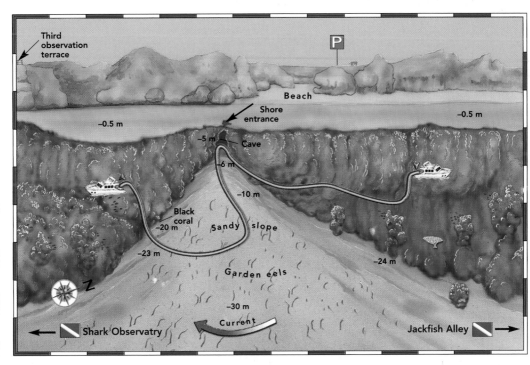

Third observation terrace
Beach
Shore entrance
−0.5 m
−0.5 m
−5 m
Cave
−6 m
−10 m
Black coral
−20 m
Sandy slope
−23 m
−24 m
Garden eels
−30 m
Current
Shark Observatry
Jackfish Alley

Comments

• *Do not dive if the sea conditions are not good and especially if there are waves.*
• *It is advisable to approach the eels from the north very slowly in order not to frighten them.*
• *The morning hours are best for taking photos of the Garden eels.*

Look out for

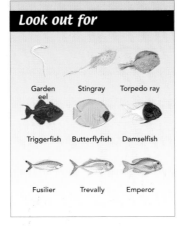

Garden eel

Stingray

Torpedo ray

Triggerfish

Butterflyfish

Damselfish

Fusilier

Trevally

Emperor

A *Panther torpedo ray* (Torpedo panthera)

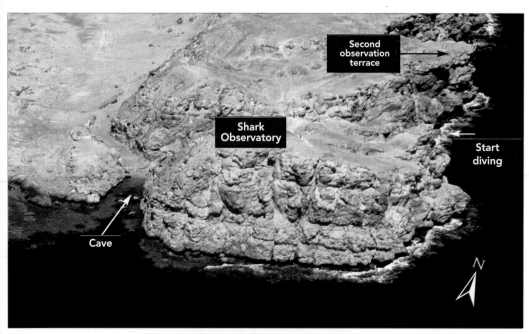

Aerial view of the promontory of Ras Mohammed with Shark Observatory

This name indicates not only the first obserbation terrace on the top of the Ras Mohammed promontory, but also the diving site that is on a level with that promontory.

This is a magnificent wall dive, also known as the *Ras Mohammed Wall*: while looking down into the deep blue, you can admire a grandiose environment and at the same time see large pelagic predators and Hawksbill turtles (*Eretmochelys imbricata*). Even a Whale shark (*Rhincodon typus*) has been seen in this area.

A pair of Common lionfish (Pterois miles)

The classic dive begins not far from the second observation terrace on the cliff.

After descending to about 15 meters (but not deeper as the route is relatively long and not all scuba divers may have sufficient air) you can explore the wall on your left, which is rich in Alcyonarians, gullies, shelters and caves swarming with life, without losing sight of the blue from which jackfish, barracuda and some sharks might suddenly appear.

On a line with the southern corner of the promontory the wall takes a sharp turn

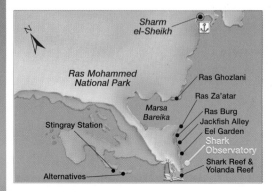

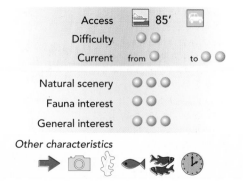

Access	🚢 85'	🚐
Difficulty	⚪⚪	
Current	from ⚪	to ⚪⚪
Natural scenery	⚪⚪⚪	
Fauna interest	⚪⚪	
General interest	⚪⚪⚪	

Other characteristics

➡️ 📷 🪸 🐟 🦈 🕐

The Whale shark (Rhincodon typus) *is the biggest fish on Earth: it has been spotted several times in the summer months along the coast of Sharm el-Sheikh*

westwards and runs towards the small beach under the observatory: here you will see some large gorgonians (*Subergorgia hicksoni*) and, further up, a majestic overhang. Continue along the wall until you enter an extremely beautiful cave that has a large fissure in its top through which light filters inside creating evocative effects.

From this cave you can exit directly onto the reef.

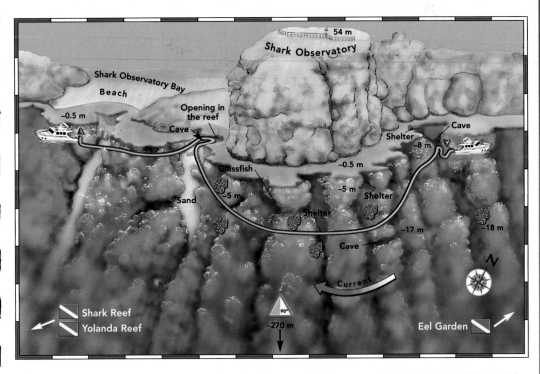

Comments

- *Check the direction of the current; it is better to dive when the tide is ebbing.*
- *Stay at a depth of 15–20 meters and ascend to 8–5 meters in the last phase of your dive.*
- *The afternoon is ideal for observing the spectacular effects of the light.*

Look out for

Gorgonian   Soft coral   Trevally

Barracuda   Whale shark   Lionfish

Turtle

Features

- *Superb marine landscape.*
- *The chance to see large pelagic predators.*

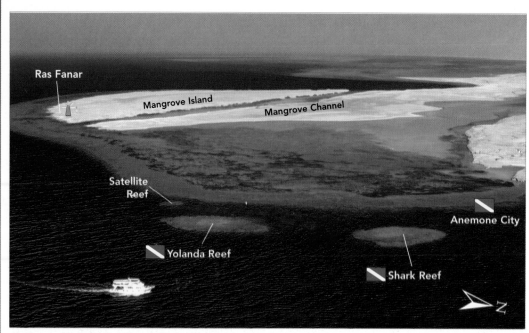

Ras Fanar

Mangrove Island

Mangrove Channel

Satellite Reef

Anemone City

Yolanda Reef

Shark Reef

Aerial view of Shark Reef and Yolanda Reef

S hark Reef is the most famous and popular dive site in the Red Sea for the variety of its marine environment and above all for the extraordinary abundance of its reef and pelagic fauna. However, to enjoy this site in all its splendour you should go there in the summer months (especially July). Another point to bear in mind is that the incredible spectacle of schools of hundreds of barracuda, jackfish and batfish that appear before your eyes can be enjoyed only by those with enough technical know-how to

face the currents, which at times are extremely strong. There are many dives you can make here – all of which are drift dives – and they can be

YOLANDA

Type of ship: merchant
Construction date: 1964
Length: 74.8 m
Width: 11.7 m
Tonnage: 1,907 t
Date of shipwreck: :
   1–2 April 1980
Date ship sank to the bottom:
   15th March 1987

varied at will, depending on different factors (weather conditions, speed and direction of the current, technical level of the divers, etc.). However, the classic and most complete dive will allow you to visit not only Shark Reef but the other two sites, Anemone City and Yolanda Reef, in one. The dive begins northeast of Shark Reef on a line with a plateau commonly known as **Anemone City**, which lies at a depth of 12–20 m and juts out like a large balcony over the blue. A large population of sea anemones (*Heteractis magnifica*

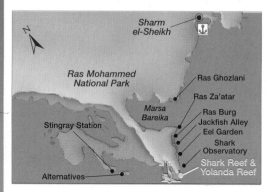

Sharm el-Sheikh

Ras Mohammed National Park

Ras Ghozlani

Ras Za'atar

Marsa Bareika

Ras Burg
Jackfish Alley
Eel Garden

Stingray Station

Shark Observatory

Shark Reef & Yolanda Reef

Alternatives

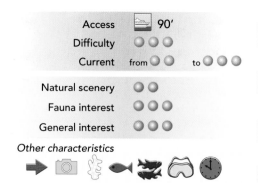

Access		90'
Difficulty	○ ○ ○	
Current	from ○ ○	to ○ ○ ○

Natural scenery	○ ○
Fauna interest	○ ○ ○
General interest	○ ○ ○

Other characteristics

Aerial view of Shark Reef and Yolanda Reef

and *Entacmaea quadricolor*), among whose stinging tentacles live multicoloured Red Sea anemonefish (*Amphiprion bicinctus*), have colonized this plateau in which the light-coloured sand is interrupted by coral formations. On this plateau, at a depth of 14 m, you will note a sort of large metal post placed in an upright position in the 1970s, it seems, to commemorate a diver who died there.

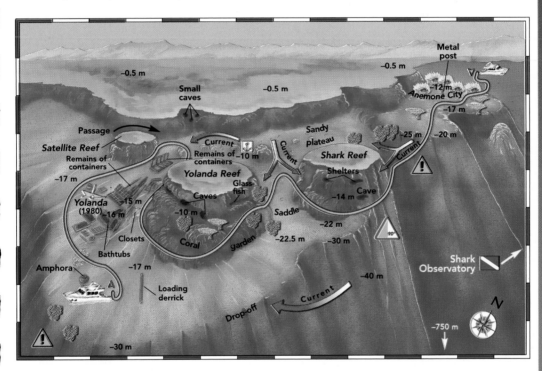

Comments

- *The site is usually overcrowded. Try to arrive early in the morning.*
- *Access and times for diving are regulated by the Ras Mohammed Park authorities.*
- *Be careful of the currents, which can be violent at times.*

Look out for

Acropora   Anemonefish   Gorgonian

Batfish   Barracuda   Trevally

Napoleonfish   Grouper   Grey reef shark

Features

- *An absolutely exceptional concentration of fauna, in particular in the summer.*
- *An extremely varied marine environment.*
- *Vast area for diving.*
- *A variety of dives.*

After exploring Anemone City you must swim in the blue for a few minutes at a depth of 20 m and at a course of 150°, which will lead you directly to **Shark Reef**, clearly recognizable by the unmistakeable profile of some gorgonians. Here a wall that descends vertically to an abyss more than 700 m deep: keeping this wall to your right, you skirt round a coral outcrop. If you observe the blue you will easily spot schools of batfish (*Platax* sp.), walls of jackfish (*Caranx* sp., *Carangoides* sp.), snappers (*Lutjanus bohar* and *Lutjanus monostigma*) and emperors

A dense school of Blackfin barracuda (Sphyraena qenie) cruising in a circle

at 14 m; this one signals the start of a splendid coral garden with mauve-coloured

The remains of the containers which once held the cargo of the Yolanda colonised by marine fauna around which a school of Onespot snappers (Lutjanus monostigma) move

(*Lethrinus nebulosus*, *Monotaxis grandoculis*) and Bluespine unicornfish (*Naso unicornis*). You easily also find big schools of small Blackfin barracuda (*Sphyraena qenie*), sometimes forming circles within which often move one or two Blacktip sharks (*Carcharhinus limbatus*). After going a few dozen meters more, you will reach the sandy and shallow saddle that connects Shark Reef and **Yolanda Reef** which silhouette takes shape right after a big gorgonian situated at a depth of 20 m and a second gorgonian

Alcyonarians contouring the eastern wall of Yolanda. After having crossed this garden, in an almost parallel direction to the reef wall and after having curved around its southern corner you will see – at a depth between 25 and 10 m – the remains of the cargo of *Yolanda*, a Cypriot merchant ship that sank here on the night of 1–2 April 1980 while on its way to Aqaba: containers, bathtubs, sanitary fixtures, wallpaper, cases of whisky and even a *BMW 320* automobile that belonged to the ship

captain. The wreckage is always surrounded by large Malabar groupers (*Epinephelus malabaricus*), Napoleonfish (*Cheilinus undulatus*), Onespot snappers (*Lutjanus monostigma*) and fusiliers (*Caesio* sp.). The ship – which stood half above the surface in an unstable vertical position since the bow was stuck in the seabed – was pushed by the waves to a depth of 50 m at the beginning of 1987 and, on the 15th March of the same year, sank into the blue during a violent storm. It lies today at a depth of around 200 m. The dive usually ends after you have finished exploring the remains of the *Yolanda*: if you still have some air left you can explore the sandy lagoon stretching out behind Yolanda Reef and the saddle between the two coral outcrops inhabited by Bluespotted stingrays (*Taeniura lymma*), scorpionfish (*Scorpae-nopsis* sp.), Stonefish (*Synanceia verrucosa*), Napoleonfish (*Cheilinus undulatus*) and Crocodilefish (*Papilloculiceps longiceps*). As an alternative you can visit the nearby **Satellite Reef** or explore the area south of Yolanda, where you can see some Grey reef sharks (*Carcharhinus amblyrhynchos*),

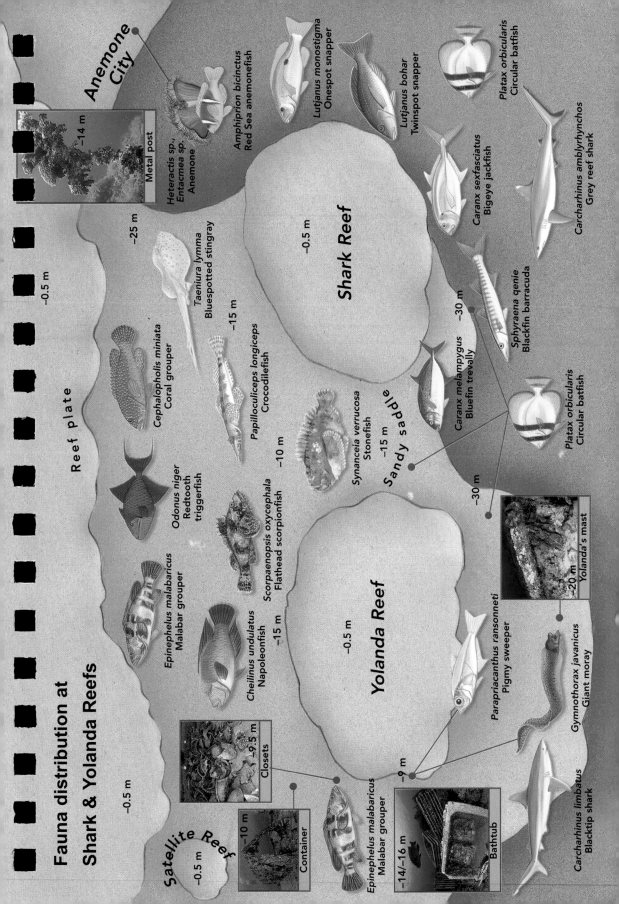

Fauna distribution at Shark & Yolanda Reefs

Anemone City

Metal post –14 m

Heteractis sp., Entacmea sp. Anemone

Amphiprion bicinctus Red Sea anemonefish

Lutjanus monostigma Onespot snapper

Lutjanus bohar Twinspot snapper

Platax orbicularis Circular batfish

Carcharhinus amblyrhynchos Grey reef shark

Caranx sexfasciatus Bigeye jackfish

Sphyraena qenie Blackfin barracuda

Platax orbicularis Circular batfish

Caranx melampygus Bluefin trevally

Shark Reef

–0.5 m

–30 m

–30 m

Sandy saddle

–15 m

Synanceia verrucosa Stonefish

–25 m

–15 m

Reef plate

Cephalopholis miniata Coral grouper

Taeniura lymma Bluespotted stingray

Papilloculiceps longiceps Crocodilefish

–10 m

Scorpaenopsis oxycephala Flathead scorpionfish

–0.5 m

Odonus niger Redtooth triggerfish

Epinephelus malabaricus Malabar grouper

Cheilinus undulatus Napoleonfish

–15 m

–15 m

–0.5 m

Yolanda Reef

–0.5 m

Parapriacanthus ransonneti Pigmy sweeper

Gymnothorax javanicus Giant moray

Yolanda´s mast –20 m

Carcharhinus limbatus Blacktip shark

Bathtub –14/–16 m

–9 m

Epinephelus malabaricus Malabar grouper

Container –10 m

Closets –9.5 m

Satellite Reef

–0.5 m

A family of Red Sea anemonefish
(Amphiprion bicinctus) around
their anemone (Heteractis
magnifica) at Anemone Reef — **1**

A big Blacktip shark
(Carcharhinus limbatus) — **2**

A dense school of Circular batfish
(Platax orbicularis) between
Shark and Yolanda Reef — **3**

The extensive plateau of sanitary
fixtures that were part of the
cargo of the ship Yolanda — **4**

A couple of Giant morays
(Gymnothorax javanicus) in a
small cave on the southern side
of Yolanda Reef — **5**

STRAIT OF GUBAL

The Strait of Gubal connects the Gulf of Suez to the Red Sea and is bordered to the west by the Egyptian coast and to the east by the Sinai peninsula. The Gulf of Suez is much shallower than the Gulf of Aqaba because of its different geological origin; its average depth is about 80 meters.

The channel through which ships pass into the Strait of Gubal – which is much wider than the Strait of Tiran – is flanked to the northeast by two outcrops, **Beacon Rock** and **Shag Rock**, both of which have beacons as well as the wrecks of the *Dunraven* and the *Kingston* respectively. To the southwest the channel is delimited by the southern tip of *Shadwan* Island (also known as *Shaker Island* on British maps), which also has a beacon, situated 15.2 miles from the one on Beacon Rock.

The southeastern section of the strait is characterized by the presence of two massive, half-outcropping coral formations (called *sha'ab* in Arabic) that create a coral reef, inside which there are shallow lagoons with sandy floors: *Sha'ab Mahmud* and *Sha'ab Ali*.

Sha'ab Mahmud stretches out in line with the western side of the Ras Mohammed peninsula and is about 6 miles long and 2.7 miles wide with a north-west to south-east orientation. Beacon Rock is situated on its southernmost point.

This long coral reef forms a wide lagoon well protected from waves, its southern entrance is marked by Beacon Rock to the west and by the reef of *Sha'ab el-Utat* to the east. Sha'ab Mahmud is interrupted by two passages called **Small Crack (Small Passage)** and **Big Crack (Big Passage)**: the first is only practical for small boats whereas the second passage, situated 27°46.540' N and 34°03.362' E, is navigable and usually used by boats cruising towards the wreck of the *Thistlegorm* and to dive sites in the area of Gubal.

There is another reef, circular in shape, directly in the north of the Big Crack called *Sha'ab Surur* or *En-Neghs* as local fishermen call it. The other important reef in the Strait of Gubal is **Sha'ab Ali**: situated to the north-west of Sha'ab Mahmud, it stretches out over 8.3 miles in a northeast-southwest direction and is separated from the Sinai coast by a deep channel with an average depth of

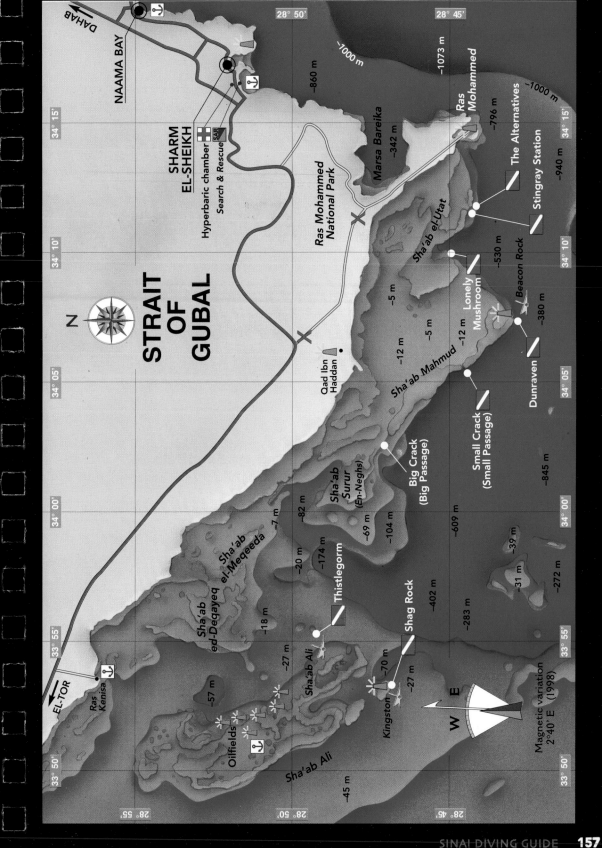

DAHAB

NAAMA BAY

28° 50'   28° 45'

~1000 m

~1073 m

~860 m

Ras
Mohammed

34° 15'

SHARM
EL-SHEIKH

Hyperbaric chamber
Search & Rescue   SAR

~796 m

The Alternatives

~1000 m

34° 15'

Marsa Bareika
~342 m

Ras Mohammed
National Park

Stingray Station

~940 m

Sha'ab el-Utat

~530 m

34° 10'

34° 10'

STRAIT
OF
GUBAL

N

Lonely
Mushroom

~5 m

Beacon Rock

~380 m

Dunraven

~5 m

~12 m   ~12 m

Sha'ab Mahmud

Qad Ibn
Haddan

34° 05'

Small Crack
(Small Passage)

~845 m

34° 05'

34° 00'

Sha'ab
Surur
(En-Neghs)

Big Crack
(Big Passage)

~82 m

~69 m

~104 m

~609 m

34° 00'

~39 m

~402 m

~283 m

~31 m

~272 m

~7 m

Thistlegorm

Sha'ab
el-Meqeeda

~20 m

~174 m

Shag Rock

Sha'ab
ed-Deqayeq

~18 m

~27 m

~70 m

33° 55'

~27 m

Kingston

~27 m

33° 55'

Sha'ab Ali

EL-TOR

Ras
Kenisa

~57 m

W   E

Oilfields

Magnetic variation
2°40' E (1998)

33° 50'

Sha'ab Ali

~45 m

33° 50'

28° 55'   28° 50'   28° 45'

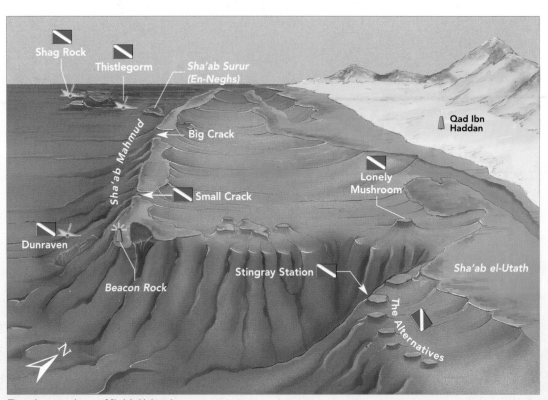

Shag Rock

Thistlegorm

Sha'ab Surur (En-Neghs)

Sha'ab Mahmud

Big Crack

Small Crack

Dunraven

Beacon Rock

Stingray Station

Lonely Mushroom

Qad Ibn Haddan

The Alternatives

Sha'ab el-Utath

N

Three-dimensional map of Sha'ab Mahmud

Strait of Gubal	Snorkeling	Open Water	Advanced Open Water
The Alternatives	●	●	
Dunraven			●
Small Crack	●		●
Shag Rock	●		●
Thistlegorm			●
Sha'ab Abu Nuhas	●		●

🤿 Snorkeling   🛢 Open Water   🛢🛢 Advanced Open Water

Aerial view of the beacon at Beacon Rock

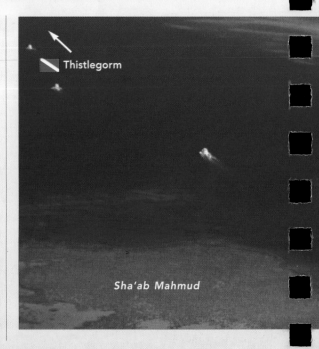

Thistlegorm

Sha'ab Mahmud

Satellite view of Sha'ab Mahmud

20–25 meters. Sha'ab Ali is best-known for the famous wreck of the Thistlegorm on its eastern side. It surrounds a lagoon with a depth of 7–10 meters, the entrance of which, marked by a series of luminous buoys, lies on its northeastern side.

Diving boats often spend the night in this lagoon so that scuba divers can be at the site of the shipwreck at dawn, thus avoiding the arrival of the many daily boats from Sharm and Hurghada later in the morning.

Aerial view of Big Crack

Sha'ab el-Utath

Aerial view of The Alternatives

Three miles west of Ras Mohammed, a series of outcropping coral pinnacles extends east-west for about 1.5 miles on the southern edge of *Sha'ab el-Utat*, flanking a large sandy lagoon with an average depth of about ten meters. Local fishermen call this site *Saba Erg* (the 'Seven Pinnacles') while divers have renamed it 'Alternatives' because, as it is so well-sheltered, it offers the opportunity to make alternative dives when conditions in the open sea are prohibitive. The classic dive goes around the two middle pinnacles, which are in line with a fixed mooring. Due to its position this site has tidal currents that greatly influence visibility, which can be quite poor when the

Leopard shark (Stegostoma fasciatum)

Thistlegorm

Ras Mohammed

Shag Rock

Stingray Station

Small Crack

The Alternatives

Dunraven

N

Access 2h

Difficulty from ○ to ○ ○ ○

Current from ○ to ○ ○

Natural scenery ○

Fauna interest ○ ○

General interest ○ ○

Other characteristics

current comes from the south, especially if accompanied by wind and waves. If, on the other hand, the sea is calm and the current is either lacking or is coming from the north, you can enjoy Alternatives swarming with fauna where you can find numerous coral genera, large groupers (*Epinephelus malabaricus, E. tauvina*), Bluespotted stingrays (*Taeniura lymma*), squids, nudibranchs and even Leopard sharks

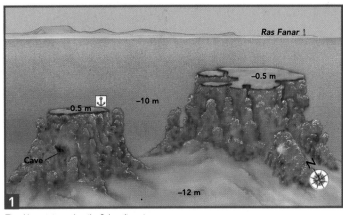

The Alternatives: detail of the dive site

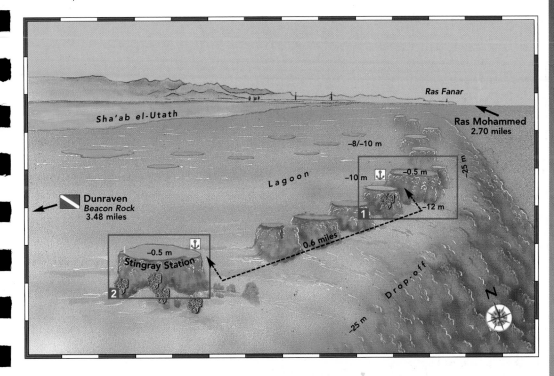

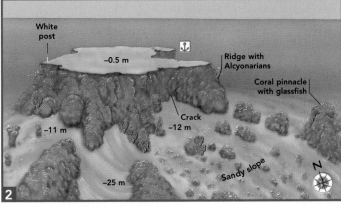

Stingray Station: detail of the dive site

A Four colour chromodoris
(Chromodoris quadricolor)

27°43.748' N — 34°11.903' E

Features

- A sheltered site offering a safe stay.
- An abundance of marine life, especially groupers and many genera of corals.
- Offers you the chance to see Leopard sharks (Stegostoma fasciatum).

A Feathertail stingray (Pastinachus sephen) accompanied by its remora

A group of anthias swarms around a red Alcyonarian and red sponge on the northeastern ridge of Stingray Station

Look out for

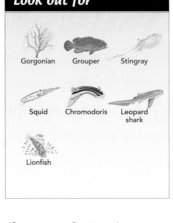

Gorgonian   Grouper   Stingray

Squid   Chromodoris   Leopard shark

Lionfish

Comments

- It is better not to dive if the sea is rough and visibility is poor.
- Night diving can be effected only in optimal conditions; make sure to bring two torches with you.

(Stegostoma fasciatum). In the north-western part of Alternatives we find a large, roughly quadrangular outcrop, known as **Stingray Station** (27° 43.845' N – 34° 11.241' E) because many Bluespotted stingrays gather here, particularly in the spring months. About 1.7 miles to the west of Stingray Station, a single, large circular tower known as **Lonely Mushroom** comes up from the sandy seabed; it is situated at 27° 43.640' N – 34° 09.293' E and has a shamandura fixed on the reef at the surface, which can sometimes be hard to locate. Despite its small dimension, this site permits short yet interesting dives, especially for the lovers of macro-photography, as nudibranchs and shrimps are hiding between the numerous soft and small hard corals.

Aerial view of Stingray Station

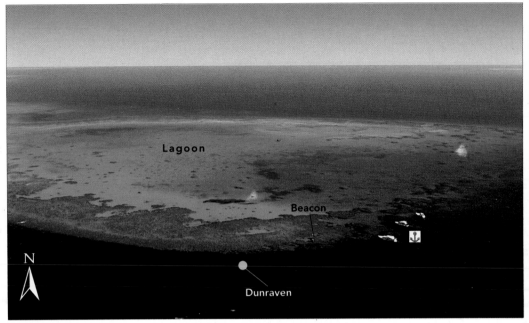

Aerial view of Beacon Rock

There is a small semi-outcropping reef situated 6.9 miles west of Ras Mohammed with a small metal beacon indicating the southern tip of Sha'ab Mahmud. In 1876 this was the site of the shipwreck of the British merchant ship *Dunraven*, built in Newcastle in 1873 by *Mitchell & Co* with mixed propulsion (sail and steam), and bound for Bombay. The wreck lies upside down at 15–29.5 meters' depth, in two sections; it was discovered only in 1977 by geologist Arye Keller and underwater cameraman Howard Rosenstein. The *Dunraven* was the subject of a memorable BBC documentary film in 1979 and has become a classic site for scuba divers. Since the cargo (timber and

DUNRAVEN

Type of ship: *steamer*
Nationality: British
Year of construction: 1873
Length: 85 m
Width: 9.7 m
Estimated tonnage: 1,800 t
Date of shipwreck:
   22nd of April 1876
Depth: 15–29.5 m

bales of cotton) was lost during the shipwreck when the ship caught fire, the wreck looks like a large, practically empty cave. You can access through the three main openings at the stern, center and the bow. You reach the *Dunraven* by zodiac if the boat is moored in the sheltered area behind the lighthouse. The dive begins from the stern, the deepest point of the wreck. After going a few dozen meters, you can penetrate the hull – populated by large groupers, lionfish and swarms of glassfish and multicoloured

Access		2h 30'
Difficulty	◐◐	
Current	from ◐	to ◐◐
Natural scenery	◐	
Fauna interest	◐◐ .	
General interest	◐◐	

Other characteristics

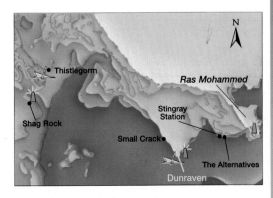

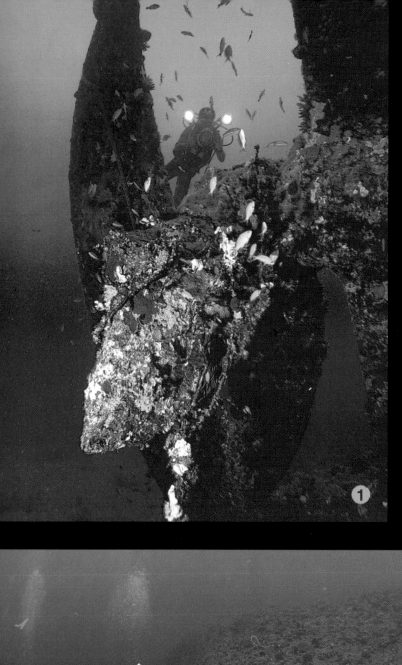

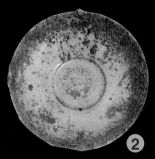

The big propeller of the *Dunraven lacking the upper blade, encrusted with soft corals, small sponges and hard corals*

1

A plate with the name of the *Dunraven in the middle that was part of the boat service*

2

View of the starboard side of the stern showing the propeller and rudder. The arrow indicates the opening to penetrate the hull

3

Drawing by the shipyard Mitchell & Co showing the Dunraven

Alcyonarians. It is best to exit through the opening amidships by the engine room, so that you can explore the outside of the bow area and the nearby coral garden.

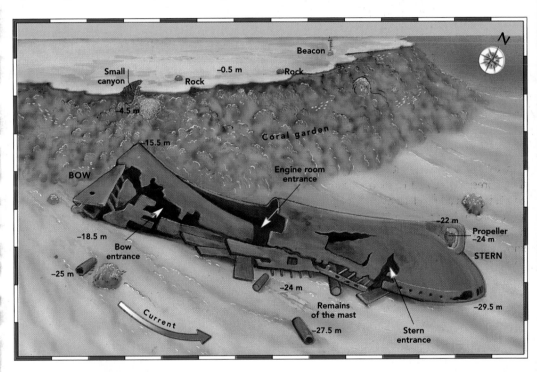

Comments
• *Dive when the sea is calm and the weather is good.*
• *There is often a current moving to the north.*
• *Even though visibility may be fairly good, it is advisable to have a torch.*

Look out for

Soft coral   Porites   Sponge

Crocodilefish Scorpionfish Glassfish

Grouper

The propeller of the Dunraven

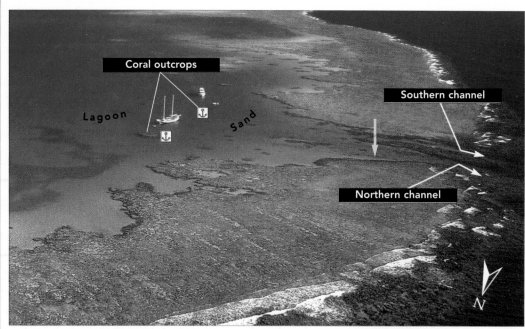

Boats moored inside the lagoon at Small Crack. The yellow arrow indicates the main passage of the reef

The long, half-outcropping coral reef running from northwest to southeast that constitutes the impressive Sha'ab Mahmud and separates a broad sandy lagoon from the open sea, is breached by two channels known as **Small Crack** (or **Small Passage**) and **Big Crack** (or **Big Passage**). Small Crack, called *Fossma Saghir* by local fishermen, is the more southerly channel. Its central body is divided by a large coral formation into two secondary channels from 5 to 8 meters deep with tidal currents that can become extremely strong. When the tide is flooding and the current it generates moves northwards, you are pushed from the lagoon out towards the open sea. If on the other hand the tide is ebbing, the current runs south towards the lagoon: it is therefore preferable to dive then, so that you can drift back to your boat moored inside the lagoon. Obviously a zodiac would be ideal for dives in Small Crack.

On the outer reef wall, which descends to a sandy floor between 18–22 meter deep, you will see gorgonians,

A school of Bluefin trevalley (Caranx melampygus)

Access	🛥 3h		
Difficulty	◐ ◐		
Current	from ◐	to ◐ ◐	

Natural scenery	◐ ◐
Fauna interest	◐ ◐
General interest	◐ ◐

Other characteristics

Alcyonarians and large table corals. Often there are turtles and also Leopard sharks (*Stegostoma fasciatum*) and Whitetip reef sharks (*Triaenodon obesus*). In the summer there are schools of barracuda and jackfish and, near the mouth of the channel, a school of breams (genus *Acanthopagrus*). Inside the northern channel there is an abundance of fire corals (*Millepora dichotoma*), typical in areas with strong currents.

Fishing boats moored inside the lagoon at Small Crack. The yellow arrow indicates the main passage of the reef

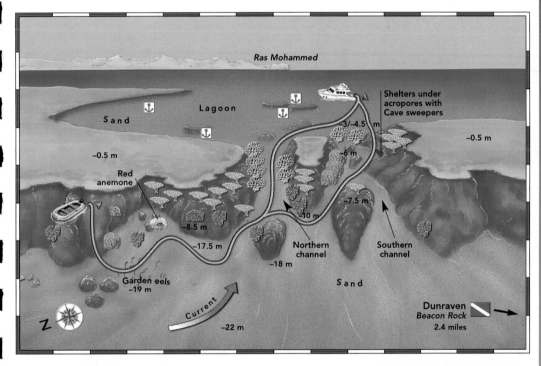

Comments

• Be sure to check the direction of the current before your dive.
• If the current is strong and running northwards, do not dive, especially if you do not have a zodiac.

Look out for

Acropora Gorgonian Soft coral

Anemonefish Porites Turtle

Whitetip reef shark Bream Trevally

Features

• A varied underwater environment rich in different fauna.
• A quiet site with few divers.
• The chance to see Leopard sharks (*Stegostoma fasciatum*).

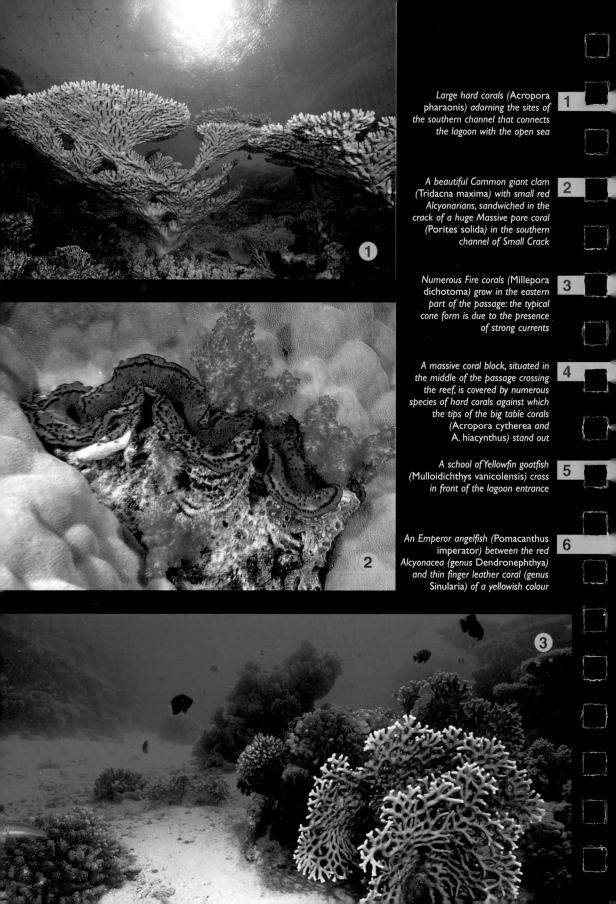

1 Large hard corals (Acropora pharaonis) adorning the sites of the southern channel that connects the lagoon with the open sea

2 A beautiful Common giant clam (Tridacna maxima) with small red Alcyonarians, sandwiched in the crack of a huge Massive pore coral (Porites solida) in the southern channel of Small Crack

3 Numerous Fire corals (Millepora dichotoma) grow in the eastern part of the passage: the typical cone form is due to the presence of strong currents

4 A massive coral block, situated in the middle of the passage crossing the reef, is covered by numerous species of hard corals against which the tips of the big table corals (Acropora cytherea and A. hiacynthus) stand out

5 A school of Yellowfin goatfish (Mulloidichthys vanicolensis) cross in front of the lagoon entrance

6 An Emperor angelfish (Pomacanthus imperator) between the red Alcyonacea (genus Dendronephthya) and thin finger leather coral (genus Sinularia) of a yellowish colour

4

5

6

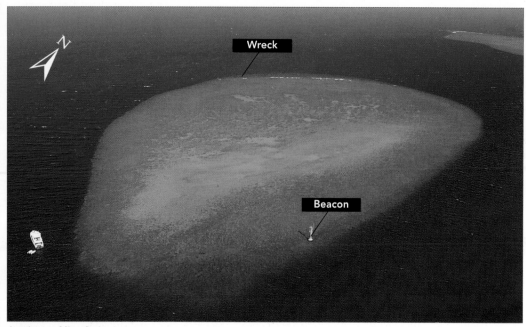

Labels on image: Wreck, Beacon

Aerial view of Shag Rock

S hag Rock, situated about a mile south of Sha'ab Ali and 6 miles away from the wreck of the *Thistlegorm*, is the name given to a shallow reef marked by a small metal lighthouse on its south-eastern side. A big sandy plateau by this lighthouse extends to a depth of 8–10 meters, with a fixed shamandura called the *Lady Jenny Mooring*.

On the northern side of the reef on the sandy seabed at a depth of 15 meters, there is a small wreck lying in a south-north direction with its bow stranded on the reef. The wreck at Shag Rock has for a long time been falsely called *Sara H.*, an imaginary name that in reality does not apply to any ship: this wreck is

KINGSTON

Type of ship: merchant
Nationality: British
Year of Construction: 1871
Length: 78 m
Width: 10 m
Tonnage: 1449 t
Date of shipwreck:
     22nd February 1881
Depth: 4–17 m

the British cargo vessel *Kingston* built in 1871 in Sunderland by *Oswald Shipbuilding Co.* which ran aground on this reef on the 22nd February 1881 whilst en route to Aden, located in southern Yemen, with its cargo of coal. The *Kingston* was 78 meters long, 10 meters wide, with a 1,449 tonnage and was equipped with a twin-cylinder engine giving the vessel a velocity of 11 knots.

The exploration of the ship starts at the stern at a depth of 15 meters where the still intact propeller can be observed. The route continues into the inside

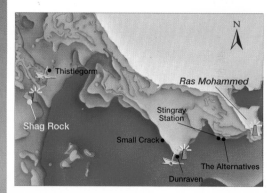

Map labels: Thistlegorm, Ras Mohammed, Stingray Station, Shag Rock, Small Crack, The Alternatives, Dunraven, N

Access	🚤 2h		
Difficulty	from ⚪	to ⚪ ⚪	
Current	⚪		

Natural scenery	⚪ ⚪	
Fauna interest	⚪ ⚪	
General interest	⚪ ⚪	

Other characteristics

➡️ 📷 🦑 🐟

of the hull, easily accessible as the wooden bridge is no longer there and the area is well illuminated by sunlight. The remains of the engine room with the boilers are still nicely visible whereas the bow area situated at a depth of 4 meters is destroyed. To the right of the wreck you can see the remains of the mast resting on the seabed. The fauna here is particularly interesting and comprises surgeonfish (genera *Acanthurus* and *Zebrasoma*), rabbitfish (genus *Siganus*) and nudibranchs.

From here you continue the dive either to the east or west to explore the reef populated by a rich fauna represented by jackfish (genera *Caranx* and *Carangoides*), groupers and snappers, turtles and Whitetip reef shark (*Triaenodon obesus*) or an Eagle ray.

Schools of dolphins are regularly spotted in this area.

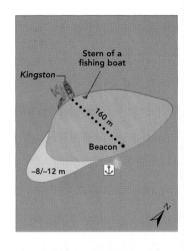

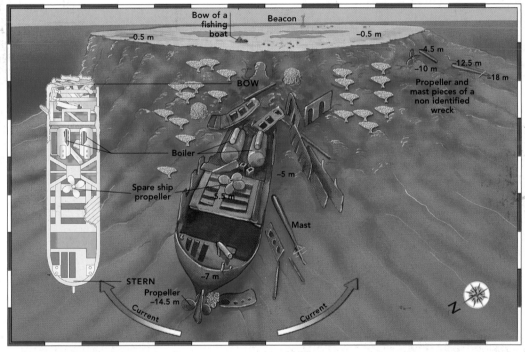

Comments

• *Dive only when the sea is calm.*
• *No torch is needed for the exploration of the wreck.*
• *Strong currents possible.*

Look out for

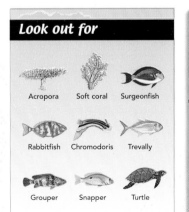

Acropora   Soft coral   Surgeonfish

Rabbitfish   Chromodoris   Trevally

Grouper   Snapper   Turtle

Features

• *Wreck is easily accessible and offers spectacular opportunities for photographers.*
• *Abundance of soft and hard corals.*
• *Numerous and varied reef fauna.*
• *Ideal site for a third dive after the Thistlegorm.*

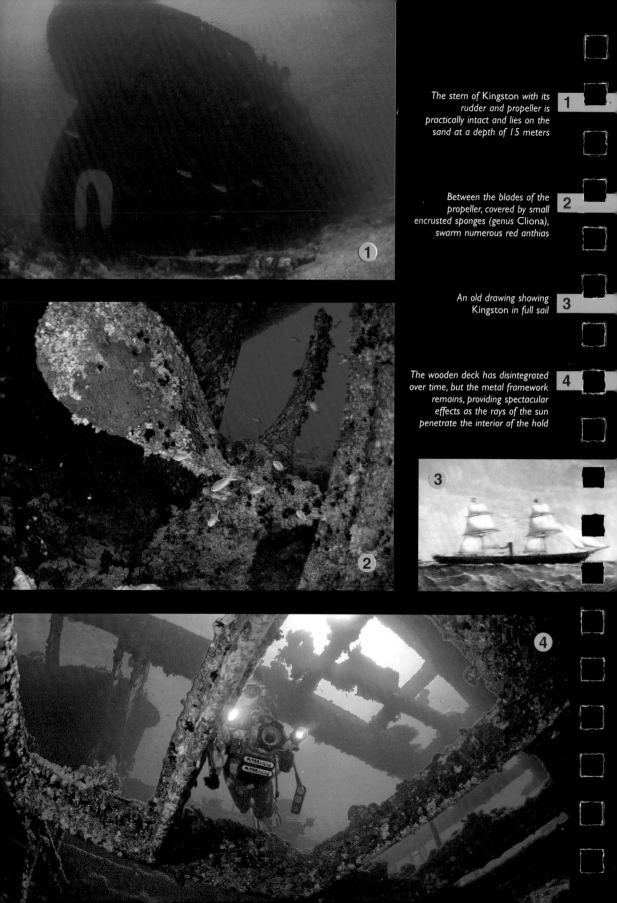

1 The stern of Kingston with its rudder and propeller is practically intact and lies on the sand at a depth of 15 meters

2 Between the blades of the propeller, covered by small encrusted sponges (genus Cliona), swarm numerous red anthias

3 An old drawing showing Kingston in full sail

4 The wooden deck has disintegrated over time, but the metal framework remains, providing spectacular effects as the rays of the sun penetrate the interior of the hold

The stern and the propeller of the Thistlegorm

The *Thistlegorm*, the Gaelic name means 'blue thistle', was a British transport ship belonging to the *Albyn Line* shipping company, was 126.5 meters long, a capacity of 4,898 tons (9,009 displacement tons), and had a three cylinder steam engine developing 1,860 HP that gave the vessel a speed of around 10 knots. The *Thistlegorm* was built to transport refurbished wartime materials for the British troops. In May 1941 with a crew of 39 men it had left the port of Glasgow, Scotland, with a cargo of munitions, bombs of different kinds, anti-tank mines, *Lee Enfield MK III* rifles, a hundred of *BSA* motor-

cycles, *BSA W–M20, Matchless G3L* and *Norton 16 H, Bedford, Morris* and *Ford* trucks, two

The launching of the Thistlegorm *on the 9th of April 1940*

Access	🚢	4h 30'
Difficulty	⚪⚪⚪	
Current	from ⚪	to ⚪⚪ ⚪
Natural scenery	⚪	
Fauna interest	⚪⚪	
General interest	⚪⚪⚪	

Other characteristics

📷 🐟

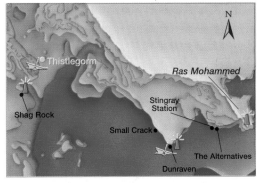

light *Bren Carrier MK II* tanks, two steam *Stanier 8 F* locomotives complete with two coal tenders and water tankers necessary for travel in desert zones, transport trucks, portable field generators, spare parts for airplanes and automobiles, medicines, tyres and rubber boots. The cargo was destined for the British 8th Army stationed in Egypt and Cyrenaica (Lybia); yet the German forces controlled the Mediterranean so circumnavigating Africa and passing through the Suez Canal to reach the port of Alexandria was considered the safer route. The *Thistlegorm* was already on its way up the Red Sea when it received the order to anchor in the Strait of Gubal and wait as the Suez Canal was temporarily obstructed by a vessel that had hit a German mine. On the night of the 5–6th October two German *Heinkel He III*

THISTLEGORM

Type of ship: steam freighter
Nationality: British
Construction date: 1940
Propulsion: steam
Max. speed: 10.5 knots
Length: 126.5 m
Width: 17.5 m
Tonnage: displacement of 9,009 t
Date of shipwreck:
 5–6 October 1941
Depth: 15–30 m

bombers, coming from their base in Crete, sighted and attacked the ship. It was hit by two bombs on hold no. 4 where the munitions deposit – among other things – was situated. The explosion was very violent and tore the ship in two whilst the locomotives,

despite their weight of 126 tons each and the fact that they were tied to the deck, were catapulted into the air, sinking to the seabed about 30 meters away. The *Thistlegorm* sank abruptly in an upright position on a flat, sandy seabed 30 meters deep at 1:30am on the 6th of October 1941. The crew and the captain were saved by the nearby vessel *HMS Carlisle*, but nine men died during the attack. It was Jacques-Yves Cousteau with his legendary oceanographic ship *Calypso*, who discovered the wreck in 1955 and who mentioned it in an article published in February 1956 in the monthly *National Geographic Magazine*. Cousteau, however, did not reveal the position of the wreck, thus it went forgotten for almost 40 years until 1992 when it was rediscovered by an Israeli skipper. In a short time the *Thistlegorm* has become a great favourite with scuba divers from all over the world and is now the most visited wreck in the whole Red Sea.

Exploration of the wreck
The *Thistlegorm* lies 19.2 miles from Ras Mohammed and 31 miles from Sharm el-Sheikh. Locating the exact site is sometimes difficult because its framework is not visible from the surface and it is wise to use GPS. As an alternative – based on an empiric system and certainly less accurate – you can use a compass and visible landmarks. Once the position of the wreck is found the diving boat needs to be moored to the wreck's framework with

two ropes along the bow and stern parallel to the wreck itself. This operation can be delicate; it should be done by dive guides and normally takes at least 15 minutes. In the course of the years incompetent or ignorant guides tied the ropes of their boats on fragile points (like small staircases, winch arms or handrails), and not on solid structures adequate to sustain strong tractions (such as bollards,

A German Heinkel He III *bomber*

winches or propeller axis), thus causing massive damage to the ship. Exploration of the ship is usually done in two phases: The first dive is a general tour of the wreck resting in its NW-SE position; the second dive includes penetration of the holds. Descents and ascents are done along the ropes with which the diving boat is moored to the wreck. Visibility is not always good (it rarely goes beyond 20 to 30 meters) and tidal currents from bow to stern can be present and sometimes very strong.

External exploration
The stern lists to port at a 46° angle and, at its deepest point of 30 meters, the four-bladed propeller and the rudder can be seen. Ascending a few meters to a depth of 25 meters, on the upper deck there is a 4.7 inch - machine-gun and directly towards the bow the 10.3 inch anti-aircraft

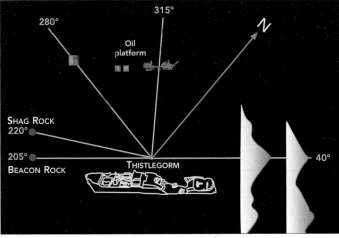

The Thistlegorm's bearings with respect to the magnetic North

gun surrounded by schools of glassfish (*Parapriacanthus ransonneti*).

You continue and examine the wide gash caused by the German bombs at hold No. 4 which contained ammunition, bombs, two *Bren Carrier MK II* tanks (which now lie on the seabed, overturned but in good condition), and trailers to transport ammunition.

The ammunition, much of which survived intact, can still be seen in situ, as can the two stumps of the propeller's axle.

One of the two *Stanier 8 F* locomotives, that were part of the cargo of the *Thistlegorm*, lies on the seabed about 30 meters away from the hull towards the south-west in line with hold no. 4. The main axis of the locomotive, of which only the front portion of the boiler and the first two pairs of wheels have survived, is resting almost parallel to the ship. Moving along the hull towards the bow you come across an open funnel vent amidst the torn wreckage of the deck.

Also located here is the opening to hold no. 3, which mainly held coal. Coming to the central and highest section of the ship, we find the bridge, from which all the contents have been removed, including the beautiful on-board telegraph used to transmit orders to the engine room. Next is the captain's cabin and further forward is the wide opening to hold no. 2, flanked by the locomotives' two coal tenders. Away from the opening of hold no. 2, approximately 20 meters to starboard, resting on the seabed at a depth of 30 meters is the second *Stanier 8 F* locomotive: different from the first in that the front boiler hatch is open. Continuing the ascent along the main deck of the ship towards the bow, one notes the two large capstans of the loading derricks serving hold no. 2, and the tilted main mast, partially supported by the port side tender. Next comes the quarterdeck, where we find the openings that provided ventilation for the

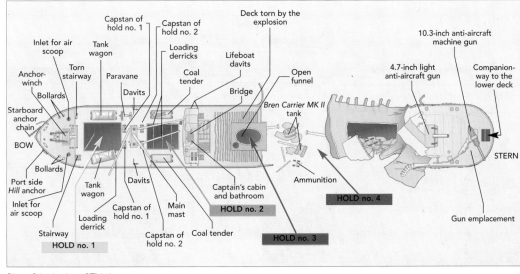

Plan of the bridge of Thistlegorm

holds. There are also two further winches before the entrance to hold no. 1, which is flanked by the two tank wagons used to transport the water supply necessary for the locomotives. On the deck, next to the starboard quarterdeck, a torpedo-shaped paravane is still visible along with the davit for lifting and lowering it into the water. These were devices on board many British vessels during the Second World War; fitted with direction-indicator fins they were paid out to stern and served to cut the cables fastening any potential deep-sea

The divergent paravane on the right side

mines to the seabed. Moving on toward the bow, at a depth of 16 meters, on the port side there is one of the two small stairways to the forecastle whereas the starboard one was torn away in 2001 and rests on the bridge not far away.
At the center of the forecastle

is the perfectly preserved large anchor winch, surrounded by dense shoals of anthias.
One may also observe the port side anchor, still in its original position, and its counterpart on the starboard side, which lies on the seabed over a hundred meters from the hull.

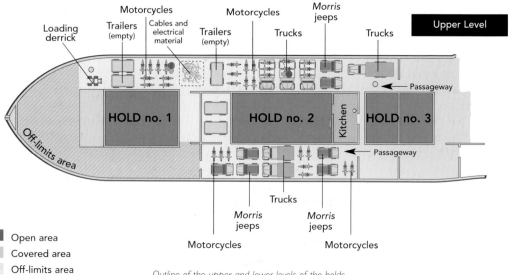

- ■ Open area
- ■ Covered area
- ■ Off-limits area

Outline of the upper and lower levels of the holds

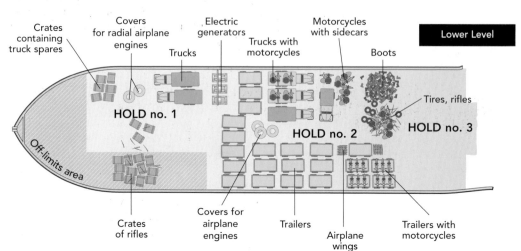

The Holds

Examining the holds and their cargo is usually the objective of the second dive on the wreck. **Hold no. 3** is of minimal interest since it contained mainly coal for the engine boiler. If the current is strong, going through this hold is the easiest way to reach hold no. 2, which is far more interesting. **Hold no. 2** is divided into two – an upper and a lower level. On the upper level you find on both sites numerous *WOT 2 Ford* trucks, *Bedford 0Y* and *MW* trucks, as well as several *Morris commercial CS 8* jeeps. There are also some *BSA W-M20* and *Norton 16H* motorcycles, some of them with sidecars. On the port side of the lower level there are many trailers (almost all of which are empty) and spare airplane wings; on the starboard side there are Bedford trucks containing some *Norton H16* motorcycles with sidecars and a supply of rubber

Motorbike BSA W-M20 in hold no. 2

boots. **Hold no. 1**, situated towards the bow and connected by two internal lateral passageways to hold no. 2, is also of considerable interest. Whilst its port side has completely collapsed, the starboard side of this hold contains, on the upper level, two empty trailers side-by-side, *Matchless G3L* and *Norton 16 H* motorcycles (some with sidecars), and, on the lower level, covers for airplane engines, crates of medicines, *Lee Enfield MK III* rifles, and several portable electric generators.

Conservation the wreck

Unfortunately, nowadays the number of scuba divers visiting the *Thistlegorm* every day has reached unsupportable levels. Their presence is jeopardizing

the fine state of preservation of the wreck's framework; the air bubbles accumulating against the metal walls are causing rapid corrosion that is endangering their very survival. Furthermore, many scuba divers cannot resist the temptation to take away

objects, parts of the motorcycles or even ammunition. The *Thistlegorm* is not only one of the most famous wrecks in the world and one of the major tourist attractions in Egypt (it generates more money than one of the Pyramids at Giza), yet it is above all an extraordinary historic relic of WW2 the conservation of which today becomes more and more urgent and should incite the Egyptian Authorities to introduce severe measures controlling scuba diving – or maybe even closure of the site.

Comments

• *The site is hard to find if you do not have a GPS.*
• *Difficult dive because of the depth and the current.*
• *Visibility often poor.*
• *Ascents and descents must be done using the mooring lines of the diving boat.*
• *Start your ascent with 80 bar.*
• *Carry a torch with you.*
• *Be careful when visiting the inner structures.*
• *Very crowed site with too many boats on surface and too many divers on the wreck.*
• *Do not take anything from the wreck.*

Features

• *Extremely interesting dives on a wreck that is exceptional for its history and preserved condition.*
• *An abundance of fauna.*

Look out for

Anemonefish Barracuda Grouper

Batfish Trevally Butterflyfish

Surgeonfish Crocodilefish Soldierfish

The bow of Thistlegorm with the big anchor winch still intact **1**

A scuba diver explores hold no. 2 containing numerous Lee Enfield MKIII rifles **2**

A motorbike BSA W–M20 identical to those transported by Thistlegorm (Sinai Heritage & Diving Museum, *Naama Bay*) **3**

One of the many motorbikes BSA W–M20 found in hold no. 2 **4**

The stern of the Thistlegorm is still intact despite the explosion of the near hold no. 4 with its bombs and munitions **5**

5

Aerial view of the northern coast of Sha'ab Abu Nuhas

The reef of Abu Nuhas, meaning 'Father of Copper' in Arabic, was named by the local fishermen who used to find many copper parts in their nets: they belonged to the *Carnatic* and to other vessels wrecked in this area. The reef is situated in the middle of the Strait of Gubal directly north of Shadwan Island which is about 3 miles away. This is a fairly sensitive position with its proximity to the major shipping lanes of the Gulf of Suez. Numerous ships were wrecked on this half-submerged reef that previously had no lighthouse, four of which are still visible today and in good condition: they transformed the coral reef of Abu Nuhas into one of the most appreciated sites amongst scuba divers in the Red Sea. All wrecks lie on the northern

The remains of the bow belonging to the Kimon M or 'Wreck of the Lentils' which ran aground in 1978

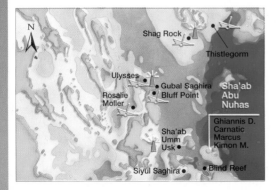

Access	105'
Difficulty	⬤ ⬤
Current	⬤
Natural scenery	⬤
Fauna interest	⬤
General interest	⬤ ⬤ ⬤

Other characteristics

	Date	Name	Cargo
SHIPWREKS AT ABU NUHAS	1869 September	Carnatic	Bottles of wine, mails, copper, silver
	1978 September	Marcus	Tiles
	1978 December	Kimon M.	Lentils
	1981 August	Chrisoula K.	Tiles
	1983 April	Ghiannis D.	Timbers
	1987 February	Olden	Lentils

boats. Further to the south, between Abu Nuhas and Shadwan, there are three small reefs called *Yellowfish Reefs* due to the presence of numerous yellow fish: butterflyfish (genus *Chaetodon*), grunts (genus *Plectorhinchus*) and goatfish (genus *Parupeneus*) and that come up from a sandy seabed at a depth of 15 meters. They can be object of an alternative dive when weather conditions do not allow wreck diving. The exploration of the wrecks has to be done with a calm sea and preferably by zodiac.

The beacon at Abu Nuhas

side of the reef exposed to prevailing winds and waves, and extending from west to east. The oldest one is the wreck of the *Carnatic* that goes back to 1869, the youngest of the still visible wrecks is *Ghiannis D.*, shipwrecked in 1983. The *Olden*, transporting lentils, sank in 1987 and has vanished, probably resting in deep waters still to be found. On the southern side of the reef, in front of a shallow lagoon that has no access, there is the only fixed mooring offering sufficient protection for

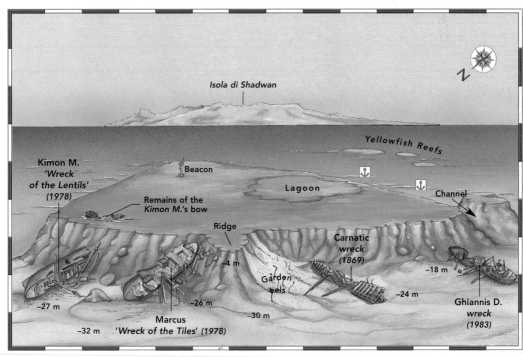

Isola di Shadwan

Yellowfish Reefs

Kimon M. 'Wreck of the Lentils' (1978)

Beacon

Remains of the Kimon M.'s bow

Ridge

Lagoon

Channel

Carnatic wreck (1869)

Garden eels

−4 m

−18 m

−24 m

−26 m

−27 m

−30 m

−32 m

Marcus 'Wreck of the Tiles' (1978)

Ghiannis D. wreck (1983)

The intact structure of the command bridge of the Ghiannis D. inclined 45° to the left side

The Greek cargo ship *Ghiannis D.* that had set sail from the Croatian harbour of Rijeka bound for Jeddah in Saudi Arabia and Hodeida in Yemen, carrying a cargo of timber crashed against the north-western corner of the reef of Abu Nuhas on 19th April 1983 as the captain of the ship was probably distracted for a moment. The *Ghiannis D.* did not sink immediately and all its crew members were rescued as Egyptian ship *Santa Fe* intervened, yet there was nothing they could do to safeguard its hull. The *Ghiannis D.* had been built and launched in 1969 in Japan under the name of 'Shoyo Maru', measured 99.5 meters long, 16 meters wide, with a capacity of 2,932 registered tons and a draught of 6.35 meters. The vessel was driven by a 6-cylinder engine producing 3,000 HP that gave the ship a speed of 12 knots. In 1975 the ship was sold and renamed in 'Markos', then in 1980 the Greek company *Dumarc Shipping and Trading Corporation* bought it and renamed it 'Ghiannis D.'. The new owner added the big 'D' – the initial of its name – on the funnel which is still visible today. This is why earlier many had mistakenly thought the name of the ship was 'Dana'.

GHIANNIS D.

Type of ship: cargo
Nationality: Greek
Year of construction: 1969
Length: 99.5 m
Width: 16 m
Tonnage: 2,932 t
Date of shipwreck:
  19th April 1983
Depth: 27 m

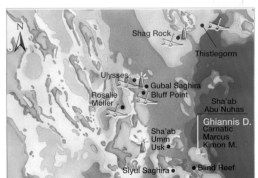

Access	95'
Difficulty	◐ ○
Current	○
Natural scenery	○
Fauna interest	○
General interest	○ ○ ○

Other characteristics

The *Ghiannis D.* lies on the bottom at 27 meters in a north-east/south-west direction with the bow separated from the stern section. Both lay on the port side and are covered with splendid soft corals whereas the center section has collapsed. The bow and stern structures of the wreck are perfectly intact and offer the possibility to explore all their details. The dive needs to be done in calm sea conditions starting from the stern section which is completely separated from the rest of the hull and is the most beautiful and interesting part of the whole wreck: it is dominated by a big winch shaped like an upside down U that reaches up to 6 meters below the surface, and in calm seas is sometimes visible from the diving boat.

The command bridge has wide openings and is well illuminated, easily accessible and represents one of the most interesting

The cargo of the ship – timber- is still visible today

points of the wreck: in the center there is the wheel house with the binnacle; however, inside the bridge scuba divers may feel disorientated due to the inclination of the ship. You enter the engine room through

an opening in the funnel which has some light rays filtering through from above and is inhabited by a school of glassfish. Inside it seems as if time has stood still: all the machinery, engines, pipes and

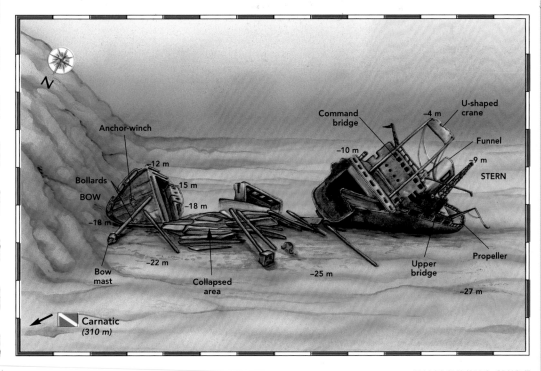

N

Anchor-winch

−12 m

Bollards

BOW

−15 m

−18 m

−18 m

−22 m

Bow mast

Collapsed area

−25 m

Command bridge

−4 m

−10 m

U-shaped crane

Funnel

−9 m

STERN

Upper bridge

Propeller

−27 m

Carnatic
(310 m)

instruments are still in perfect condition. Exit the stern section and continue your exploration towards the bow crossing the middle part of the hull which is completely destroyed. Pay close attention and you can find numerous wooden planks that were part of the ship's cargo. The bow of *Ghiannis D.* is cut off and bowed to its left side at a depth of 18 meters on its middle part but perfectly intact. There is a big mast in the center and the anchor chain comes out through one of the two hawse holes. During the exploration of the wreck colonized by red soft corals, small table corals (*Acropora* sp.), Raspberry corals (genus *Pocillopora*), sponges and anemone with their Red Sea anemonefish (*Amphiprion bicinctus*), you come across numerous schools of anthias and glassfish (*Parapriacanthus ransonneti*), whereas on the upper bridge groups of Common lionfish (*Pterois miles*) swarm. Some huge groupers and batfish are always there (genus *Platax*) accompanied by great many parrotfish and in the crevices of the hull some Giant moray has found its den (*Gymnothorax javanicus*).

Details of the engine room are still in perfect condition

Comments

• *With rough sea, diving is only possible with a zodiac.*
• *Visibility is usually always good, but take a torch to explore inside.*

Look out for

Soft coral   Anemonefish   Anthias

Glassfish   Batfish   Lionfish

Grouper   Parrotfish   Moray

Features

• *The best-conserved and maybe the most interesting of the wrecks at Abu Nuhas.*
• *A great number of soft corals and reef fish. You almost always find a school of lionfish on the bridge close to the funnel.*
• *At mid morning the sunlight penetrates through the port-holes producing spectacular light effects.*

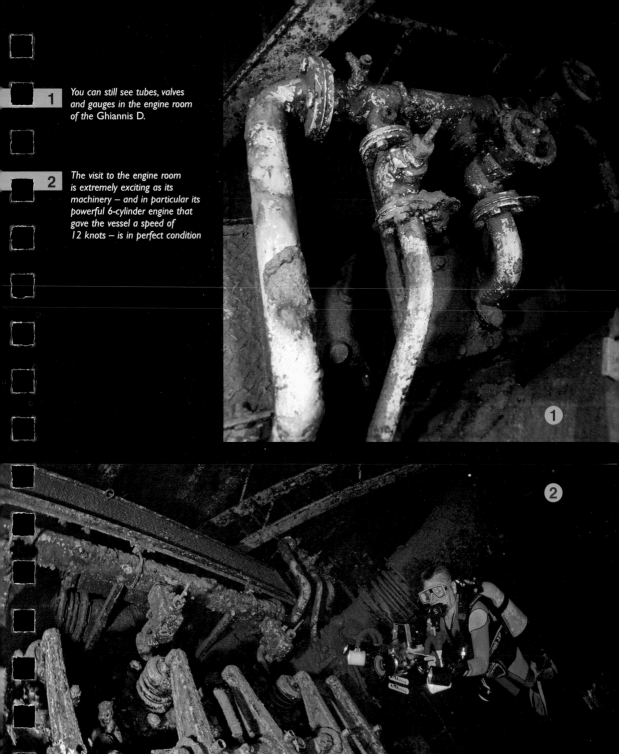

1 You can still see tubes, valves and gauges in the engine room of the Ghiannis D.

2 The visit to the engine room is extremely exciting as its machinery – and in particular its powerful 6-cylinder engine that gave the vessel a speed of 12 knots – is in perfect condition

The bridge with
the wheel house and
the binnacle **1**

The funnel clearly shows a big
letter 'D' standing for the initial of
the Greek company Dumarc,
owner of the ship. An arrow
indicates the access route for
penetration into the engine room **2**

The bow, although detached
from the hull, is still intact, with
the anchor chain coming out
from the starboard bow-eye.
The anchor was thrown in an
attempt to save the ship **3**

The stern of the Ghiannis D.
is perfectly conserved and resting
on its portside on the sandy seabed **4**

4

27°34.746' N — 33°55.546' E

The stern of the Carnatic perfectly intact

The wreck of the *Carnatic* is situated immediately to the east of *Ghiannis D.* and lies almost parallel to the Greek cargo vessel.

An old photo showing the Carnatic docked at Calcutta

The *Carnatic* was an elegant British vessel, built in 1862 by the London shipyard *Samuda Bros*, it measures 89.9 meters long and 11.6 meters wide with a tonnage of 1,776 and belonged to the first generation of those 'steamers' with mixed propulsion, i.e. sail and steam. The engine was fuelled by a boiler in the center of the hull, with a 4-cylinder engine that supplied the vessel with a power of 2,422 HP.
The *Carnatic*, operated by *P&O (Peninsular and Orient)*, serviced the Suez-Bombay route and sometimes went as far as

China. Weighing anchor in Suez on the 12 September 1869 on its way to Bombay, the *Carnatic* ran aground on reef of Abu Nuhas in the night of the 12–13th September despite

CARNATIC

Type of ship: *steamer*
Nationality: British
Year of construction: 1862
Length: 89.8 m
Width: 11.6 m
Tonnage: 1,776 t
Date of shipwreck:
        12–13th September 1869
Depth: 27 m

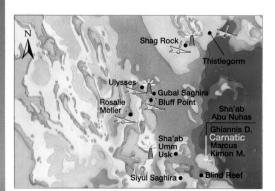

Access	🚢 85'
Difficulty	⚪⚪
Current	⚪
Natural scenery	⚪
Fauna interest	⚪
General interest	⚪⚪

Other characteristics

📷 🐟

The Carnatic *in full sail on the drawing belonging to the ship: it was retrieved together with the treasure by Lloyds of London after the shipwreck*

good weather conditions: the inquiry of the Board of Trade in London revealed that a strong current caused the ship to deviate from its route. Apart from 34 passengers and 176 crew members on board, the *Carnatic* was transporting cotton bales, the mail destined for British troops in India, and a cargo of the finest bottles of wine and soda water, still visible until a few years ago. One of the holds also

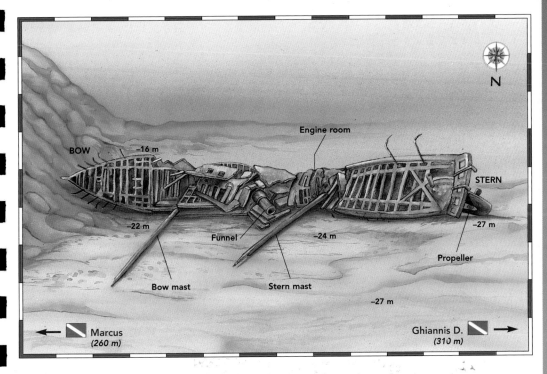

Engine room

BOW   −16 m

STERN

−22 m

Funnel   −24 m   −27 m

Propeller

Bow mast   Stern mast

−27 m

Marcus
(260 m)

Ghiannis D.
(310 m)

contained 40,000 sterling in gold that was retrieved at the beginning of November 1869: but the legend lives on that some of the bullion still remains inside the hold…
Despite the impact, Captain Philip Buton Jones did not deem the situation to be dangerous for passengers and crew, so all stayed on board waiting for assistance from another *P&O Liner* called *Sumatra* that was operating the

The Carnatic *run aground on the reef of Abu Nuhas in a lithography published by the* Illustrated London News

Comments

• Relatively easy diving, only to be effected in calm seas.
• Be careful of sharp pieces of metal.
• Dive preferably in the morning.

The tapered bow of the Carnatic with the copper ring (indicated by the arrow) where the bowsprit was integrated

Features

• Wreck of significant historical interest as it is the most important steamer found in the Red Sea.
• Superb bunches of soft corals growing on the metal structures of the deck.
• A gigantic umbrella-shaped Acropora is situated in the center section of the wreck, a huge Malabar grouper often rests under its branches.

same route. But at 2am on the 14th September, the water level inside the hull rose suddenly and the situation became worse in the following hours as the wind rose and the waves grew. At 11am, the captain gave order to abandon ship but the Carnatic suddenly snapped into two sections, taking with it 31 lives. Parts of the hull were left on the reef for a couple of months until after a strong storm it glided to the seabed at a depth of 27 meters and shattered into a third section. Most of the ship's structure today is corroded and covered by soft corals. Its exploration starts from the stern with the big propeller with three blades. Continue along the deck to reach the bridge and the engine room situated at a depth of 25 meters with the boiler and propulsion machinery; on the seabed rest the two masts. The holds are easily accessible and host dense schools of glassfish (Parapriacanthus ransonneti) best observed in the early morning hours when the sunlight filters through the distinctive square portholes. The bow with its unmistakable elegant and tapered line rests on the reef at a depth of 16 meters. Groupers, trevalleys and lion fish swarm around the wreck whose structure has become home for hard corals, sponges and numerous soft corals.

An important part of the cargo of the Carnatic were wine bottles

Look out for

Acropora   Soft coral   Sponge

Glassfish   Grouper   Trevally

Lionfish

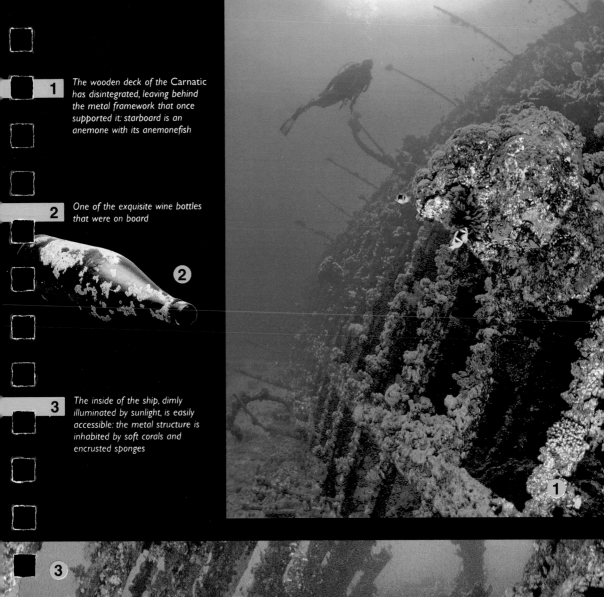

1 The wooden deck of the Carnatic has disintegrated, leaving behind the metal framework that once supported it: starboard is an anemone with its anemonefish

2 One of the exquisite wine bottles that were on board

3 The inside of the ship, dimly illuminated by sunlight, is easily accessible: the metal structure is inhabited by soft corals and encrusted sponges

The rudder and propeller with four blades from the 'wreck of the tiles'

27°34.795' N — 33°55.693' E

The third wreck of Abu Nuhas – also known as 'wreck of the tiles', is situated to the east of *Carnatic*, separated by a small reef ridge. What is the true identity of this ship? According to general opinion we deal with the *Chrisoula K*.

The *Chrisoula K*. was built in the harbour of Lubecca in 1954 with a tonnage of 3,720, a length of 98 meters, a width of 14.8 meters and a 9-cylinder engine supplying 2,700 HP. The ship was launched with the name 'Dora Oldendorf', renamed 'Anna B' in 1970, and

CHRISOULA K.

Type of ship: cargo
Nationality: German
Year of construction: 1954
Length: 98 m
Width: 14.8 m
Tonnage: 3,720 t
Date of shipwreck:
    31st of August 1981
Depth: 4–26 m

then given the name 'Chrisoula K.' when the Greek *Clarion Marine Company* bought it in 1979. The vessel was on its way to Jeddah in Saudi Arabia with its cargo of 3,700 tonnes of Italian tiles. It ran aground on the north-eastern side of Abu Nuhas on 31st August 1981 whilst navigating at maximum speed and during a time when the captain had handed command to one of his officers and withdrawn to his cabin. A picture taken shortly after the shipwreck shows the bow of the *Chrisoula K*. smashed by the violent impact and stranded on

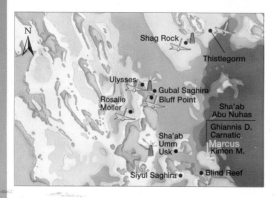

Access	🚢 80'
Difficulty	⚪⚪
Current	⚪
Natural scenery	⚪
Fauna interest	⚪
General interest	⚪⚪

Other characteristics

📷 🐟 🕐

The bow of the Chrisoula K. on the reef at Abu Nuhas visible until 1986.
The arrow indicates the anchor chain coming out of the port hawse hole

the reef. An examination of the 'wreck of the tiles' reveals however, that the bow is still almost intact and the anchor chain comes out of

The tiles constituted the cargo of the ship and are still numerous

The tiles with the inscription 'Made in Italy'

Pay close attention to the bow of the 'wreck of the tiles', today inhabited by a great number of small table corals (Acropora sp.), you see that it does not have the anchor chain on the port side, but on the starboard: so it cannot be the Chrisoula K.

The big propeller with four blades lies at a depth of 27 meters

and one of the two masts. Very interesting, but only for experienced wreck divers, is a visit to the engine room which is still in excellent condition even if the components, including a huge diesel engine, are covered by a thin muddy layer. The ship's cargo still in the holds, comprised of banks of tiles stacked chaotically due to the terrible impact with the reef, is surrounded by glassfish. Apart from the encrusting red sponges and table corals, there are also some anemones with their Red Sea anemonefish (*Amphiprion bicinctus*) on the outside plates

the starboard hawse hole, whereas on the photo showing the bow of the *Chrisoula K.* the anchor chain is on the port side. Additionally, the serial number of the engine corresponds to that of the cargo ship *Marcus* that was shipwrecked some years earlier than the *Chrisoula K.* In May 1978, 'Marcus' came from Suez and was on its way to Saudi Arabia with a cargo of tiles produced in Italy, just like the *Chrisoula K*, when it had some problems with the rudder during a storm and ran aground on the reef of Abu Nuhas. The violence of the impact caused the torsion of the quarterdeck now resting on the right side with the propeller at a depth of 27 meters, whereas the rest of the ship, intact, lies on the sandy seabed with the bow just below the surface at a depth of 4 meters. The exploration starts at the stern where you can see the enormous propeller with four blades and the rudder, intact. Proceed to starboard where you find a big loading derrick reclining on the bottom

A big ventilator in the center of the stern section of the wreck

Marcus

and batfish (genus *Platax*) often pass by. The funnel rests on the sand (-19 m) and further on, towards the reef, you see another loading derrick (-15 m), whilst close to the bow on the starboard side a few meters from the surface, is the anchor chain laying on the reef. And the *Chrisoula K.*? The hull can be found on the sandy seabed at a depth of 60 meters, resting on its starboard site about 400 meters to the north of the reef.

The top of one of the ship masts reclined on the sandy bottom

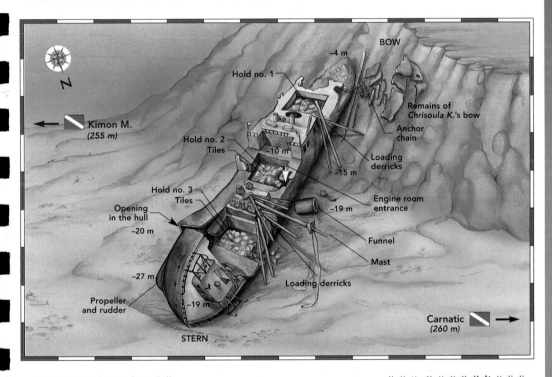

N

BOW

-4 m

Hold no. 1

Remains of
Chrisoula K.'s bow

Kimon M.
(255 m)

Anchor
chain

Hold no. 2
Tiles

-10 m

Loading
derricks

-15 m

Hold no. 3
Tiles

Engine room
entrance

Opening
in the hull
-20 m

-19 m

-27 m

Funnel

Mast

Loading derricks

Propeller
and rudder

-19 m

Carnatic
(260 m)

STERN

27°34.795' N — 33°55.693' E

Comments

• *In case of rough sea divers should use a zodiac.*
• *Use a good torch when penetrating the holds.*
• *Make sure not to stir up the thin muddy layer in the inside of the holds.*

Look out for

Acropora   Soft coral   Sponge

Anemonefish   Batfish   Garden
eel

Glassfish

Features

• *Well conserved wreck, rich in reef fish, hard and soft corals.*
• *There are some Garden eels coming out of the sand close to the anchor.*
• *Substantial amount of glassfish in many parts of the ship.*

1

The bow of the Marcus with the anchor chain visible to the starboard side

1

The entry to the engine room with its machinery still in good condition

2

The bridge of the Marcus obstructed by pieces of wreckage and big metal tubes

3

An Arabian angelfish (Pomacanthus maculosus) swims around the metal structures of the bridge inhabited by small table corals and soft corals

4

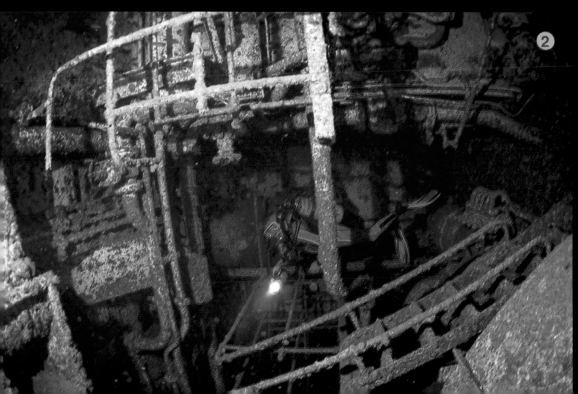

2

3

4

The port side, the propeller and the rudder of Kimon M. at a depth of 27 meters

The so called 'wreck of the lentils' is situated around 250 meters to the east of the 'wreck of the tiles', at the north-eastern point of Abu Nuhas. Its name is based on the cargo of the ship wrecked here, comprising 4,500 tonnes of these pulses. The wreck was falsely identified as the 'Seastar' or the 'Olden', but is in reality the *Kimon M.*, a cargo ship coming from Suez, which was stranded on the reef in 1978. The vessel was built in Germany in 1952 at the *Stuicken & Sohn* shipyards and was originally named 'Bruns-

büttel' and then 'Ciudad de Cucuta', followed by 'Angela'. It was 106.4 meters long and 6.8 meters wide with a tonnage of 3,714 and equipped with an 8-cylinder diesel engine. At the

time of the shipwreck, the vessel – renamed *Kimon M.* – belonged to the Greek-Panama company *Janissios Shipping*. The *Kimon M.* had left the Turkish harbour of Iskandarun where it had loaded its cargo of lentils bound for Bombay. It hit the north-eastern point of the reef at Abu Nuhas on the 12th December 1978 whilst navigating at full speed. The crew were rescued thanks to the intervention of the vessel *Interasia* cruising nearby. For a long time the bow of the *Kimon M.* was visible on the reef and was a precious

KIMON M.
Type of ship: cargo
Nationality: German
Year of construction: 1952
Length: 106.4 m
Width: 6.8 m
Tonnage: 3,714 t
Date of shipwreck:
   12th December 1978
Depth: 4–32 m

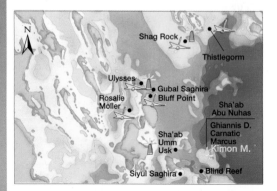

Access 🚤 75'
Difficulty ⚫⚫
Current ⚫
Natural scenery ⚫
Fauna interest ⚫
General interest ⚫⚫
Other characteristics

warning signal for vessels passing by. The remainder of the hull sank slowly down the plateau and now rests on its starboard side with the stern on the sandy bottom at a depth of 32 meters.

Today, the first hold is situated at 16 meters whereas the bow mast is on the reef only 4 meters deep together with numerous pieces and the massive anchor.

Start the dive at the stern, still intact with its propeller and the rudder.

Then proceed along the port side of the ship to observe the entries of the holds with the winches often surrounded by schools of anthias.

Turn to the bow area, completely destroyed, where you can see the anchor.

The ship has become unstable and thus the exploration of its holds might be dangerous and should be avoided.

One of the winches on the deck

Comments

• It is possible to reach the Kimon M., *starting from the 'wreck of the tiles' or Marcus, by finning eastwards.*
• *Current and poor visibility possible.*
• *In case of rough sea it is practically impossible to dive as the wreck is situated at the extreme eastern point of the reef.*

Look out for

Acropora   Soft coral   Anthias

Batfish

Features

• *The enormous engine room is particularly interesting.*
• *Rich in reef fauna.*
• *Impressive colonization of hard and soft corals.*
• *A great number of Alcyonarians grow along the metal cables.*

The mast of the Kimon M. resting on the sandy seabed **1**

The engine of the ship, an 8-cylinder diesel built by the company Waggon & Masch, is still well preserved **2**

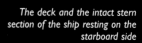

The port side of the stern with a big bow-eye through which the mooring ropes were passed **3**

The deck and the intact stern section of the ship resting on the starboard side **4**

4

DAHAB

The small city of Dahab lies 80 kilometers north of Sharm el-Sheikh and has seen considerable tourist development in the last few years. The number of scuba divers visiting its diving sites has risen amazingly, yet many of these divers are not clients of the over 30 local dive centers here but come from Sharm looking for different dives in a more relaxed and calm atmosphere.

Dahab is divided into two parts, the southern part comprises the big, shallow **bay of El-Qura** bordered by a sandy tongue that forms a hook, sheltered from waves and dominating winds that blow almost constantly from the north; this is the more modern and touristic part with big 4 and 5 star hotels and a concentration of numerous windsurfers who find ideal conditions for their preferred sport (fresh wind and few waves).

Less than 3 kilometers to the north is the 'old' part with a typical Bedouin slant that has grown up around a second bay, even wider than the previous one called **Assalah**: this used to be the original Bedouin village that gave birth to the tourist center we know today.

Assalah is also divided into two parts: *Mashraba* in the south and *Masbat* in the north.

The Assalah bay is bordered by a splendid palm grove and a beach with fine sand of a golden

Aerial view of the bay of El-Qura

The bay of Assalah with the area of Masbat in the north and Mashraba in the south

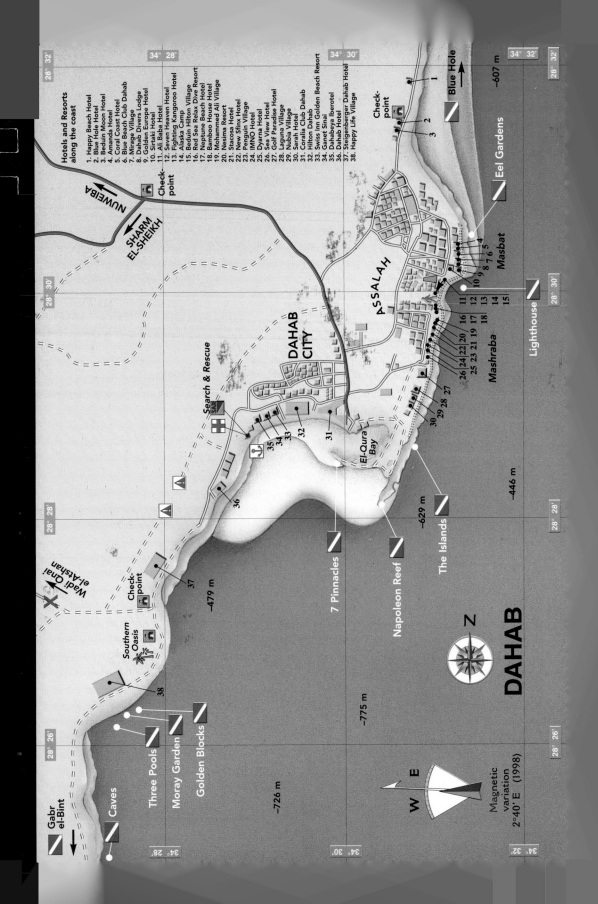

Hotels and Resorts
along the coast

1. Happy Beach Hotel
2. Blue Hole Hotel
3. Beduin Moon Hotel
4. Amanda Hotel
5. Coral Coast Hotel
6. Blue Beach Club Dahab
7. Mirage Village
8. Dahab Divers Lodge
9. Golden Europe Hotel
10. Sirtaki Hotel
11. Ali Baba Hotel
12. Seven Heaven Hotel
13. Fighting Kangoroo Hotel
14. Alaska Camp
15. Beduin Hilton Village
16. Red Sea Relax Dive Resort
17. Neptune Beach Hotel
18. Bamboo House Hotel
19. Mohammed Ali Village
20. Nesima Resort
21. Stacosa Hotel
22. New Sfinx Hotel
23. Penguin Village
24. IMNO Hotel
25. Dyarna Hotel
26. Sea View Hotel
27. Golf Paradise Hotel
28. Laguna Village
29. Nubia Village
30. Sarah Hotel
31. Coralia Club Dahab
32. Hilton Dahab
33. Swiss Inn Golden Beach Resort
34. Ganet Sinai
35. Dahabeya Iberotel
36. Dahab Hotel
37. Steigenberger Dahab Hotel
38. Happy Life Village

Blue Hole

–607 m

Eel Gardens

Masbat

Check-
point

Lighthouse

ASSALAH

Mashraba

DAHAB
CITY

Search & Rescue

El-Qura
Bay

–446 m

–629 m

7 Pinnacles

Napoleon Reef

The Islands

–775 m

N

DAHAB

W   E

Magnetic
variation
2°40' E (1998)

NUWEIBA

Check-
point

SHARM
EL-SHEIKH

Caves

Three Pools

Moray Garden

Golden Blocks

Gabr
el-Bint

Southern
Oasis

Wadi Qnai
el-Atshan

Check-
point

–479 m

–726 m

The bay of Assalah bordered by a nice palm grove: most of the diving centers are situated here

colour. Maybe this particularity is the origin of the name 'Dahab' meaning in the local language 'gold', according to tradition the name was given by Bedouins here who were fascinated by this golden sand. Many bungalows, camps, a myriad of small restaurants, a lot of small and medium sized hotels and most of the diving centers are concentrated in the Assalah area. The numerous diving sites, at least

Dahab	Snorkeling	Open Water	Advanced Open Water
N. Ras Abu Galum	●	●	
S. Ras Abu Galum	●	●	
Blue Hole – El Bells	●		●
The Canyon	●		●
Ras Abu Helal	●		●
Eel Gardens	●	●	
Lighthouse	●	●	
The Islands	●	●	
Napoleon Reef	●	●	
Moray Garden	●	●	
Golden Blocks	●	●	
Three Pools	●	●	
The Caves			●
North Gabr el-Bint	●	●	

The bay of Assalah is very busy full of bars and small restaurants along the sea promenade

fifteen, are divided into two groups: those in the north of Assalah with sites between this bay and the famous Blue Hole (the most known diving site in Dahab) from where you reach the area of Ras Abu Galum; and those diving sites to the south of El-Qura bay with sites between this bay and the area of Gabr-el Bint, accessible by foot, camel or boat.

In contrast to Sharm el-Sheikh where scuba diving is mainly by boat, in Dahab the sites are easily accessible by land and boats are rare. The tourist development in Dahab may be a recent phenomenon, yet in reality the small city has a deeply rooted history, going back as far as the Nabateans, the legendary traders of old times who had their base close to Petra in Jordan, less than 150 kilometers from Dahab as the crow flies.

Recent archaeological excavations in the center of Assalah reveal traces of a port and Nabatean trading center dating back to 1st-2nd century AD.

The excavations of the Nabatean port of Assalah

Numerous shops and small restaurants bordering the bay of Assalah

Camels are a daily sight in Dahab reaffirming its Bedouin origin

Scuba divers kitting up at the Lighthouse dive site

Aerial view of the south of the site of Ras Abu Galum: on the right is the Bedouin village of El-Omeyid

Ras Abu Galum is situated around 8 kilometers north of Blue Hole with which it is connected by a path along the rocky coast, a walk or camel ride that will take an hour and a half. The road is fascinating and leads to the Bedouin village of El-Omeyid that over the last few years has experienced an incredible development thanks to the many tourists who visit this place in increasing numbers either for scuba diving or to stay a day or two trekking in the hinterland to reach the ancient Bedouin settlement (now abandoned) called *Bir Oqda* close to a spring.

Ras Abu Galum can also be reached by car (four wheel drive is necessary) following the track that goes off the asphalted road 20 kilometers before Nuweiba and driving along the splendid and very long Wadi Rasasa.

You can also take the track along the coast that starts south of the village of Nuweiba (*Nuweiba Muzeina*) and before reaching Ras Abu Galum you can admire beautiful bay called 'El-Gardud' by the locals: the bay is closed to the west by a narrow strip of land with a hook shape that recalls the bay of El-Qura.

A young Bedouin woman on the beach of Ras Abu Galum

Aerial view of the site of El-Gardud, north of Ras Abu Galum

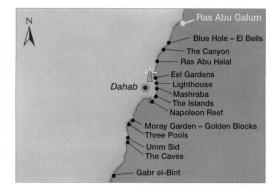

THE PROTECTED AREA OF RAS ABU GALUM

The area of Ras Abu Galum was declared Abu Galum Managed Resource Protected Area in 1992 and covers a territory of 500 square kilometers. Different and important ecosystems are present in Ras Abu Galum such as a rich and well developed coral reef, a practically intact coastline bordered by high mountains furrowed with deep wadis: these are the elements that distinguish this region and conserve its wildness and beauty. Recent studies reveal that in Ras Abu Galum there are more than 165 plant species of which 44 are endemic (only found in this area).

There is the Zigophyllum coccineum (in Arabic rotrait) among the shrubs which are particularly plentiful here. This richness seems to be due to the fact that Ras Abu Galum represents a transitional zone where its tropical climate interacts with the Mediterranean climate. The fauna includes Nubian Ibex (Capra hibex nubiana), the Red fox (Vulpes vulpes), hyrax (Procavia capensis), lizards (Agama sinaitica, Uromastix ornatus) and some snakes including the Horned rattlesnake (Cerastes cerastes).

The local Bedouin community used to live by fishing and sheep-farming but has now found a new and a growing important economic resource in tourism.

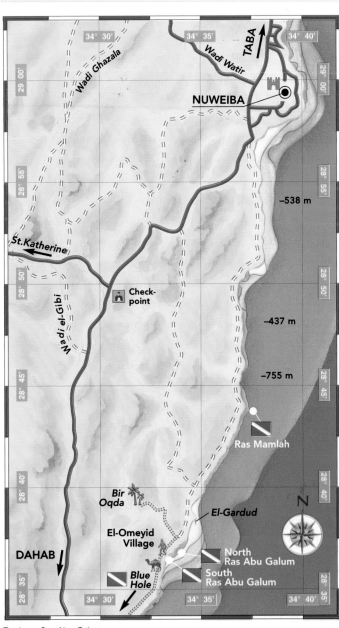

Tracks to Ras Abu Galum

One of the most common shrubs is the Zigophyllum coccineum

The camel is the most popular mode of transport to reach Ras Abu Galum

Aerial view of North Ras Abu Galum

Ras Abu Galum

South Ras Abu Galum

Shore entrance

The site is situated north of the cape in front of the Bedouin huts that extend up to this area that a few years ago were still desert. This dive is the most beautiful and interesting you can do at Ras Abu Galum and allows a chance to observe a fantastic underwater landscape with huge hard coral blocks, table corals and soft corals.

The entry is at the level of a split in the reef. After passing a big Massive pore coral (*Porites solida*) and some flat fire corals (*Millepora platyphylla*) on the right, descend onto a sandy bottom towards a big madrepore tower, the top of which is just a few meters below water level and surrounded by red Scalefin anthias (*Pseudanthias squamipinnis*): its crevices accommodate a colony of Pigmy sweepers (*Parapriacanthus ransonneti*) and Cave sweepers (*Pempheris vanicolensis*). Continue the descent along the reef slope surrounded by Masked butterflyfish (*Chaetodon semilarvatus*) and around which swarm some calm, silvery snappers (genus *Lethrinus*),

A Flat fire coral (*Millepora platyphylla*)

groups of Doublebar breams (*Acanthopagrus bifasciatus*) and some Circular batfish (*Platax orbicularis*) while near the surface cruise Cornetfish (*Fistularia commersoni*) in search of food.

A red fan coral of the genus *Acabaria* with expanded polyps

Access
Difficulty
Current

Natural scenery
Fauna interest
General interest

Other charactestics

Fire corals, Raspberry corals, small table corals and Broccoli soft corals are the main elements that form the reef of Ras Abu Galum

After descending to 10–15 meters first explore the southern part of the reef keeping the reef to your right, then make a large anticlockwise loop to the north until you reach a group of madrepore towers with numerous Massive pore corals (genus *Porites*) and an enormous Salad coral (*Turbinaria mesenterina*) Start your return from here: you exit through the same split from which you entered.

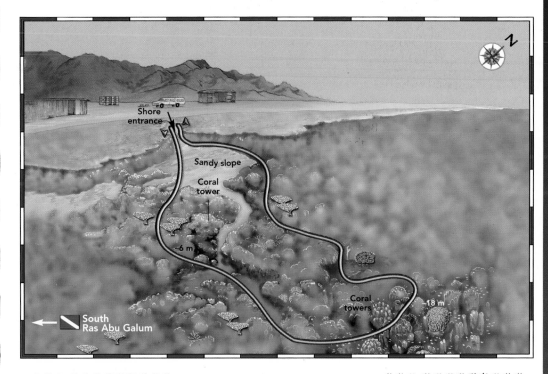

Comments

• Camels are required to reach this site from Dahab.
• Site is exposed to winds and waves.
• Avoid diving here when the sea is rough.
• Try entering the water at high tide.

Look out for

Acropora
Turbinaria
Fire coral

Angelfish
Anthias
Glassfish

Butterflyfish
Batfish
Snapper

Features

• Varied and interesting underwater landscape.
• Plentiful reef fauna.
• Site is less damaged than South Ras Abu Galum.

Aerial view of the site of South Ras Abu Galum

The site of South Ras Abu Galum is situated by the Bedouin village of El-Omeyid at the end of the track connecting it with the Blue Hole. You enter from the beach close to the small Visitor Center in the Park.
After having skirted a cave that opens at a depth of 4 meters, descend to 10–12 meters while passing by the spur that defines the boundary of the coral reef and continue with the reef to your left.
The first part of the dive is unfortunately disfigured by the proliferation of empty bottles

An enormous bank of Lobophyllia hemprichii

A Salad coral *(genus* Turbinaria)

Access		
Difficulty	○	
Current	○	
Natural scenery	○	
Fauna interest	○	
General interest	○	

Other charactestics

and other plastic waste objects. Continuing eastwards along the reef you will see some Salad corals (genus *Turbinaria*) and, a bit deeper, some Massive pore corals (*Porites solida*) before reaching some madrepore towers. From this point turn westwards to come back to the starting point, stay at a depth of 6–4 meters and you will cross a beautiful hard coral plateau on which enormous banks of *Lobophyllia hemprichii* stand out.

The camel, which you can load with all scuba diving equipment, represents the best means of transportation to reach Ras Abu Galum

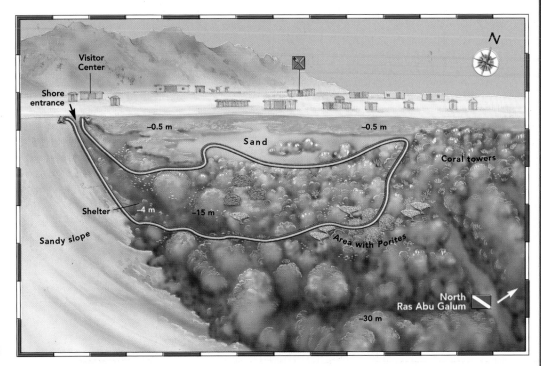

Comments

• *Easy dive site presenting no particular problems.*
• *Entry to the water can be independent to the tides.*
• *Site is disfigured at the beginning of the dive by waste.*

Look out for

Turbinaria   Porites   Rose coral

Anemonefish   Cornetfish   Bream

Damselfish   Sergeantfish

Features

• *Site protected from waves and currents.*
• *Also suitable for snorkeling.*
• *The hard coral formations are rich and well developed, especially on the plateau.*

Aerial view of the Blue Hole and the site that is today called 'El Bells'

T he Blue Hole is one of the most famous diving sites in the whole the Red Sea, not because of its beauty but unfortunately because it is associated with a high number of fatal incidents. The Blue Hole is situated 12 km north of Dahab and 1.5 km north of another famous site called 'The Canyon' from where the track to this site starts and which is accessible by any vehicle. Until 2003 a narrow passage through two rocks situated a few hundred meters away from the site made access to Blue Hole complicated, but with the opening of the new route in 2004 these difficulties have definitely ceased. The

beauty of the site has a special appeal and attracts hundreds of tourists every day, among which

The most difficult passage of the track leading to Blue Hole (A) and the new route (B) allowing access for all kinds of vehicles

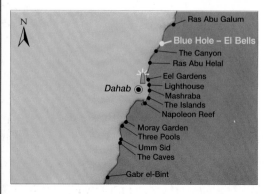

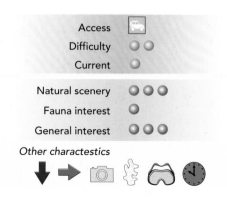

Access			
Difficulty	○	○	
Current	○		
Natural scenery	○	○	○
Fauna interest	○		
General interest	○	○	○

Other charactestics

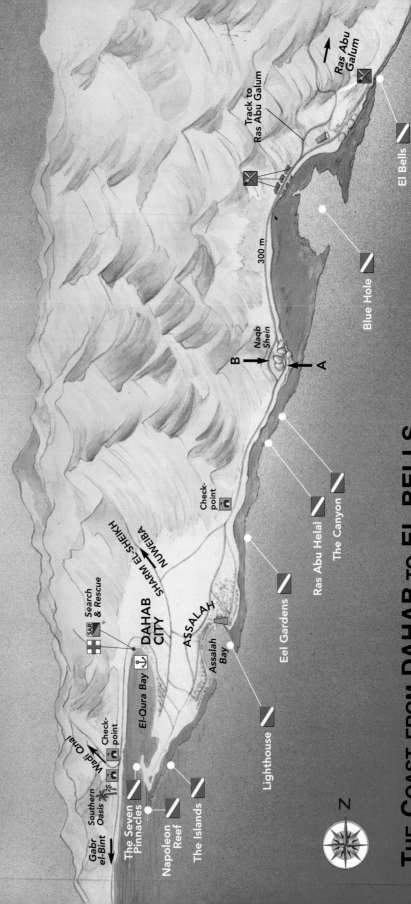

THE COAST FROM DAHAB TO EL BELLS

Ras Abu Galum

Track to Ras Abu Galum

El Bells

300 m

Blue Hole

Naqb Shein

B

A

Check-point

NUWEIBA

SHARM EL-SHEIKH

Ras Abu Helal

The Canyon

Eel Gardens

Search & Rescue

SAR

DAHAB CITY

ASSALAH

Assalah Bay

Lighthouse

Wadi Qnai

Check-point

El-Qura Bay

Southern Oasis

Gabr el-Bint

The Seven Pinnacles

Napoleon Reef

The Islands

N

scuba divers now count for only a small part: the shingle beach and the barrier reef separating the Blue Hole from the open sea are perfect for bathing and snorkeling in waters that are always calm. A huge number of small and friendly Bedouin restaurants opened along the shore of the Blue Hole with the tourist influx over the last few years. The site is a madrepore formation with special characteristics: it has an almost circular shape, 150 meters wide and 110 meters deep and connects with the open sea through a tunnel 26 meters long and whose ceiling starts at a depth of 52 meters. The interest in diving the Blue Hole is in reality relatively small, its walls are plain with few hard corals, its fauna very limited and the underwater landscape insignificant. Yet the site can be very interesting when doing a drift dive starting from the nearby site called '**El Bells**' (from the original name 'The Bells') situated 250 meters to the north and accessible from the

One of the many Bedouin restaurants that borders the Blue Hole

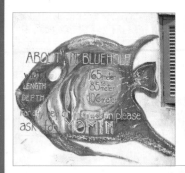

The ascent in the crystal clear waters of the Blue Hole

The crack in the reef that permits entry to El Bells

Blue Hole by foot along a track. El Bells is a sort of chimney in the reef and is open at the upper part towards the sea, that widens and narrows forming cavities in the shape of bells: the third one of these starts at 26 meters after a big arch and is 6–7 meters high. You enter through a crack in the reef from where you jump into the blue: a few meters below the surface the spectacle is magnificent and the chimney is lightened by sun

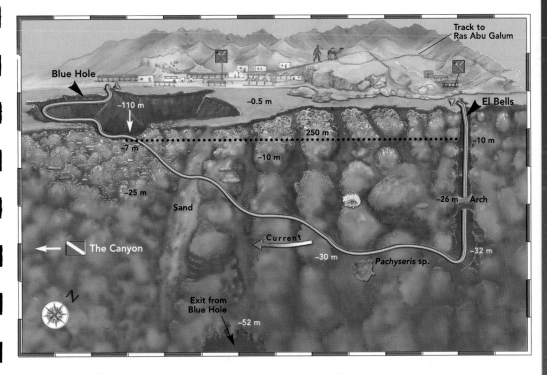

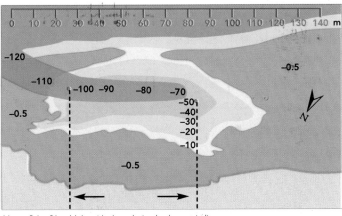

Map of the Blue Hole with the relative bathymetric lines

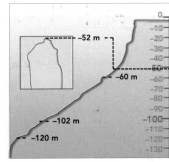

Section of the tunnel, 26 meters long and 52 meters deep, connecting the Blue Hole to the open sea

DANGEROUS CHALLENGES

On the rocky wall of the northern side of the Blue Hole, nearby the narrow track leading to El Bells, there are the memorial tablets to commemorate the too many scuba divers, almost all of them young and without any doubt experienced divers, who aimed to challenge their limits or to satisfy their adventurous instincts but never found their way back to the surface from this vertiginous pit.
Why does the Blue Hole claim so many victims?
The upper part of the gallery to exit to the open sea is situated at a depth of 52 meters: at this depth – diving on compressed air without the use of suitable gas mixes including inert gases like helium – a minimal effort is enough to increase the respiratory rhythm.

The inhalation of oxygen and nitrogen at hyperbaric pressure can have dramatic consequences; oxygen becomes toxic once the partial pressure rises above 1.4 to 1.6 atm.
Sometimes you come upon a counter current in the 26 meters long gallery leading to the

external reef wall, especially close to the exit: in this case the diver needs to exercise more thus increasing the risk of hyperventilation with disastrous consequences including loss of orientation, convulsions, visual disturbances and respiratory failure.

rays that give life to the whole spectrum of blue. Here you descend into this extraordinary universe to a depth of 30 meters around the third and big bell. Then abandon the chimney and proceed towards the south with the reef on your right while ascending slightly. The beautiful wall falls vertically into the blue and is often encrusted with big colonies of Star coral

(*Pachyseris speciosa*) of a brownish colour and bordered by gorgonians, soft corals, black corals, anemones (genus *Heteractis*) with their anemonefish, and animated by some more or less deep shelters over which schools of red Scalefin anthias (*Pseudanthias squamipinnis*), butterflyfish (genus *Chaetodon*) and angelfish (genus *Pomacanthus*) swim. After around half

an hour at a depth of 7 meters you reach the saddle that allows the entrance to the inside of the Blue Hole situated by a beautiful coral garden teeming with life. At this point you just need to skirt around the madrepore walls in which you can observe some big sponges called Elephant ear sponge (*Ianthella basta*) before exiting the water to the western part of the Blue Hole.

Comments
- *The entry at El Bells may be a little difficult.*
- *Sometimes the site is overcrowded.*
- *Pay attention not to exceed the max. allowed depth of 30 meters.*

Look out for

Anemone   Gorgonian   Anthias

Butterflyfish   Angelfish   Sponge

Features
- *Spectacular diving, especially the beginning of the dive.*
- *The coral garden on the saddle at the entry to Blue Hole is extremely beautiful and colourful.*
- *The site is in general pleasant with a relaxing atmosphere.*
- *An ideal site for snorkelling.*

1 The spectacular chimney illuminated by sun rays which characterises El Bells

2 Groups of Elephant ear sponges (Ianthella basta) are visible on the walls of Blue Hole

3 A red Alcyonarian (genus Dendronephthya) on the wall of the reef at the exit of El Bells

Aerial view of the Canyon dive site

T he Canyon is situated 1.5 kilometers south of Blue Hole and is easily reachable from Dahab (10 kilometers) thanks to the nice asphalt coastal road finished in 2004. There is a restaurant with a small diving center opposite the entrance to the site. The access to the site is easy over the shingle beach in front of which you can park your car. You need to cross the reef platform for a dozen meters before you reach the lagoon that then opens to the sea, so it is best to start the dive at high tide to avoid damaging the reef.

The sandy lagoon has an average depth of about 3 meters and is inhabited by a rich fauna comprising of goatfish, butterfly fish, dominos and pullers and on its most

The entry to the Canyon site as seen from the coast

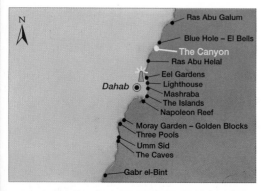

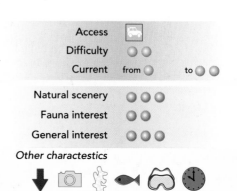

Access				
Difficulty	◯ ◯			
Current	from ◯		to ◯ ◯	
Natural scenery	◯ ◯ ◯			
Fauna interest	◯ ◯			
General interest	◯ ◯ ◯			

Other charactestics

western point there is a saddle serving as exit (and entry) point to the sea. Here you reach a nice and very lively coral garden which stretches out between 5 and 10 meters deep (you will admire this on your way back), head straight to the canyon following an 80° heading and the small reef wall on your left. The canyon is a deep fissure that opens in a north-south direction within the reef slope and descends to a depth of

54 meters. The entry is done through its largest point: here you ascend down to a sandy bottom 28 meters deep admiring the light effects caused by the sun rays in a surreal world. Then turn northwards (the southern area of the fissure is not only too deep but also is of no specific interest) and, ascending about 10 meters, you enter a small cave situated at a depth of 17 meters. This small cave is open on two sides and

Scuba divers kiting up on the shore

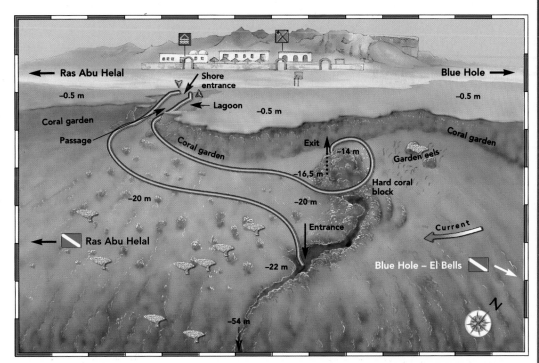

Ras Abu Helal ←

Blue Hole →

–0.5 m

Shore entrance

–0.5 m

Lagoon

–0.5 m

Coral garden

Coral garden

Passage

Coral garden

Exit

–14 m

Garden eels

–16,5 m

Hard coral block

–20 m

–20 m

← Ras Abu Helal

Entrance

Current

–22 m

Blue Hole – El Bells

–54 m

N

Comments

- Site is often overcrowded, especially in the morning.
- Enter the water preferably at high tide.
- In case of rough sea visibility may be poor in the lagoon and strong currents at the saddle of the lagoon are possible.
- The best time for diving is at midday.

Look out for

Acropora   Glassfish   Lionfish

Goatfish   Damselfish   Puller

Features

- Spectacular landscape.
- Rich and plentiful fauna in the coral gardens.

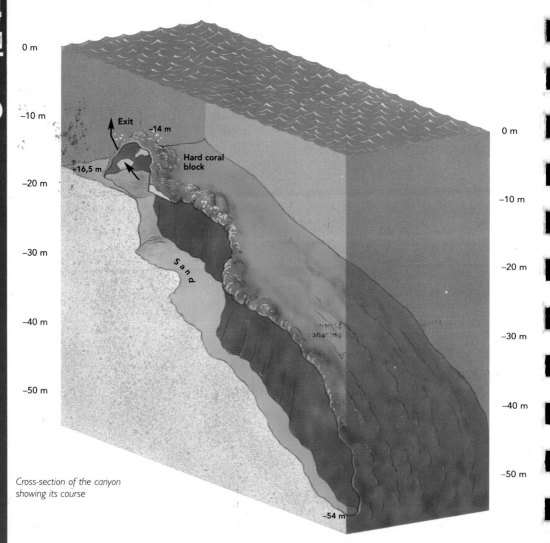

0 m

–10 m

Exit

–14 m

–16,5 m

Hard coral
block

–20 m

S a n d

–30 m

–40 m

–50 m

0 m

–10 m

–20 m

–30 m

–40 m

–50 m

–54 m

*Cross-section of the canyon
showing its course*

*The big madrepore block marking the cave through which you exit from the canyon:
the numerous small cracks of the vault allow the air bubbles emitted by scuba divers
to escape*

accommodates a dense school of glassfish (Pigmy sweepers, *Parapriacanthus ransonneti*) which literally wrap around the divers. You exit the cave back out onto the sandy plateau through its main opening at a depth of 16.5 meters; outside you notice that from here it looks like a huge madrepore block encrusted with table and soft corals teeming with life. After having skirted around its perimeter turn keeping the reef on your right to get back to the lagoon, but take your time at the coral garden close to the passage before you re-enter the lagoon.

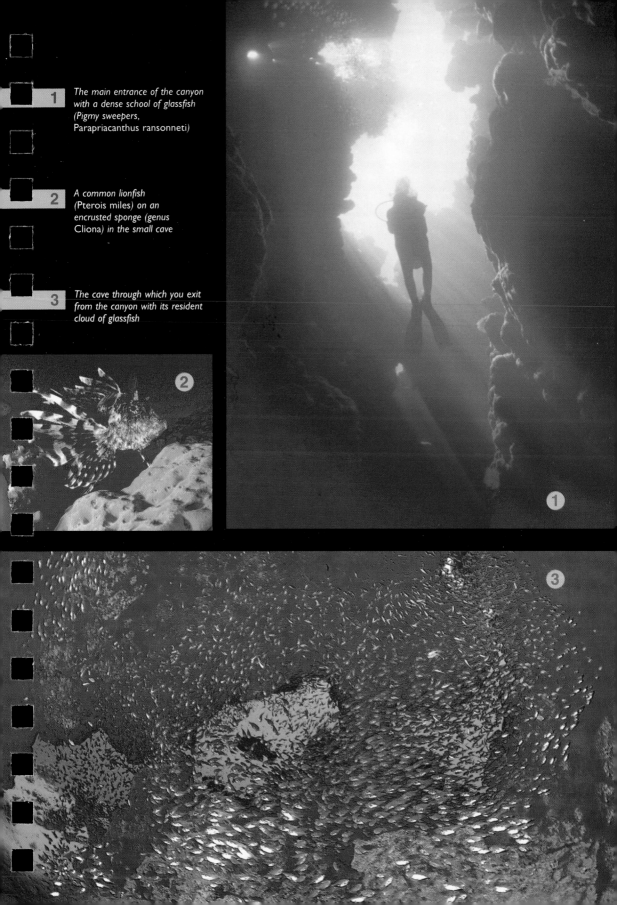

1 The main entrance of the canyon with a dense school of glassfish (Pigmy sweepers, *Parapriacanthus ransonneti*)

2 A common lionfish (*Pterois miles*) on an encrusted sponge (genus *Cliona*) in the small cave

3 The cave through which you exit from the canyon with its resident cloud of glassfish

Aerial view of Ras Abu Helal

Ras Abu Helal, which means 'Cape of the growing moon', is situated 3 kilometers south of the Canyon. At this point the coast actually has a slight indentation but the reef forms an underwater buttress around which diving takes place. The shore entry to the site is by an old sign immediately south of the buttress. You descend to a sandy lagoon with a semicircular shape at a depth between 7 and 12 meters; keeping the reef to the left, explore the underwater promontory with its beautiful

A common lionfish (Pterois miles) swims between the table corals

coral garden that represents the true interest of this dive site. The western wall of the promontory descends into the blue and at a depth of 30 meters it is ploughed by a straight split that gave this site the nickname 'small canyon'. Yet exploring this canyon is not only dangerous but it is also not particularly interesting; it is best to stay on the surrounding coral garden that extends into a second immersed bay with a sandy seabed from where you exit. The fauna is abundant on the coral garden and you find

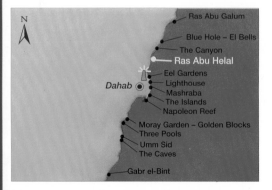

N
Ras Abu Galum
Blue Hole – El Bells
The Canyon
Ras Abu Helal
Eel Gardens
Dahab — Lighthouse
Mashraba
The Islands
Napoleon Reef
Moray Garden – Golden Blocks
Three Pools
Umm Sid
The Caves
Gabr el-Bint

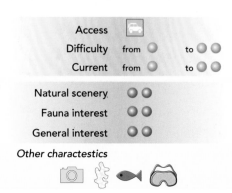

Access

Difficulty   from ○   to ○○

Current   from ○   to ○○

Natural scenery   ○○

Fauna interest   ○○

General interest   ○○

Other charactestics

lionfish, some groupers, the ever-present anthias, triggerfish, unicornfish and butterflyfish: sometimes turtles are drawn to this site where they find tender Broccoli-corals (*Lithophyton arboreum*) and other Alcyonarians. You might come across a strong current from the north (the direction of the dominant winds) by the tip of the promontory. If sea conditions dictate, the route can be inversely dived.

A Hawksbill turtle (Eretmochelys imbricata)

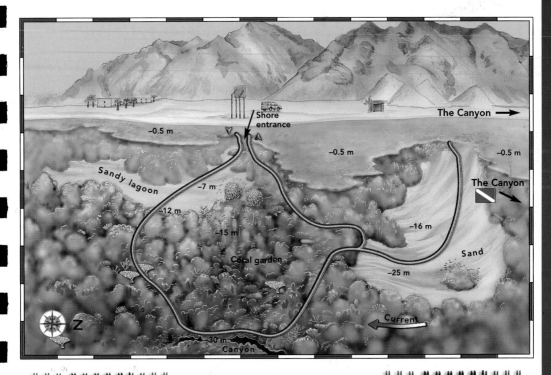

Comments

• *Pay attention to the strong currents from the north at the tip of the immersed promontory.*
• *Avoid exploring the canyon.*
• *In case of rough sea, entry into the water may be difficult.*

Look out for

Acropora — Broccoli coral — Anthias — Grouper — Unicornfish — Lionfish — Turtle — Triggerfish

Features

• *The coral garden is extremely interesting and teeming with life.*
• *Plentiful fauna.*
• *Easy and entertaining diving when the sea conditions are ideal.*
• *Interesting site for snorkelling.*

Aerial view of Eel Gardens

Seagrass

Passage

El Gardens owes its name to a huge population of Garden eels (*Gorgasia sillneri*) and are the main attraction for scuba divers. Eel Gardens is situated about 1.5 kilometers north of Lighthouse in the Assalah bay to which it is connected by a pedestrian walkway surrounding the bay.
Access by vehicle is allowed through a small internal asphalted road. Eel Gardens is well frequented, yet it is a small, peaceful oasis shaded by some palm trees with two or three pleasant restaurants that

The small palm grove at Eel Gardens

make it enjoyable.
A sign shows the diving map of the site with its precise entry point.

The reef platform here is about 60 meters wide and as always it is wise to enter the water at high tide so that you can swim over the reef rather than walking on it.
After having passed an extensive zone colonized by marine plants or sea grass on your right, you reach a winding channel at 2–3 meters through which you exit to the outside of the reef beside a small madrepore promontory.
You bypass this keeping it on you left and then after a dozen meters you come to a

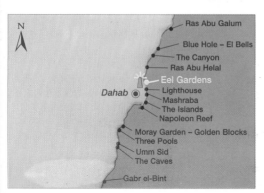

N

Ras Abu Galum
Blue Hole – El Bells
The Canyon
Ras Abu Helal
Eel Gardens
Dahab — Lighthouse
Mashraba
The Islands
Napoleon Reef
Moray Garden – Golden Blocks
Three Pools
Umm Sid
The Caves
Gabr el-Bint

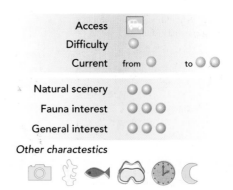

Access			
Difficulty	○		
Current	from ○	to ○ ○	
Natural scenery	○ ○		
Fauna interest	○ ○ ○		
General interest	○ ○ ○		

Other charactestics

vast slope covered by light sand from where hundreds of Garden eels come out and wave with the waters.

You can stop at the coral garden situated close to the channel on your way back: here, between table corals and some Massive pore corals, swim unicornfish (genus *Naso*), butterflyfish (genus *Chaetodon*) and in the crevices some small Grey morays (*Siderea grisea*) find shelter.

The sandy slope with the Garden eels (Gorgasia sillneri)

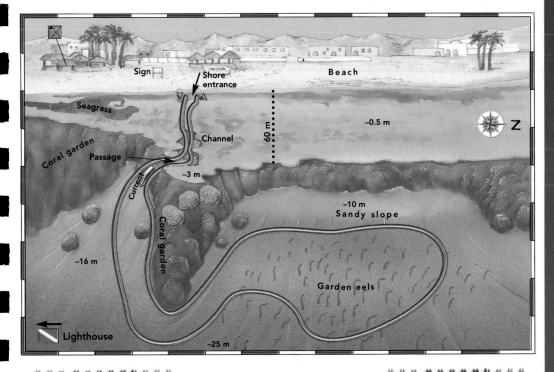

Comments

• *Best to avoid entering the water at low tide.*
• *Strong currents possible by the exit point.*
• *Best time to observe and photograph the Garden eels is in the afternoon.*
• *Approach the Garden eels slowly and cautiously as they are extremely shy.*

Look out for

Acropora   Porites   Garden eel

Unicornfish   Butterflyfish   Moray

Features

• *Watching the Garden eels is really extraordinary.*
• *Easy and relaxed diving.*
• *Suitable snorkeling site and extremely pleasant in its entirety including the facilities on land.*

Aerial view of the Lighthouse

Labels: Lighthouse, Eel Gardens, Entrance, Seagrass, N

Lighthouse is situated on the northern point of the Assalah bay in the area known as 'Masbat'. Despite its name, you will not find a lighthouse here that indicates the entry to the bay as it is a few hundred meters away to the west. Lighthouse may be the most frequented site in Dahab due to its proximity to the majority of the dive centers. Different diving routes can be chosen, ideal for beginners as well as experienced divers. Entry into the water is very easy in all sea conditions and is from the beach packed with

parasols, sun beds and bathers. The site embraces the extreme point of the bay descending into the blue to a depth of more than 25 meters creating two huge inlets. The western one has a sandy bottom with many hard coral towers. The classic route winds along the sandy ledge, going around the towers that reach up to a depth of 30 meters and then ascend slowly to a level of 8–12 meters following the reef wall rich with shelters inhabited by plentiful fauna that comprises of breams, parrotfish, lionfish and groupers.

In this way you come back to your starting point.
An alternative route and less frequented than the first one is highly recommended for

An octopus (genus Octopus)

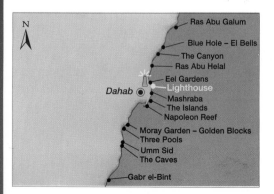

Map labels: Ras Abu Galum, Blue Hole – El Bells, The Canyon, Ras Abu Helal, Eel Gardens, Lighthouse, Dahab, Mashraba, The Islands, Napoleon Reef, Moray Garden – Golden Blocks, Three Pools, Umm Sid, The Caves, Gabr el-Bint

Access
Difficulty
Current

Natural scenery
Fauna interest
General interest

Other charactestics

photographers and naturalist divers. This dive site is called 'The Dump' where you dive to the west over a sandy slope covered by a thick blanket of sea grass belonging to the genus of *Halophila* (*H. stipulacea* and *H. ovalis*). Take your time observing the abundant fauna: some octopus (genus *Octopus*), pufferfish (family of Tetradontidae) and juvenile forms of many other fish genera that find safe shelters here.

White-spotted pufferfish (Arothron hispidus)

Comments

• Site is often overcrowded.
• Avoid arriving after 10am when the masses of scuba divers are getting ready to enter the water.
• Pay attention to the many windsurfers, especially when you surface after the dive.

Look out for

Acropora   Gorgonian   Turbinaria

Bream   Parrotfish   Lionfish

Grouper   Octopus

Features

• Dive site right in the center of Dahab close to most of the dive centers, protected from wind and waves.
• Site is suitable for divers of all experience levels.
• Entry into water is very easy.
• Underwater landscape varies a lot with plentiful fauna.

Aerial view of The Islands site

Entrance

Pools

Submerged small island

Napoleon Reef

The Islands dive site is an absolutely extraordinary site for its richness and development of its coral reef. It is situated south of Assalah at the beginning of the sand strip that later bends into a hook, limited to the north by the El-Qura bay. The entry is marked by a signboard on the beach detailing the topography of the site which starts at a small cleft in the reef. The reef platform is relatively wide so it is best to enter the sea at high tide. A series of three hard coral pools with sandy bottom situated straight after the small reef edge greets the diver. After having passed these pools, around 7–10 meters deep,

One of the numerous Massive Pore corals (genus Porites) typical for this site

leave the reef edge to your left and dive into the adventure of a real hard coral labyrinth consisting foremost of Massive pore corals belonging to the genus of *Porites*. Here you can get easily and enjoyably lost whilst admiring the rich fauna of this place. There is a small immersed, hard coral island further to the east beyond the sandy road which you can identify from the surface, especially at low tide, and that gave the site its name.
A resident school of juvenile Yellowtail barracuda (*Sphyraena flavicauda*) frequents this site

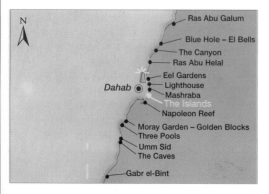

N

Ras Abu Galum
Blue Hole – El Bells
The Canyon
Ras Abu Helal
Eel Gardens
Dahab   Lighthouse
Mashraba
The Islands
Napoleon Reef
Moray Garden – Golden Blocks
Three Pools
Umm Sid
The Caves
Gabr el-Bint

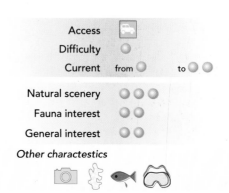

Access
Difficulty
Current   from   to

Natural scenery
Fauna interest
General interest

Other charactestics

which is also inhabited by most common representatives of the reef fauna as well as Napoleonfish (*Cheilinus undulatus*), snappers (genus *Lutjanus*), groupers (genera *Plectropomus*, *Cephalopholis*, *Variola*) and Blackspotted pufferfish (*Arothron stellatus*). Exit through the same cleft you used for entry or alternatively swim through a small tunnel that opens at a depth of 2 meters and comes up to the reef platform.

The resident school of Yellowtail barracuda (Sphyraena flavicauda)

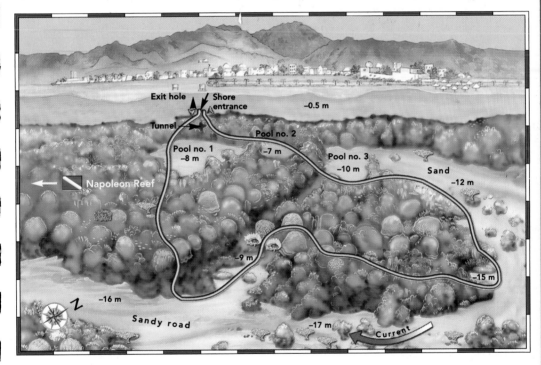

Comments

• *Enter the sea preferably with high tide.*
• *Site exposed to waves: avoid diving with choppy sea.*

Look out for

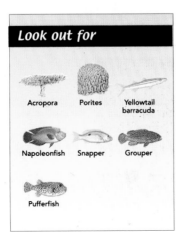

Acropora Porites Yellowtail barracuda

Napoleonfish Snapper Grouper

Pufferfish

Features

• *Exceptional richness of hard coral formations that create a real labyrinth.*
• *Numerous and interesting fauna.*
• *Easy diving, suitable for all scuba divers.*
• *Also snorkelers will not become bored.*

Aerial view of Laguna area with Napoleon Reef and The Seven Pinnacles

Track

The Islands

Salty Lake

L a g u n a

El-Qura Bay

The Seven Pinnacles

Napoleon Reef

N

T his site is situated a few hundred meters from the Islands by the sandy tongue that borders the north of the El-Qura bay, and in front of the huge tourist hotel structures built on the other side of the bay. The area is called **Laguna** ('Lagoon') and also comprises a second site called 'The Seven Pinnacles'. **Napoleon Reef** is best reached by boat or zodiac as it lies around 450 meters away from the beach. This huge madrepore tower is separated by a channel from the half submerged reef: it comes up from a sandy seabed

A Diadem sea urchin (Diadema setosum) and an octopus (genus Octopus)

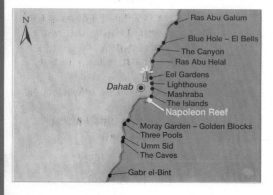

N

Ras Abu Galum
Blue Hole – El Bells
The Canyon
Ras Abu Helal
Eel Gardens
Lighthouse
Mashraba
The Islands
Napoleon Reef
Moray Garden – Golden Blocks
Three Pools
Umm Sid
The Caves
Gabr el-Bint

Dahab

Access

Difficulty

Current   from   to

Natural scenery

Fauna interest

General interest

Other charactestics

at around 20 meters depth and is frequented by plentiful fauna and some Napoleonfish (*Cheilinus undulatus*) to whom this site owes its name.

West from Napoleon Reef are **The Seven Pinnacles** which are of little interest, yet accessible by shore and characterised by an incredible number of Diadem sea urchins (*Diadema setosum*), and sometimes an octopus (genus *Octopus*) swims between them.

A Napoleonfish (Cheilinus undulatus)

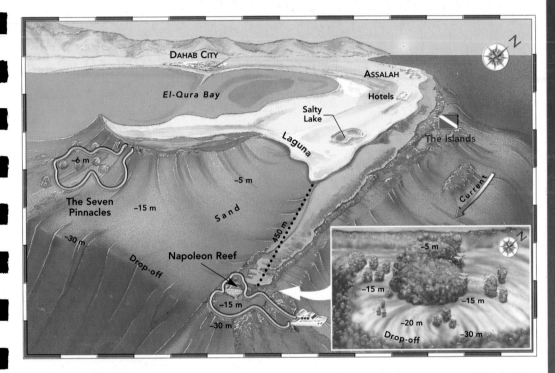

Comments

• *Site is best accessible by boat.*
• *Pay very close attention to windsurfers and kite surfers who frequent this area in high numbers.*
• *Site exposed to wind effects and sometimes has strong currents.*

Look out for

Acropora   Octopus   Napoleonfish

Features

• *Numerous fauna can be seen.*
• *Easy diving without any problems.*
• *Site suitable for snorkeling.*

Three Pools

Golden Blocks

Aerial view of the Moray Garden site

This site is situated some hundred meters south of *Happy Life Village* tourist hotel in front of the small Bedouin restaurant called *Wadi Qnai*. **Moray Garden** is also known as 'Shark's Cave' and is reached by car taking the coastal road from El-Qura bay, a distance of approximately 10 kilometers. The truth is that there are neither caves nor sharks, yet some Giant morays (*Gymnothorax javanicus*) might be seen here, especially in the northern area. Entering the water is easy from the shingle beach, and protected from waves. The diving route permits exploration of another site at the same time which is situated about a hundred meters further to the north called **Golden Blocks** due to its two hard coral towers of a golden colour that you can just see from the shore at low tide. Descend over a sandy slope passing an extensive area with sea grass (*Halophila stipulacea*) on the right, then proceed northwards to a depth of 16–20 meters where an interesting reef area starts characterised by numerous pinnacles and madrepores around which swarm shoals of fusiliers and trevallies. Continue northwards with the reef on your left and you reach the

Bedouin restaurant at Moray Garden

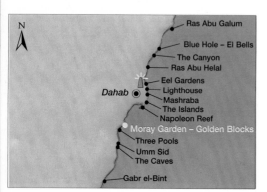

N

Ras Abu Galum
Blue Hole – El Bells
The Canyon
Ras Abu Helal
Eel Gardens
Lighthouse
Mashraba
The Islands
Napoleon Reef
Moray Garden – Golden Blocks
Three Pools
Umm Sid
The Caves
Gabr el-Bint

Dahab

Access	
Difficulty	
Current	
Natural scenery	
Fauna interest	
General interest	

Other charactestics

towers of Golden Blocks marked by a big gorgonian at a depth of 18 meters. There are anemones with their anemonefish around these blocks, as well as Red Sea bannerfish (*Heniochus intermedius*), Broccoli soft corals (*Lithophyton arboreum*) and Stalked alcyonarians (genus *Sarcophyton*).

If you still have air in your tank you may return to your starting point, otherwise end the dive and exit the water here.

A *Giant moray* (Gymnothorax javanicus)

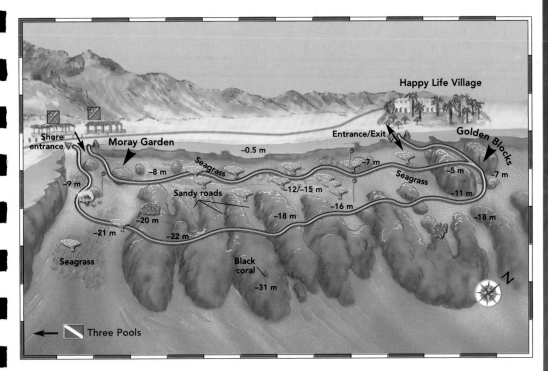

Happy Life Village

Shore entrance ▽   Moray Garden   −0.5 m   Entrance/Exit   Golden Blocks

−9 m   −8 m   Seagrass   −7 m   −5 m   −7 m

Sandy roads   −12/−15 m   Seagrass   −11 m

−20 m   −18 m   −16 m   −18 m

−21 m   −22 m

Seagrass   Black coral   −31 m

N

◀ [dive flag] Three Pools

Comments

• *The dive can be very long if the circular route is fully completed.*

Look out for

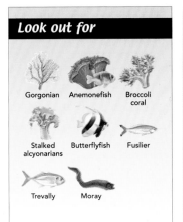

Gorgonian   Anemonefish   Broccoli coral

Stalked alcyonarians   Butterflyfish   Fusilier

Trevally   Moray

Features

• *Easy diving in a sheltered place from waves and currents.*
• *Huge variety of underwater landscape and fauna.*
• *Pleasant site with small friendly restaurant.*
• *Is very close to other interesting places.*

Aerial view of Three Pools dive site

The Caves

Pools

Moray Garden

Umm Sid
The Caves

N

Three Pools is 300 meters south of Moray Garden and is also situated just in front of a small Bedouin restaurant. The sea entry is marked by a big signboard that details the diving topography of the site. Its name derives from three real natural pools formed in the reef plate that have a sandy bottom with a depth between 3 and 4 meters aligned one after the other. You best start your dive at Three Pools with high tide as you pass from one pool to the other much easier; after the exploration of the third – and biggest – one, exit into open water. You might come across small Red Sea Moses sole (*Pardachirus marmoratus*), half hidden in the sand on the clear seabed of this last pool and some Blackspotted pufferfish

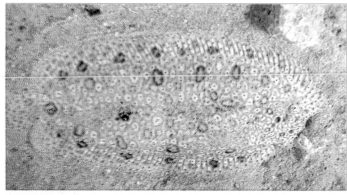

Red Sea Moses sole (Pardachirus marmoratus) in the sand of one of the pools

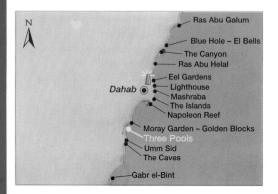

N

Ras Abu Galum
Blue Hole – El Bells
The Canyon
Ras Abu Helal
Eel Gardens
Dahab
Lighthouse
Mashraba
The Islands
Napoleon Reef
Moray Garden – Golden Blocks
Three Pools
Umm Sid
The Caves
Gabr el-Bint

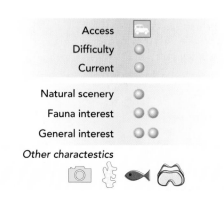

Access
Difficulty
Current

Natural scenery
Fauna interest
General interest

Other charactestics

A group of Banded dascyllus (Dascyllus aruanus)

(*Arothron stellatus*). Once out into the open sea you find a hard coral slope with Massive pore corals (*Porites solida*) and small pinnacles between which there are Salad corals (*Turbinaria mesenterina*) and Brain corals (genus *Platygyra*). Descend to a depth of 15–20 meters and start a big anticlockwise circle keeping the reef on your left: you admire this marvellous coral garden where – between

multicoloured soft corals and anemones guarded by their anemone fish – swim butterflyfish (genus *Chaetodon*), Bluespine unicornfish (*Naso unicornis*), parrotfish (genera *Scarus*, *Chlorurus* and *Cetoscarus*), as well as blue triggerfish(genera *Odonus* and *Balistapus*). End the dive by coming back to your starting point or if sea conditions permit you can continue your dive up to Moray Garden.

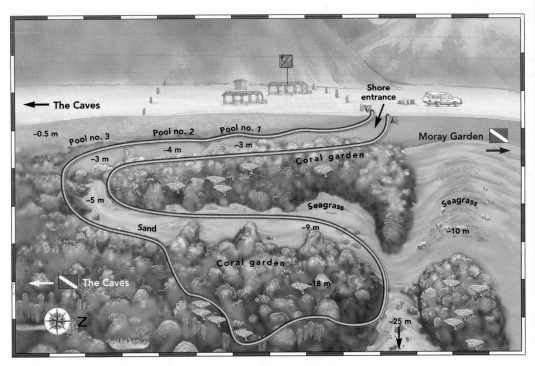

Comments

• It is a good idea to dive at high tide.
• Drift dive possible towards (and from) Moray Garden.

Look out for

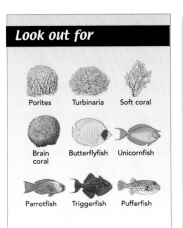

Porites Turbinaria Soft coral

Brain coral Butterflyfish Unicornfish

Parrotfish Triggerfish Pufferfish

Features

• Easy diving that offers an opportunity to admire an incredible variety of hard and soft corals.
• The pools are interesting for snorkelers.
• If you look carefully you find many nudibranchs.

28°25.000' N — 34°27.364' E

Aerial view of The Caves site

T he Caves is the last of the series of sites on the southern coast of El-Qura bay, before Gabr el-Bint and 2.2 kilometers south of Three Pools.
The entry, which is not marked by any sign, is in front of a small Bedouin restaurant at a crack in the reef plate.
Usually a drift dive is done here with the exit 120 meters to the south where a small bay opens in the reef.
Descend on a gravely slope on which at a depth of 3 meters two caves open up, thus giving the site its name

and represents its major attraction.
The southern cave especially,

straight to your right, is well worth a visit: it is covered with soft corals (Alcyonarians),

The natural pool at the exit of the dive

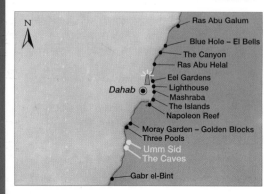

N

Ras Abu Galum

Blue Hole – El Bells

The Canyon

Ras Abu Helal

Eel Gardens

Dahab Lighthouse

Mashraba

The Islands

Napoleon Reef

Moray Garden – Golden Blocks

Three Pools

Umm Sid

The Caves

Gabr el-Bint

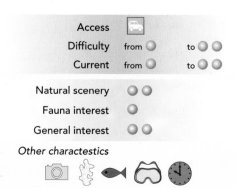

Access

Difficulty from ◯ to ◯ ◯

Current from ◯ to ◯ ◯

Natural scenery ◯ ◯

Fauna interest ◯

General interest ◯ ◯

Other charactestics

sponges and black corals (genus *Antipathes*).

After the visit to the caves, descend to a depth of 16–22 meters. Keep the reef to your right and turn south until you reach the immersed bay with the exit.

The dive site **Umm Sid** (N 28°25.654'–E 34°27.352') is 470 meters to the north of The Caves and is interesting for its fauna as well as for its hard coral formation.

View of the southern cave with branches of black coral (genus Antipathes*)*

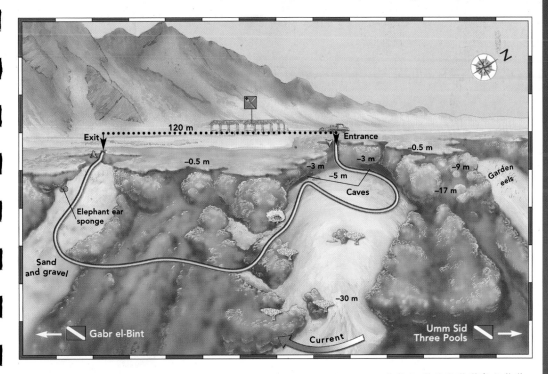

Comments

• *Site is exposed to waves.*
• *Diving should be avoided with choppy sea as the waves might considerably complicate the exit.*

Look out for

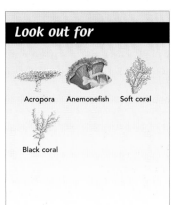

Acropora   Anemonefish   Soft coral

Black coral

Features

• *The caves are very interesting.*
• *The site is still undamaged and less frequented than others previously described.*
• *Nice developmen of soft and hard corals.*

Aerial view of Gabr el-Bint

Hard coral buttress

The Caves

Gabr el-Bint means 'the Tomb of the girl' and is situated 7.5 kilometers south of The Caves: this site is only accessible by foot, camel or boat (one hour navigation from Dahab). The track along the coast is interrupted after 1.5 kilometers from The Caves where Bedouins hire out camels on which the equipment can be loaded to reach the site in about one hour and a half. Gabr el-Bint is part of the protected area of Nabq and is very interesting for its landscape and from its naturalistic point of view.

The atmosphere is harsh and magnificent, dominated by impressive mountains higher than 1,000 meters (*Gebel Umm Isheirat*): you immediately get the impression you are visiting one of the few places unspoiled by tourism. The coral reef of Gabr el-Bint is basically intact and, beyond the common and numerous reef fauna, it is also visited by pelagic species.

Soft corals (Alcyonarians), anthias and glassfish on the wall of Gabr el-Bint

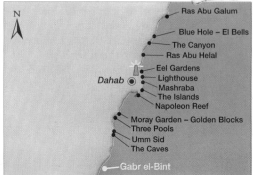

N
- Ras Abu Galum
- Blue Hole – El Bells
- The Canyon
- Ras Abu Helal
- Eel Gardens
- Dahab
- Lighthouse
- Mashraba
- The Islands
- Napoleon Reef
- Moray Garden – Golden Blocks
- Three Pools
- Umm Sid
- The Caves
- Gabr el-Bint

A Grooved mosaic coral (genus Favites)

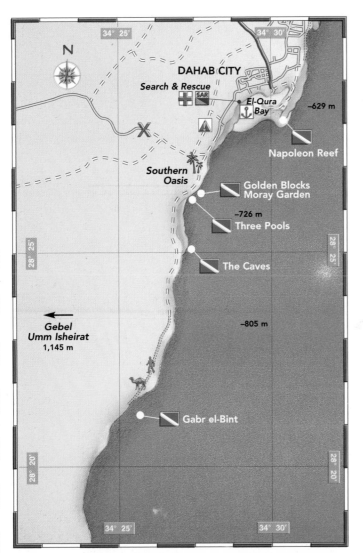

*Branches of black coral
(Antiphates dichotoma)*

The expanded polyps of the Goniopora
columna *that look like daisies*

*Red Sea bannerfish (*Heniochus intermedius*), a Coral grouper (*Cephalopholis miniata*) and a Lined butterflyfish (*Chaetodon
lineolatus*) under the umbrella of a table coral (*Acropora sp.*)*

The site of Gabr el-Bint seen from the sea

A big hard coral buttress thrusting out of the coast for a dozen of meters distinguishes the site of Gabr el-Bint. This site offers two dives: the dive to the north of the buttress is the more interesting, the second is done southwards. The landscape is fantastic both below and above water level, dominated by a splendid wall that descends into the blue decorated with table corals, Alcyonarians, fan and black corals that give life to shelters and small caves. You dive south of the hard coral buttress and descend to a

A big Gorgonian (Subergorgia hicksoni) on the wall of Gabr el-Bint

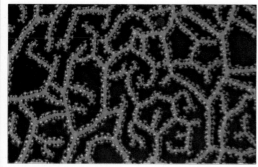

Delicate structure of a red fan coral (genus Acabaria)

Access		
Difficulty		
Current	from	to
Natural scenery		
Fauna interest		
General interest		

Other charactestics

depth of 20 meters where there are some beautiful gorgonians and a shelter, then continue northwards skirting around the madrepore wall directly on your right. Schools of red anthias, parrotfish (familiy Scaridae), Common lionfish (*Pterois miles*) and sometimes a Hawksbill turtle (*Eretmochelys imbricata*) swim close to the wall: shoals of trevallies, snappers and emperorfish pass by in the blue. After having passed a double line of nice gorgonians, ascend to 10 meters to enter a sort of sandy valley that you cross in southerly direction and come back to your starting point. An encounter with triggerfish and crocodilefish are guaranteed on this splendid section of the route as well as Bluespotted stingrays (*Taeniura lymma*) and Cornetfish (*Fistularia commersoni*) that swim close to the surface.

A finger leather coral (genus Sinularia*)*

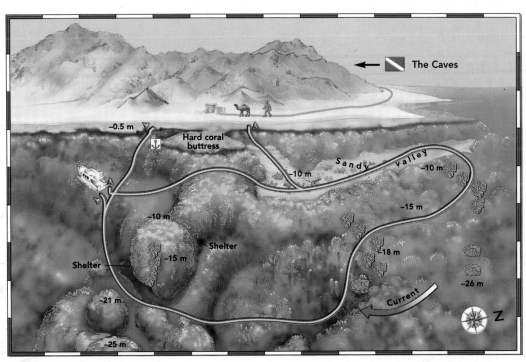

The Caves

−0.5 m

Hard coral buttress

Sandy valley

−10 m   −10 m

−15 m

−10 m

Shelter

−18 m

Shelter

−15 m

−26 m

−21 m

Current

−25 m

Z

Comments

• *Occasional current from the north.*
• *If arriving by land, make sure to follow the track and do not forget to bring along plenty of water and provisions.*
• *Excursions organized by local diving centers take a full day with a second dive south of the hard coral buttress.*

Look out for

Gorgonian   Turbinaria   Anthias

Parrotfish   Lionfish   Stingray

Snapper   Crocodilefish   Trevally

Features

• *Diving suitable for all levels of divers.*
• *The wall descending to more than 50 meters of depth is of outstanding beauty.*
• *Big variety and abundance of fauna.*
• *You can admire big Gorgonian sea-fans, red gorgonians and a forest of Alcyonarians.*

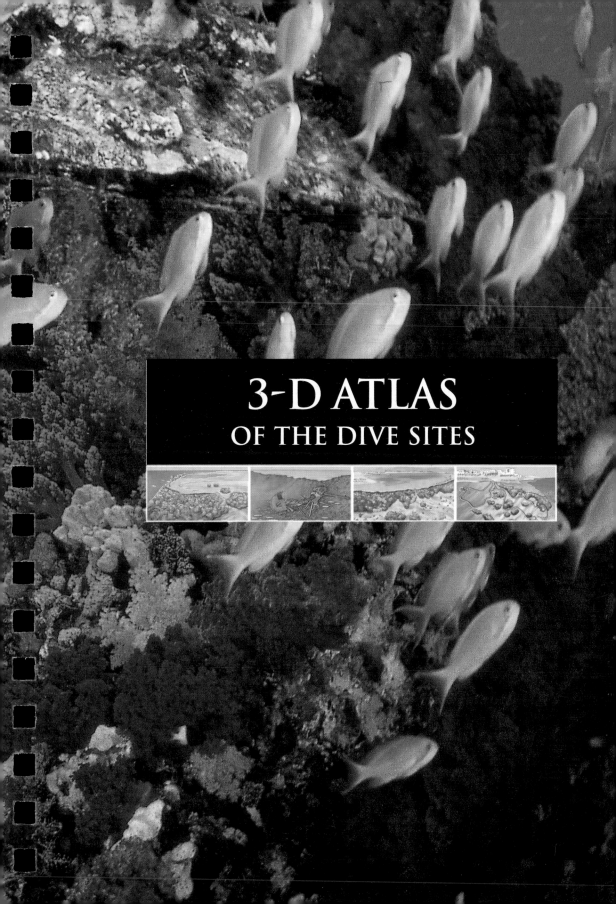

3-D ATLAS
OF THE DIVE SITES

1	Jackson Reef	2	Kormoran	3	Laguna Reef	4	Woodhause Reef	5	Thomas Reef
6	Gordon Reef	7	Ras Ghamila	8	Ras Nasrani	9	Ras Bob	10	White Knight
11	Shark's Bay	12	Far Garden	13	Fiddle Garden	14	Middle Garden	15	Near Garden
16	Sodfa	17	Tower	18	Pinky Wall	19	Amphoras	20	Turtle Bay
21	Paradise	22	Ras Umm Sid	23	Temple	24	Ras Katy	25	Ras Ghozlani
26	Ras Za'atar	27	Ras Burg	28	Jackfish Alley	29	Eel Garden	30	Shark Observatory
31	Shark & Yolanda Reef	32	The Alternatives	33	Dunraven (Beacon Rock)	34	Small Crack	35	Shag Rock (Kingston)
36	Thistlegorm	37	Ghiannis D.	38	Carnatic	39	Marcus	40	Kimon M.
41	North Ras Abu Galum	42	South Ras Abu Galum	43	Blue Hole – El Bells	44	The Canyon	45	Ras Abu Helal
46	Eel Gardens	47	Lighthouse	48	The Islands	49	Napoleon Reef	50	Moray Garden
51	Three Pools	52	The Caves	53	North Gabr el-Bint				

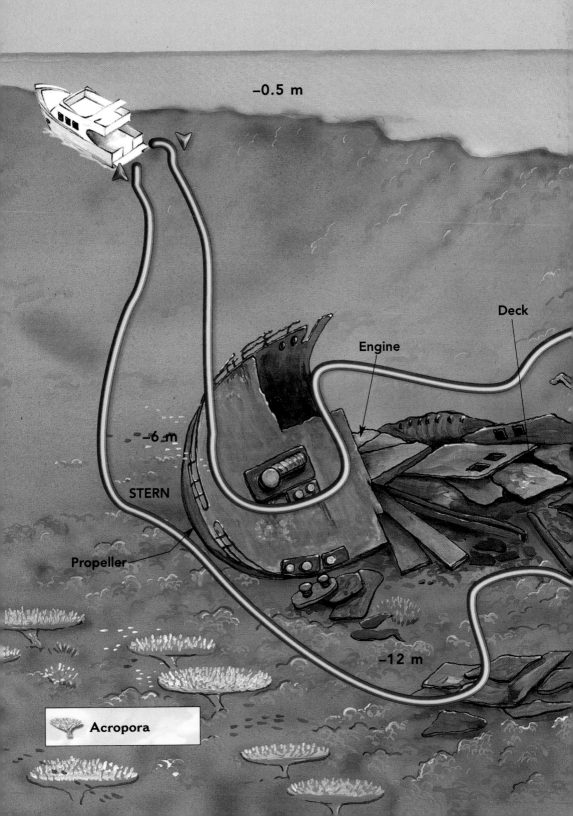

−0.5 m

Deck

Engine

−6 m

STERN

Propeller

−12 m

Acropora

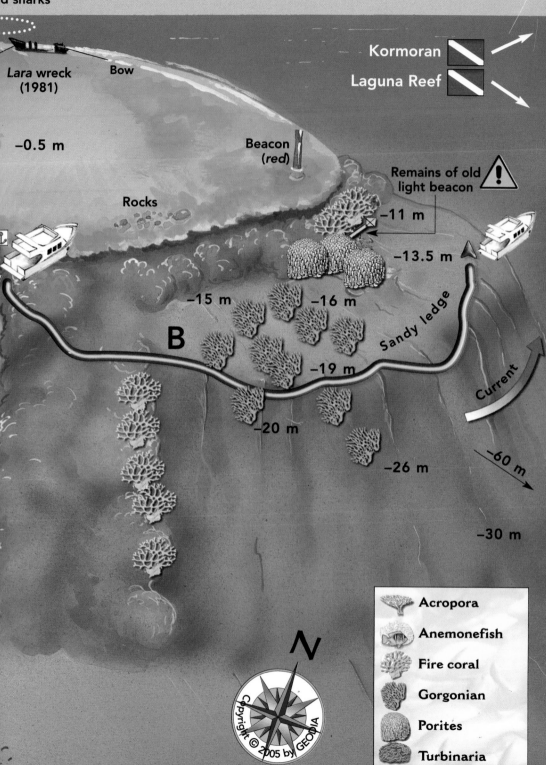

area for
d sharks

Kormoran
Laguna Reef

Lara wreck
(1981)   Bow

−0.5 m

Beacon
(*red*)

Remains of old
light beacon ⚠

Rocks

−11 m

−13.5 m

−15 m   −16 m

Sandy ledge

B

−19 m

Current

−20 m

−60 m

−26 m

−30 m

N

Copyright © 2005 by GEODIA

Acropora
Anemonefish
Fire coral
Gorgonian
Porites
Turbinaria

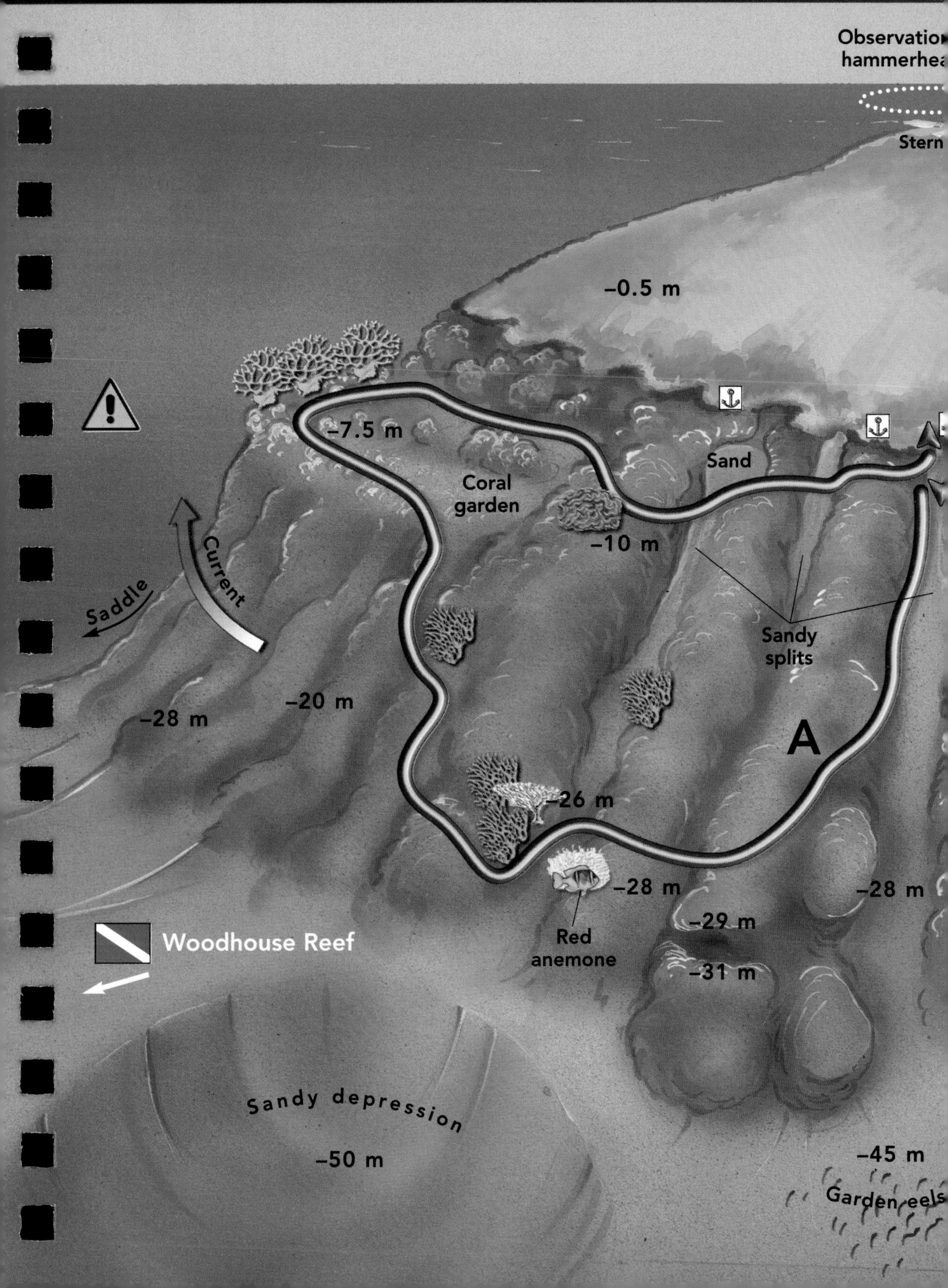

Observation
hammerhea

Stern

−0.5 m

−7.5 m

Coral
garden

Sand

−10 m

Current

Saddle

Sandy
splits

−28 m

−20 m

A

−26 m

−28 m

−28 m

−29 m

Woodhouse Reef

Red
anemone

−31 m

Sandy depression

−50 m

−45 m

Garden eels

−0.5 m

−0.5 m

Jackson Reef

BOW   −3 m

Hand-winch

Mast

Copyright © 2005 by GEODIA

N

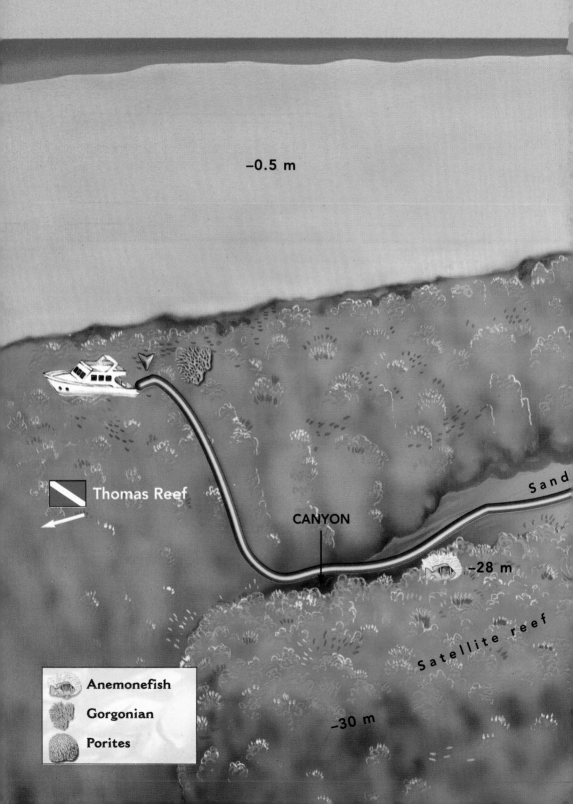

−0.5 m

Thomas Reef

CANYON

Sand

−28 m

Satellite reef

−30 m

Anemonefish

Gorgonian

Porites

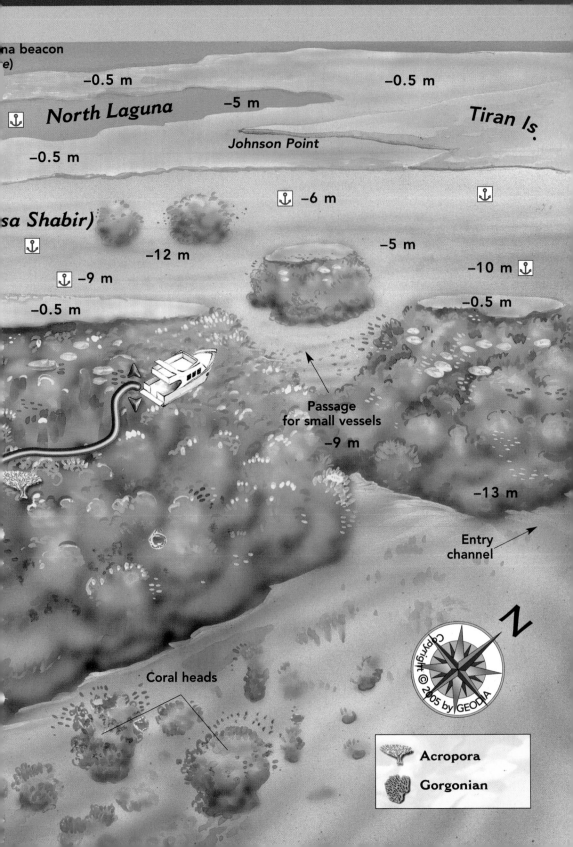

na beacon
e)

−0.5 m   −0.5 m

North Laguna   −5 m   *Tiran Is.*

Johnson Point

−0.5 m

⚓ −6 m

sa Shabir)   −5 m

⚓   −10 m ⚓

⚓ −12 m   −0.5 m

⚓ −9 m

−0.5 m

Passage
for small vessels
−9 m

−13 m

Entry
channel

Coral heads

Copyright © 2005 by GEODIA

Acropora

Gorgonian

Metallic
post

Entry
channel

North Lagu
(green/whi

South Laguna
beacon (green)

−30 m

−8 m

−12 m

1 mile

−8 m

South Laguna (Mar

−0.5 m

Coral garden

−19 m

Current

Current

−20 m

Jackson Reef

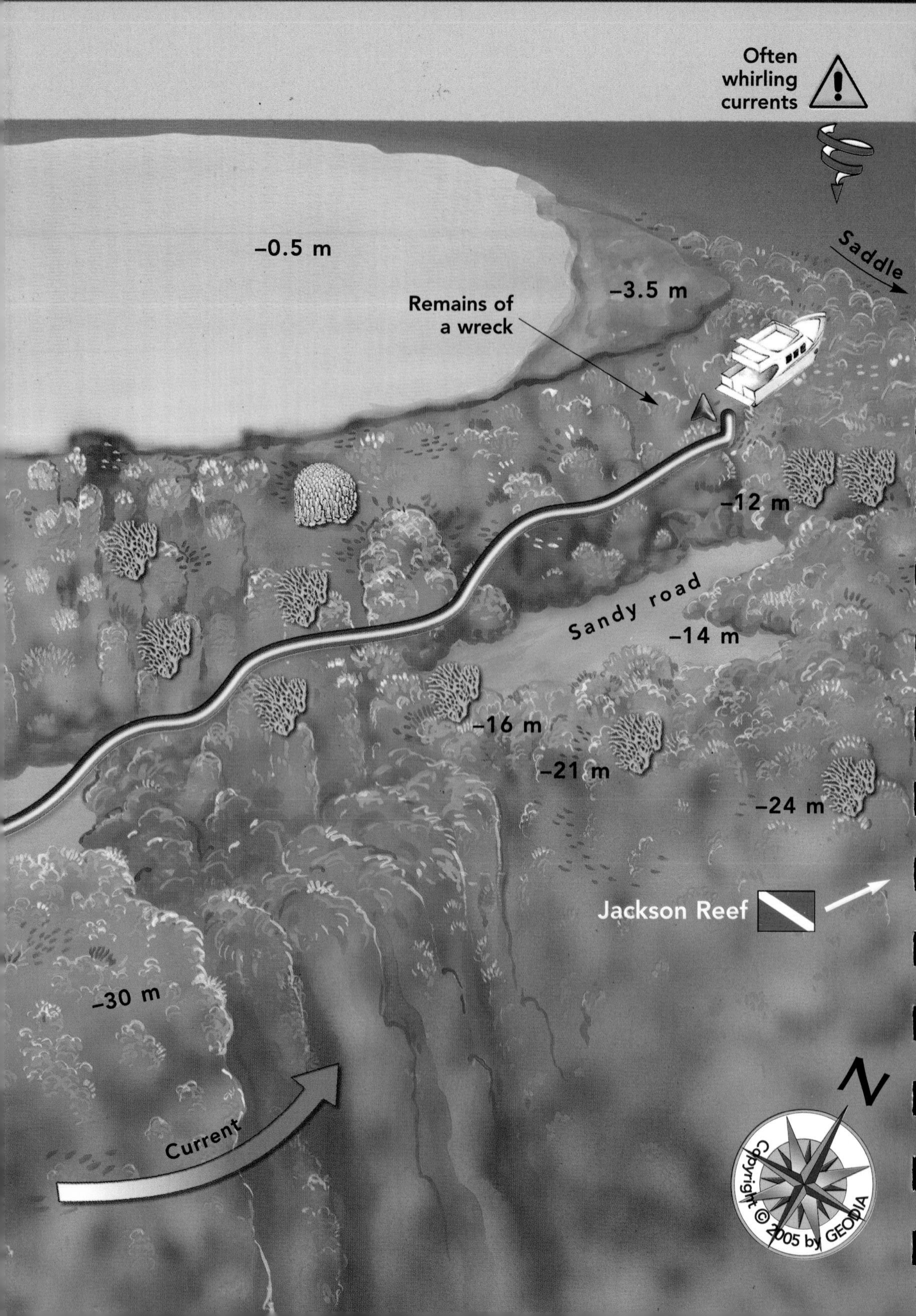

Often
whirling
currents

Saddle

−0.5 m

−3.5 m

Remains of
a wreck

−12 m

Sandy road

−14 m

−16 m

−21 m

−24 m

Jackson Reef

−30 m

Current

N

Copyright © 2005 by GEODIA

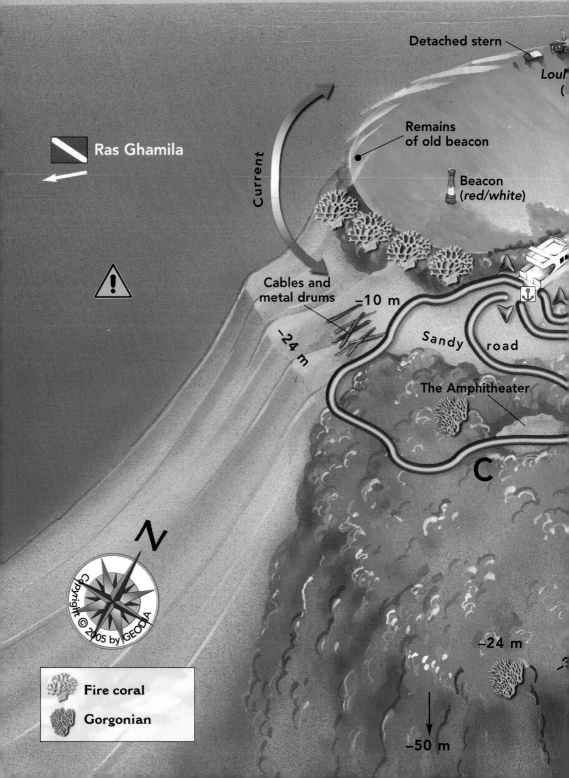

Detached stern

Loul

Ras Ghamila

Current

Remains
of old beacon

Beacon
(red/white)

Cables and
metal drums

−10 m

−24 m

Sandy road

The Amphitheater

C

N

−24 m

−50 m

Fire coral

Gorgonian

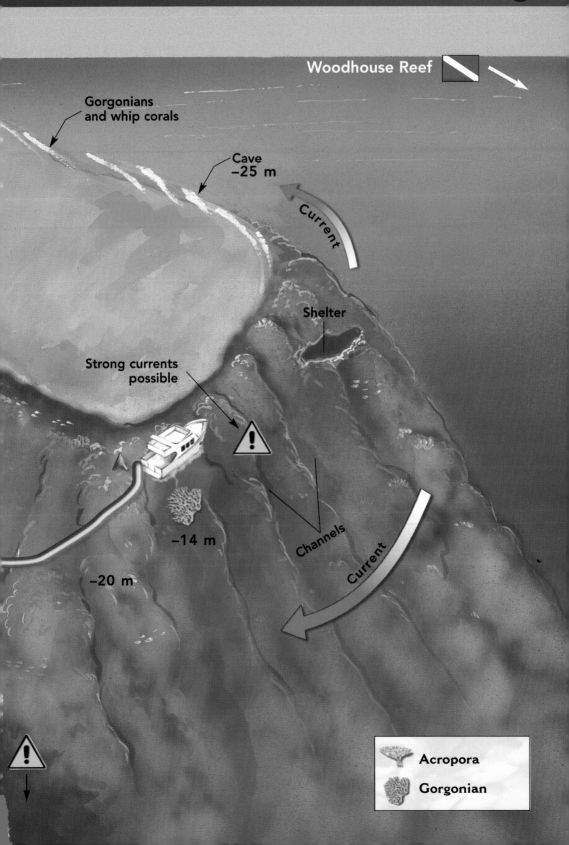

Woodhouse Reef

Gorgonians
and whip corals

Cave
−25 m

Current

Shelter

Strong currents
possible

Channels

Current

−14 m

−20 m

Acropora

Gorgonian

N

−0.5 m

−25 m
Sandy plateau

−30 m

−5 m

Cave

Coral garden

−35 m

CANYON

Current

Drop-off

−52 m

Copyright © 2005 by GEODIA

Gordon Reef

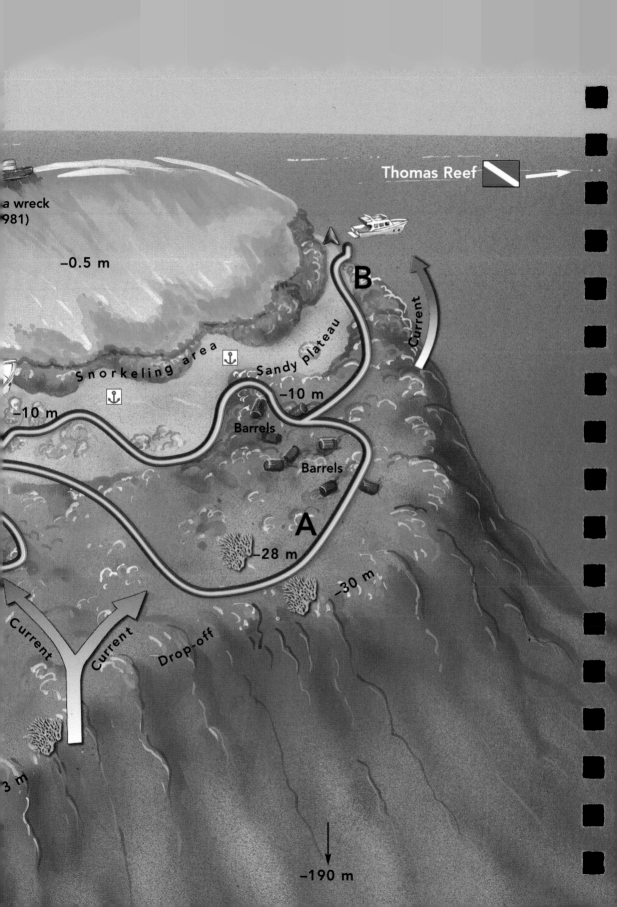

Thomas Reef →

...a wreck
...981)

−0.5 m

B

Current

Snorkeling area

Sandy plateau

−10 m

−10 m

Barrels

Barrels

A

−28 m

−30 m

Current

Current

Drop-off

...3 m

−190 m

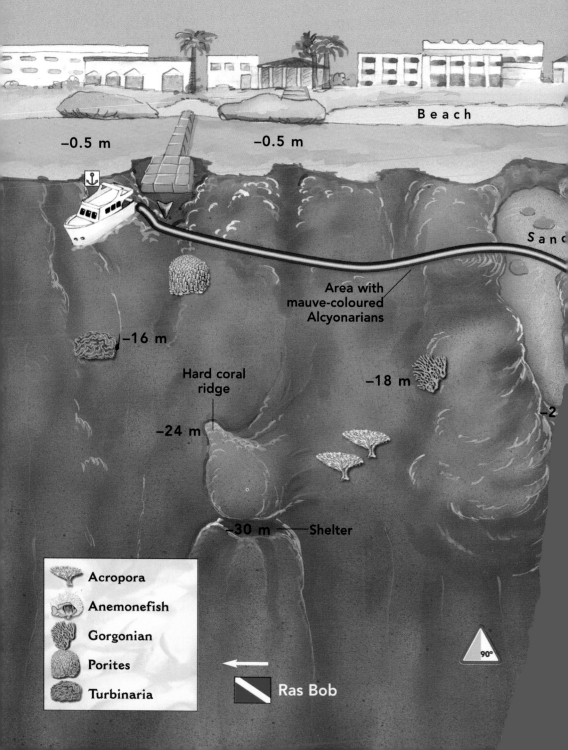

Melia Sinai Resort

The "
b

Beach

−0.5 m   −0.5 m

Sand

Area with
mauve-coloured
Alcyonarians

−16 m

Hard coral
ridge

−18 m

−2

−24 m

−30 m ——— Shelter

Acropora

Anemonefish

Gorgonian

Porites

Turbinaria

90°

Ras Bob

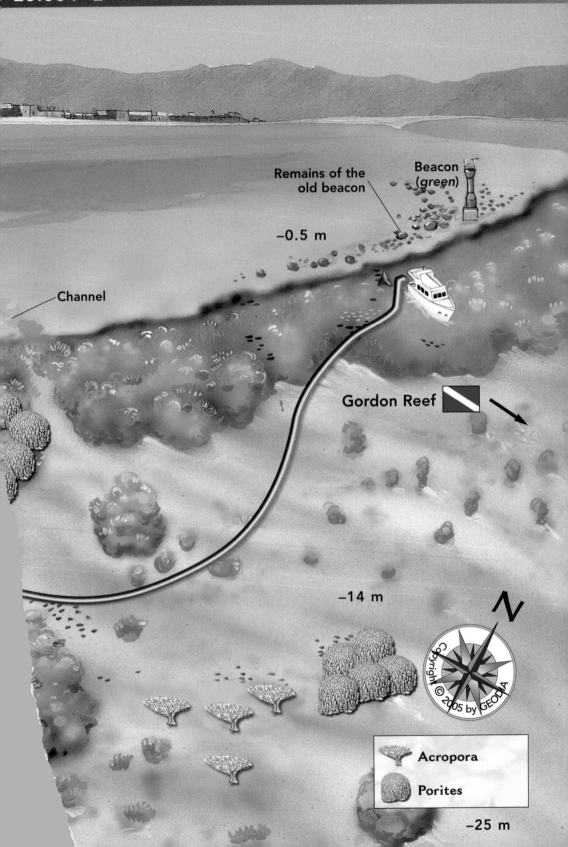

Remains of the
old beacon

Beacon
(*green*)

−0.5 m

Channel

Gordon Reef

−14 m

N

Copyright © 2005 by GEODIA

Acropora

Porites

−25 m

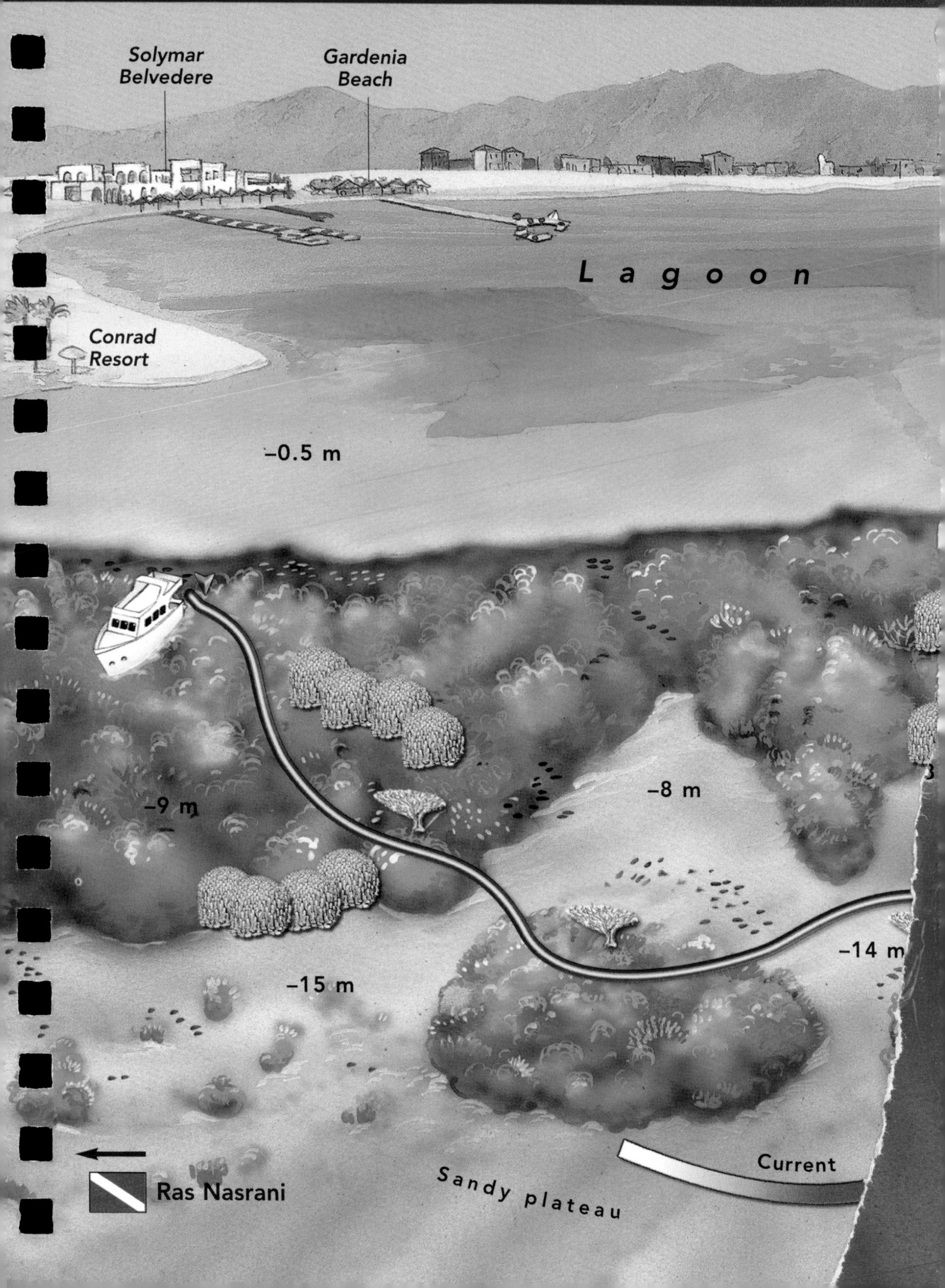

Solymar
Belvedere

Gardenia
Beach

L a g o o n

Conrad
Resort

−0.5 m

−9 m

−8 m

−15 m

−14 m

Current

Ras Nasrani

Sandy plateau

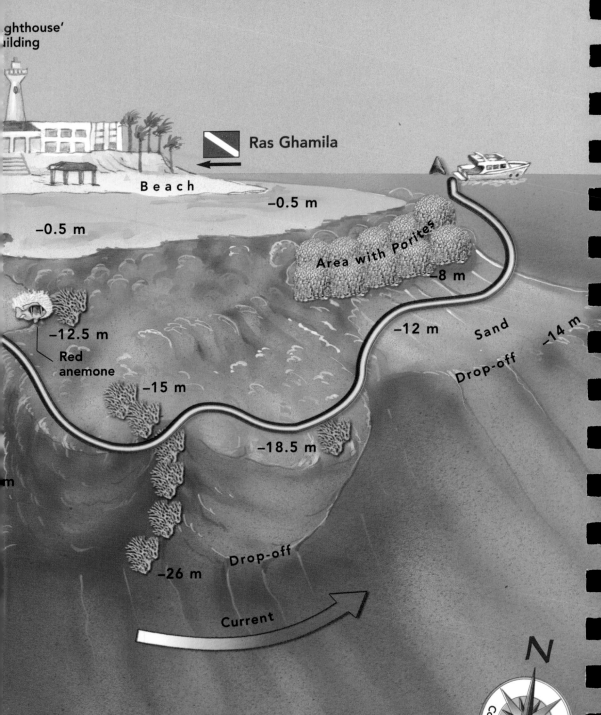

34°24.938' E

Ras Ghamila

Beach

−0.5 m

−0.5 m

Area with Porites

−8 m

Red anemone

−12.5 m

−15 m

−18.5 m

−12 m

Sand

Drop-off

−14 m

Drop-off

−26 m

Current

N

Copyright © 2005 by GEODIA

10 White Knight 27°57.627′

Crack
–0.5 m
First cave
Shark's Bay
Barrel
–15 m
Metallic fragments and remains of *Noose One*
Acropora
Anemonefish
Gorgonian
Turbinaria

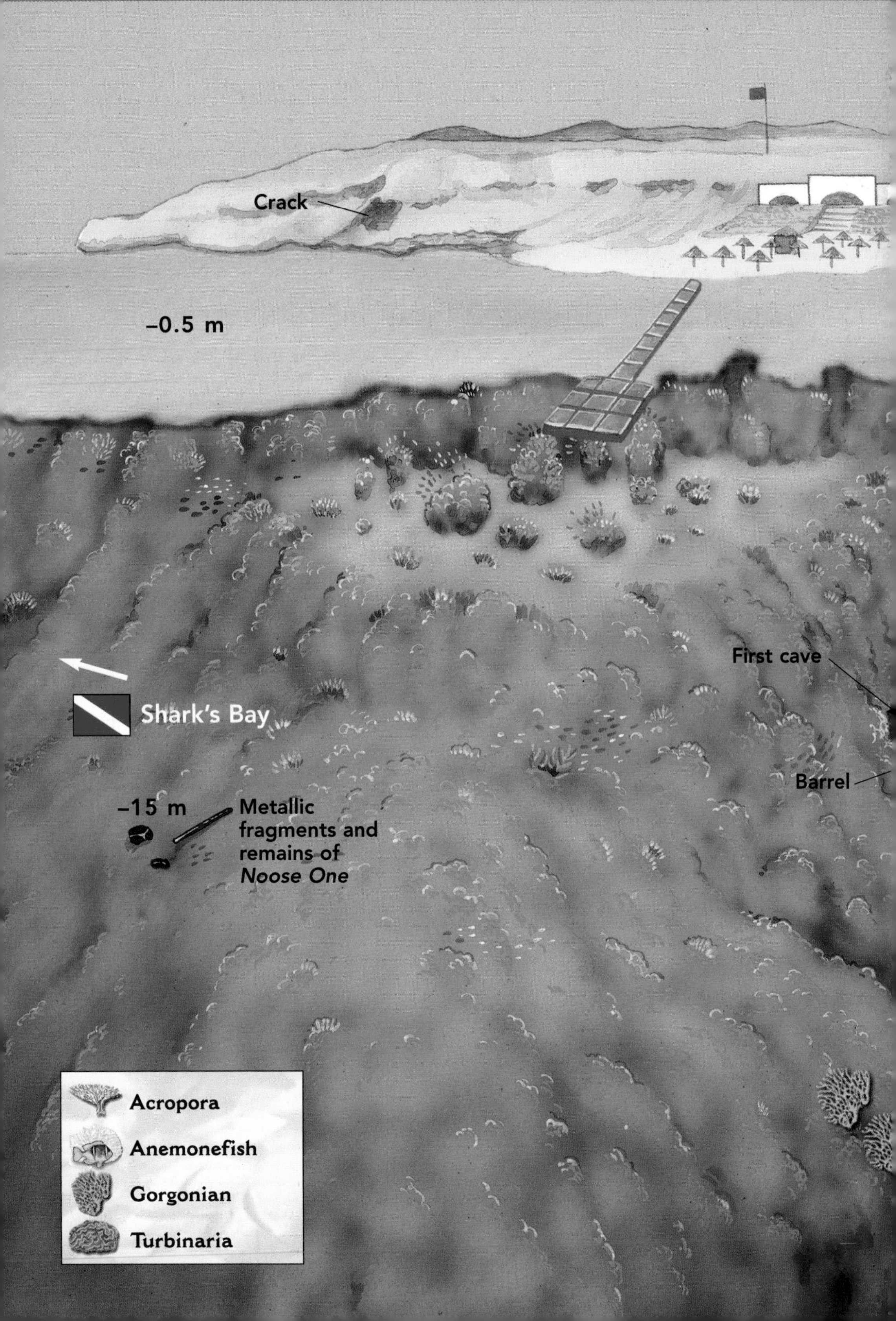

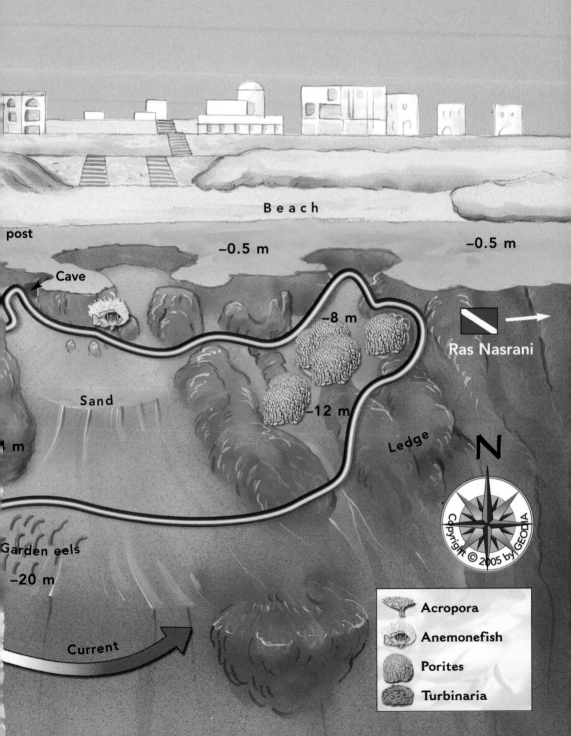

Beach

post

−0.5 m

−0.5 m

Cave

−8 m

Ras Nasrani

Sand

−12 m

Ledge

m

N

Garden eels

−20 m

Copyright © 2005 by GEODIA

Current

Acropora

Anemonefish

Porites

Turbinaria

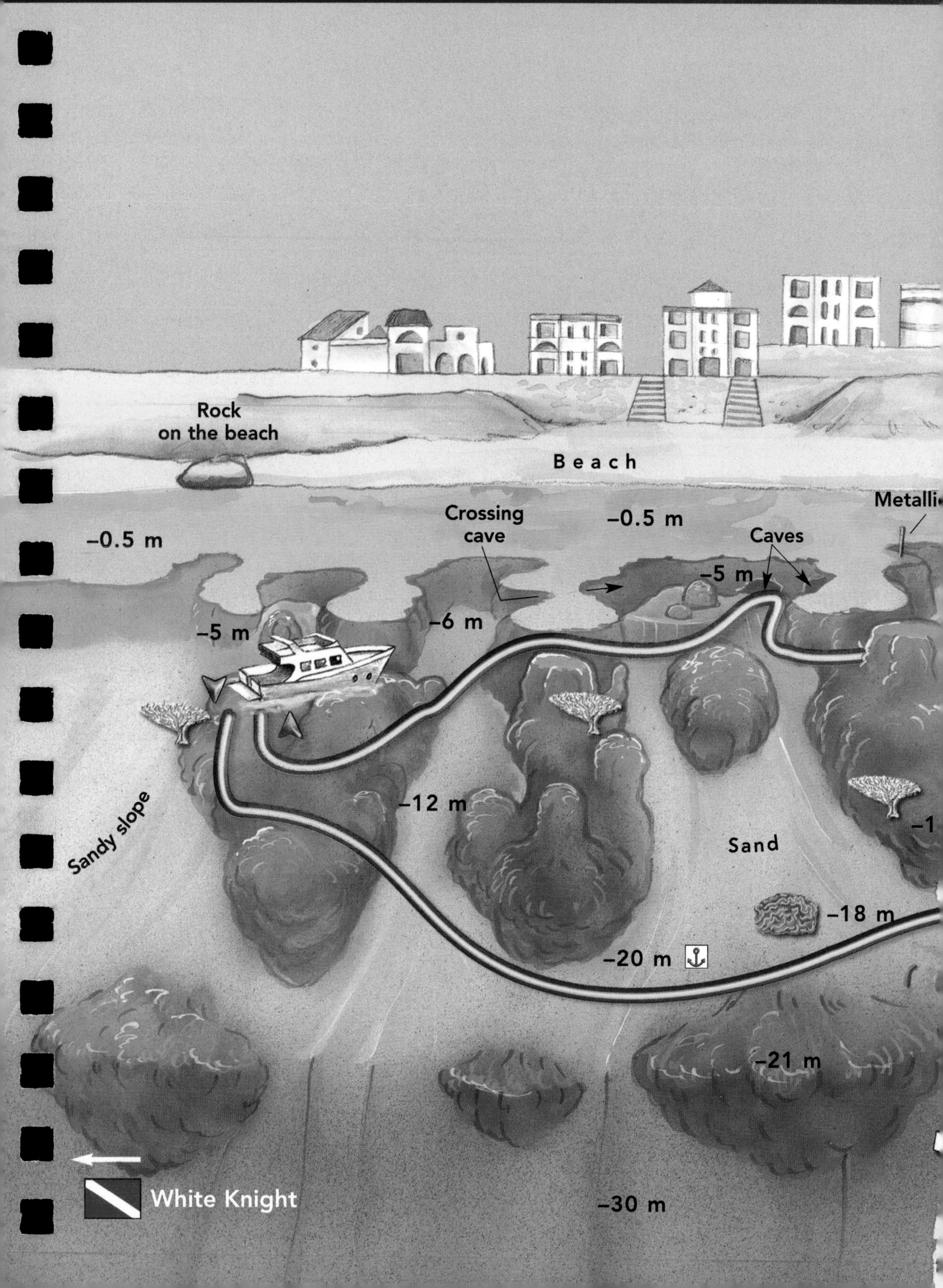

Rock
on the beach

B e a c h

Crossing
cave

−0.5 m

Metalli

Caves

−0.5 m

−5 m

−5 m

−6 m

−5 m

Sandy slope

−12 m

Sand

−1

−18 m

−20 m ⚓

−21 m

→ White Knight

−30 m

Savoy Hotel

Maxim Plaza Resort

Crack
in the reef

−0.5 m

−3 m

−6 m

−0.5 m

Snorkeling area

−8 m

−10 m

Passage

−13 m

−10/15 m

−19 m

−8 m

Second
cave

−21 m

Garden eels

Third
cave

−18 m ⚓

Ledge

−27 m

Ras Bob

N

90°

−38 m

Copyright © 2005 by GEODIA

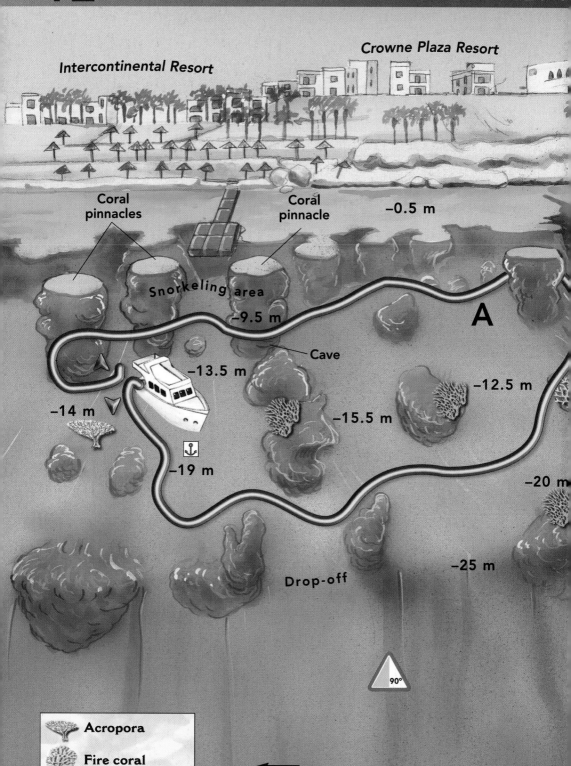

Intercontinental Resort

Crowne Plaza Resort

Coral pinnacles

Coral pinnacle

−0.5 m

Snorkeling area

−9.5 m

Cave

A

−13.5 m

−12.5 m

−14 m

−15.5 m

−19 m

−20 m

−25 m

Drop-off

90°

Acropora

Fire coral

Gorgonian

Fiddle Garden

23.097' E

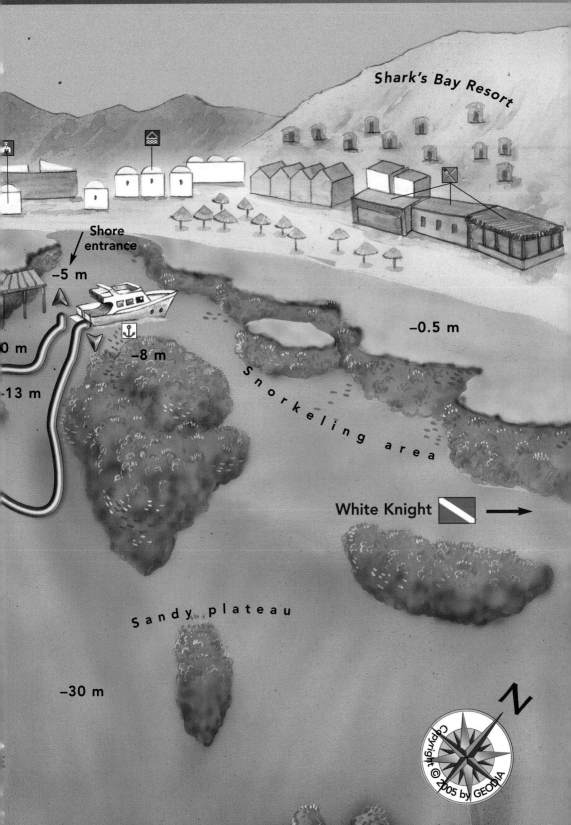

Shark's Bay Resort

Shore
entrance

−5 m

−0 m

−13 m

−8 m

−0.5 m

S n o r k e l i n g   a r e a

White Knight

S a n d y   p l a t e a u

−30 m

N

Copyright © 2005 by GEODIA

Jump
About
Gib

Pyramisa Resort

Sand

−6 m

−1

−14 m

−0.5 m

Canyon

Coral garden

90°

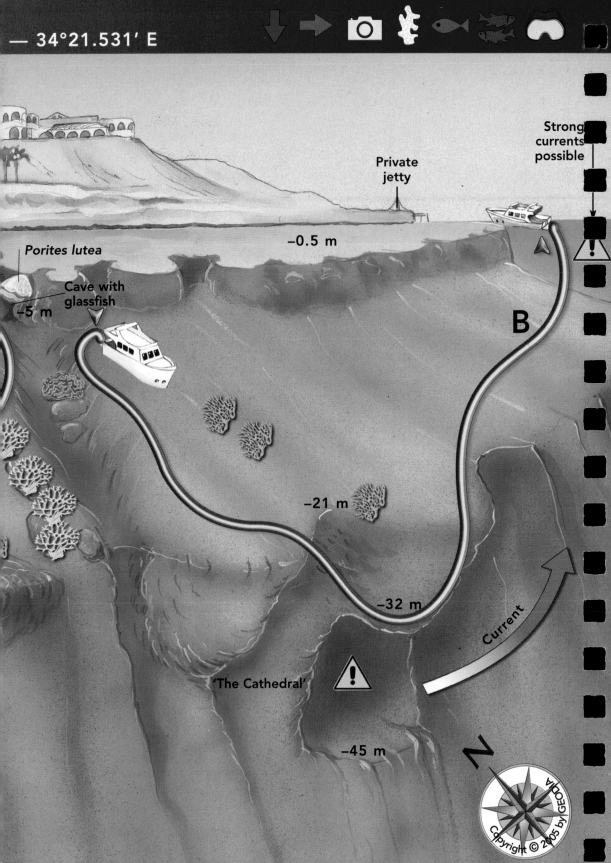

— 34°21.531' E

Strong
currents
possible

Private
jetty

−0.5 m

Porites lutea

Cave with
glassfish

−5 m

B

−21 m

−32 m

Current

'The Cathedral'

−45 m

N

Copyright © 2005 by GEO

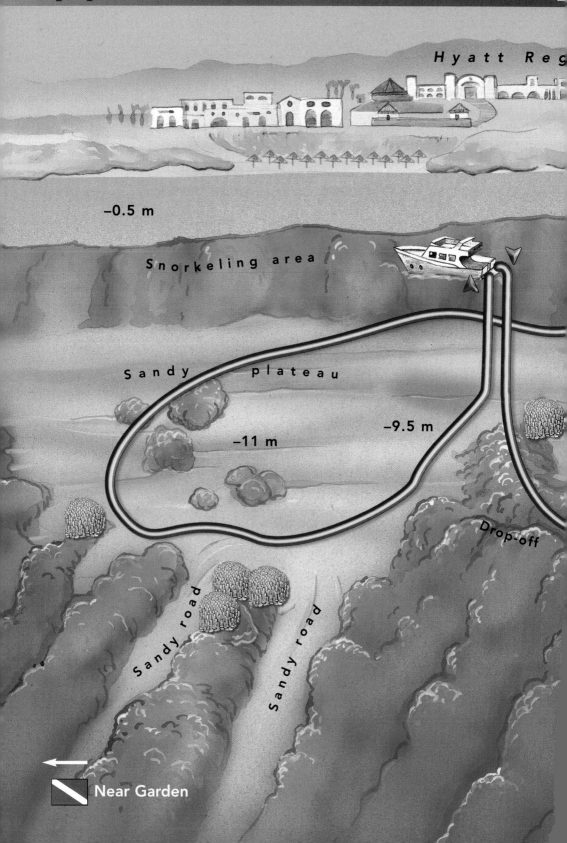

Hyatt Reg

−0.5 m

Snorkeling area

Sandy   plateau

−11 m

−9.5 m

Drop-off

Sandy road

Sandy road

Near Garden

451' E

FIDDLE GARDEN 13

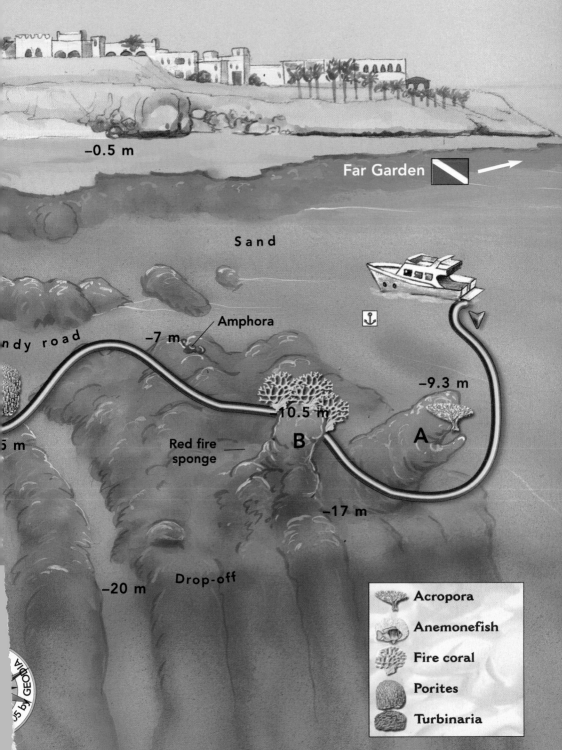

Crowne Plaza Resort

−0.5 m

Far Garden

Sand

Amphora

−7 m

ndy road

−10.5 m

−9.3 m

Red fire sponge

B

A

−5 m

−17 m

Drop-off

−20 m

Acropora
Anemonefish
Fire coral
Porites
Turbinaria

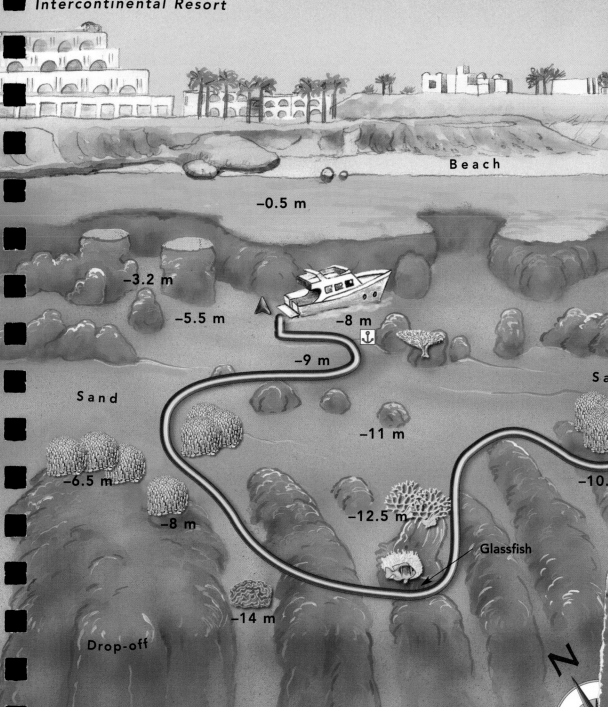

Intercontinental Resort

Beach

−0.5 m

−3.2 m

−5.5 m

−8 m ⚓

−9 m

Sand

S

S

−11 m

−6.5 m

−8 m

−10.

−12.5 m

Glassfish

−14 m

Drop-off

N

Middle Garden

Copyright

ency Resort

−0.5 m

Snorkeling area

−6 m

−8 m

Sandy road

Fiddle
Garden

−14 m

Acropora

Porites

−35 m

Copyright © 2005 by GEODIA

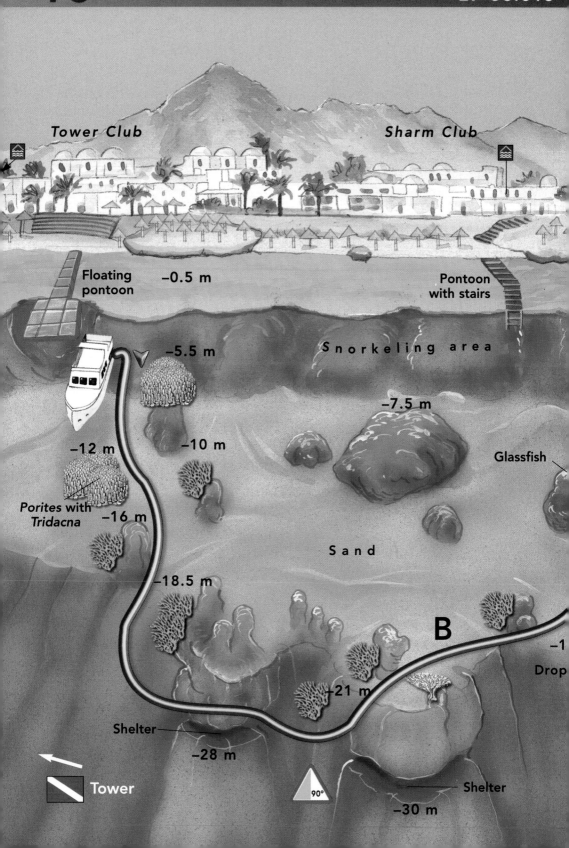

Tower Club

Sharm Club

Floating
pontoon

−0.5 m

Pontoon
with stairs

Snorkeling area

−5.5 m

−7.5 m

−10 m

Glassfish

−12 m

Porites with
Tridacna

−16 m

Sand

−18.5 m

B

−1

Drop

−21 m

Shelter

−28 m

90°

Tower

Shelter

−30 m

NEAR GARDEN 15

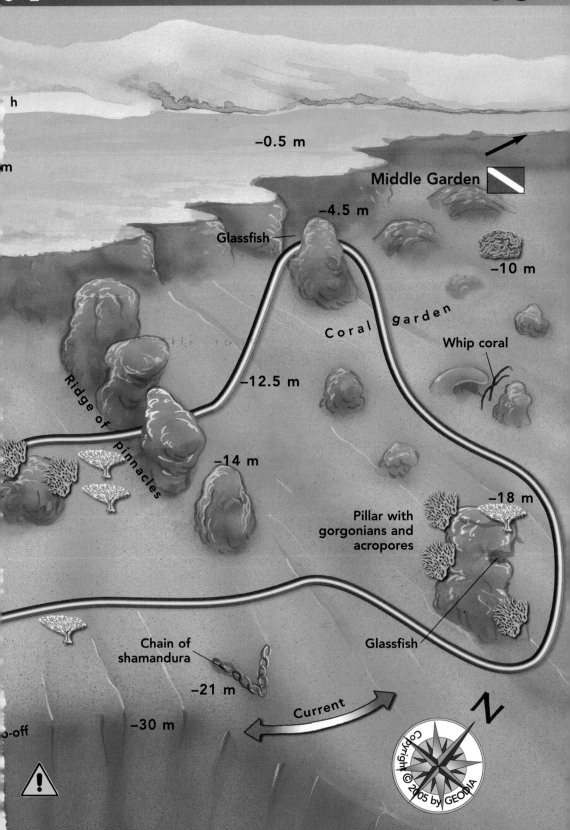

−0.5 m

Middle Garden

−4.5 m

Glassfish

−10 m

Coral garden

Whip coral

−12.5 m

Ridge of pinnacles

−14 m

−18 m

Pillar with gorgonians and acropores

Glassfish

Chain of shamandura

−21 m

Current

−30 m

N

Copyright © 2005 by GEObIA

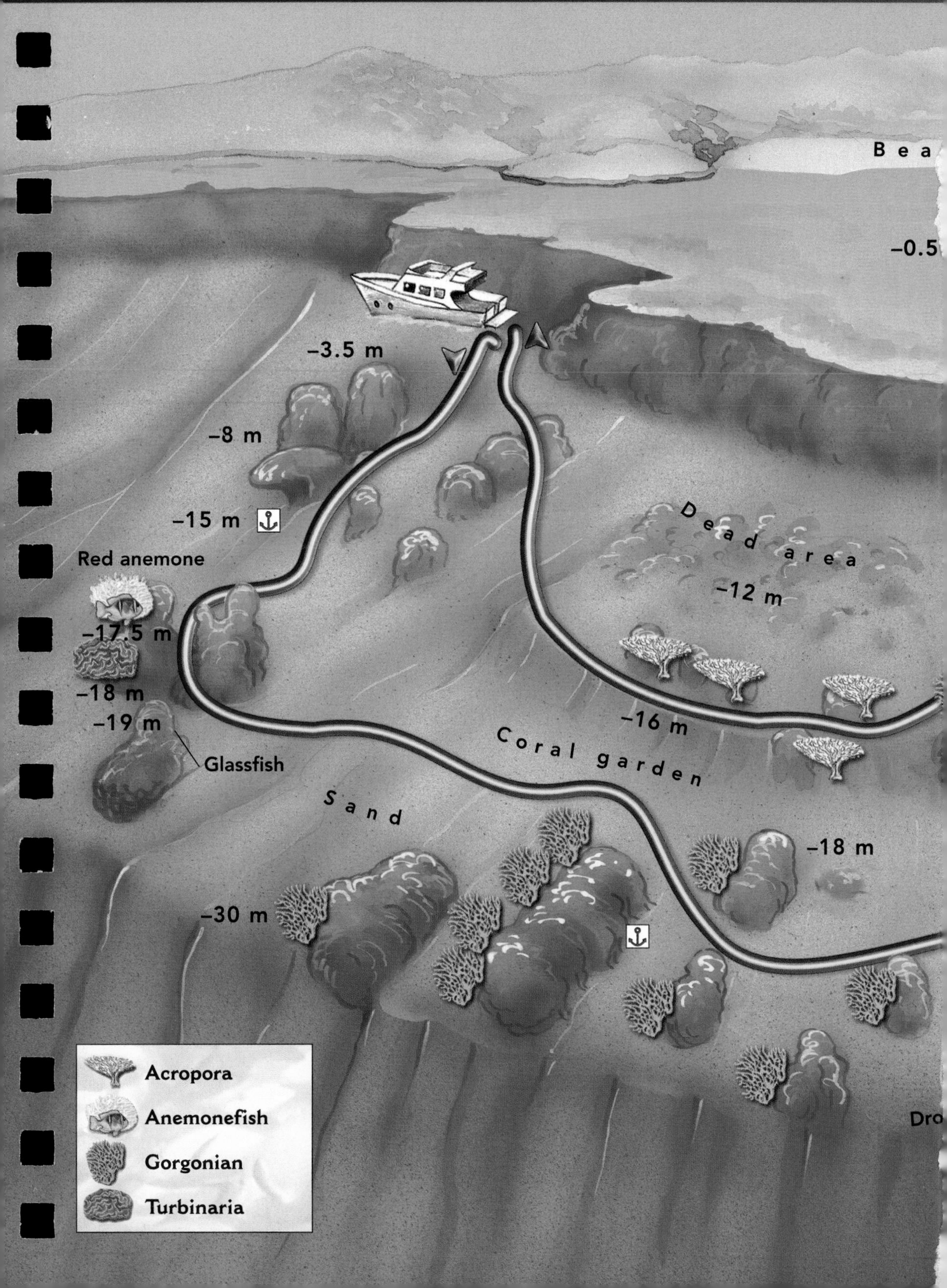

B e a

−0.5

−3.5 m

−8 m

−15 m ⚓

Red anemone

−17.5 m

−18 m

−19 m

Glassfish

S a n d

−30 m

D e a d   a r e a

−12 m

−16 m

C o r a l   g a r d e n

−18 m

⚓

Dro

🪸	**Acropora**
🐠	**Anemonefish**
🪸	**Gorgonian**
🪸	**Turbinaria**

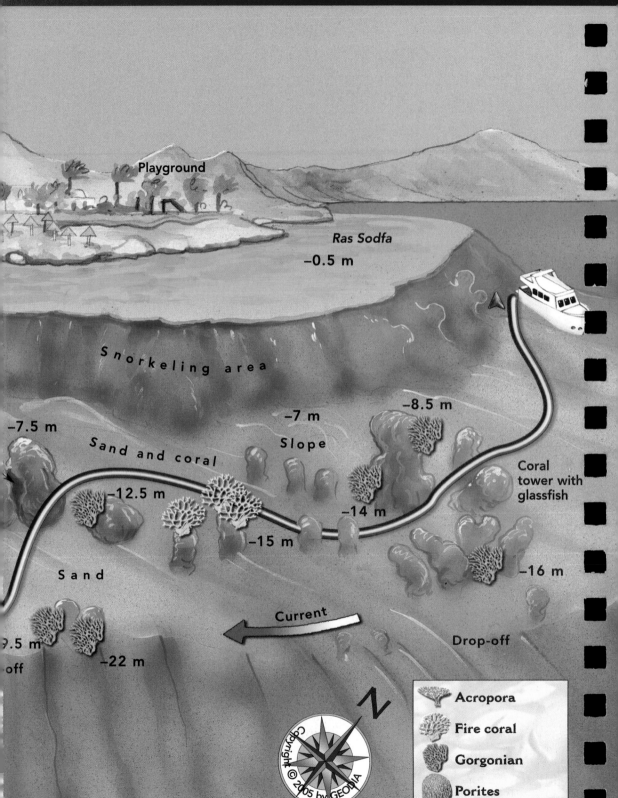

Playground

Ras Sodfa
−0.5 m

Snorkeling area

−8.5 m

−7 m

−7.5 m

Slope

Sand and coral

Coral tower with glassfish

−12.5 m

−14 m

−15 m

−16 m

Sand

−9.5 m

−22 m

off

Current

Drop-off

N

Copyright © 2005 by GEODIA

Acropora
Fire coral
Gorgonian
Porites

Sharm Reef
Beach

Dreams Beach Resort

Shore
entrance

−0.5 m

Cave

−16 m

−26 m

← Amphoras

Gorgonian

90°

−180 m

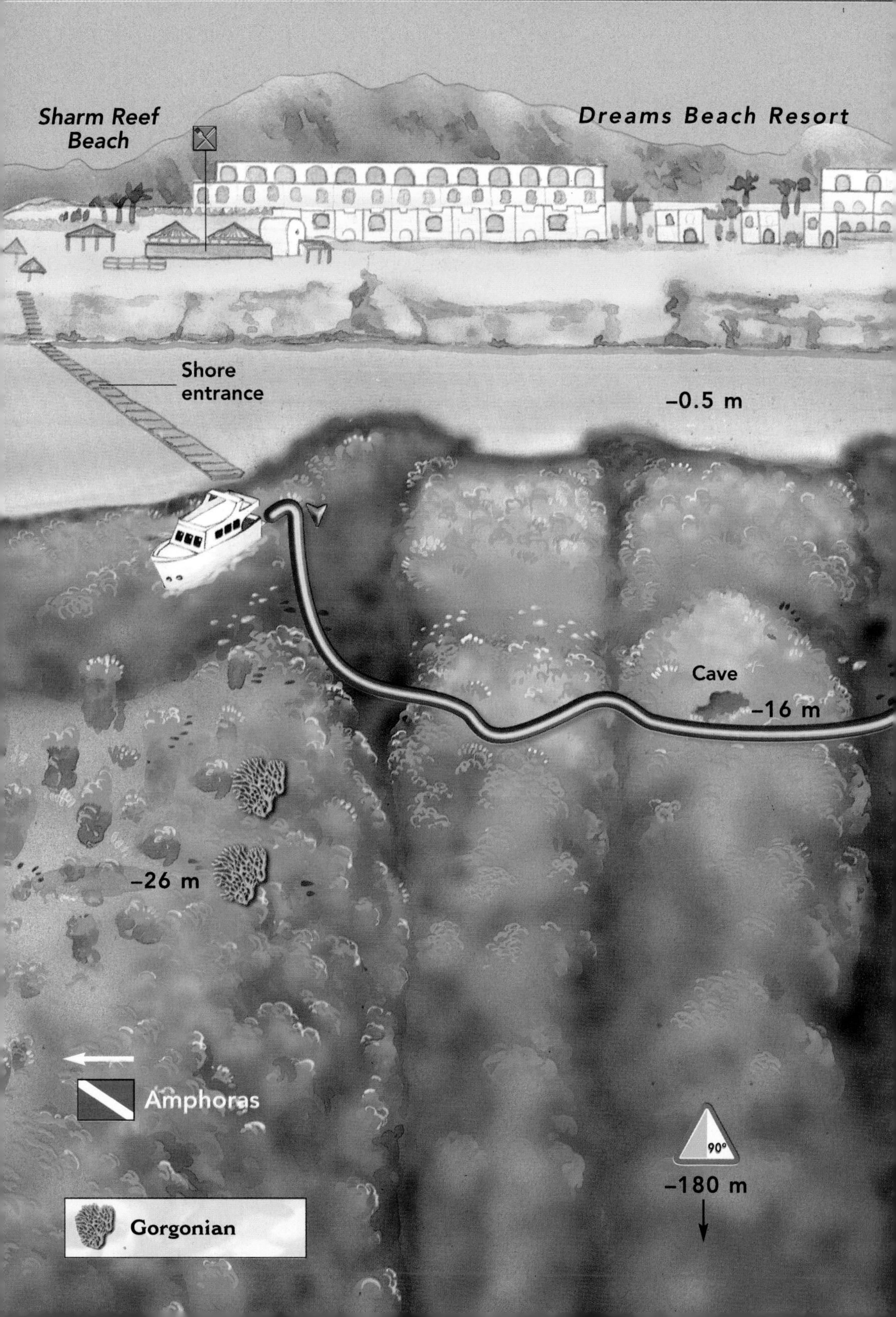

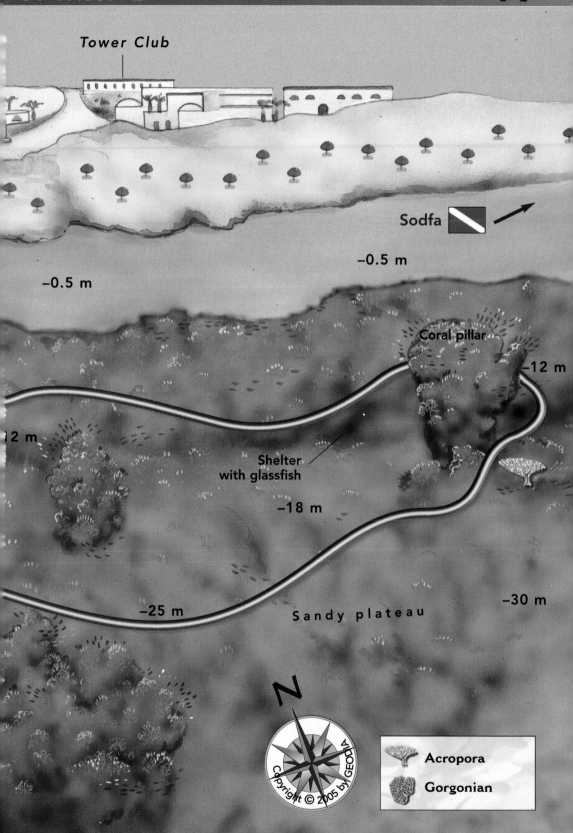

Tower Club

Sodfa

−0.5 m

−0.5 m

Coral pillar

−12 m

12 m

Shelter
with glassfish

−18 m

−25 m

Sandy plateau

−30 m

N

Copyright © 2005 by GEODIA

Acropora

Gorgonian

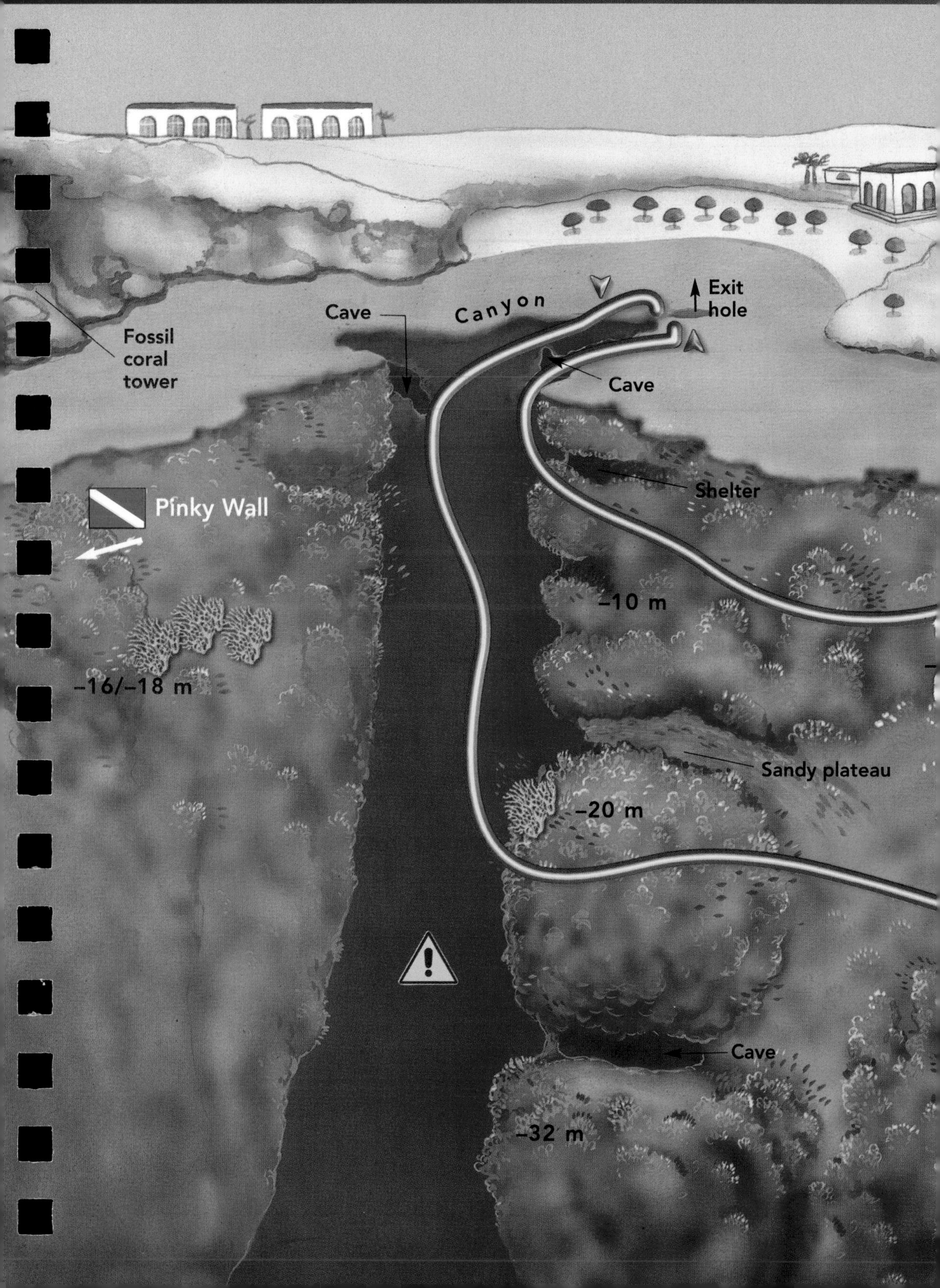

Fossil
coral
tower

Cave

C a n y o n

Exit
hole

Cave

Shelter

Pinky Wall

−10 m

−16/−18 m

Sandy plateau

−20 m

Cave

−32 m

242' N — 34°19.389' E

Exit hole

Cave

−5 m

−0.5 m

−10 m

−15 m

Tower

−30 m

−30 m

90°

Copyright © 2005 by GEODIA

20 Turtle Bay

27°51.

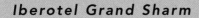

Iberotel Grand Sharm
–0.5 m
Snorkeling area
–7 m
–6 m
–10 m
–18 m
–20 m
Coral tower with glassfish
Sandy slope
Copyright © 2005 by GEODIA
N
Drop-off
–26 m
Current
Paradise

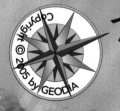

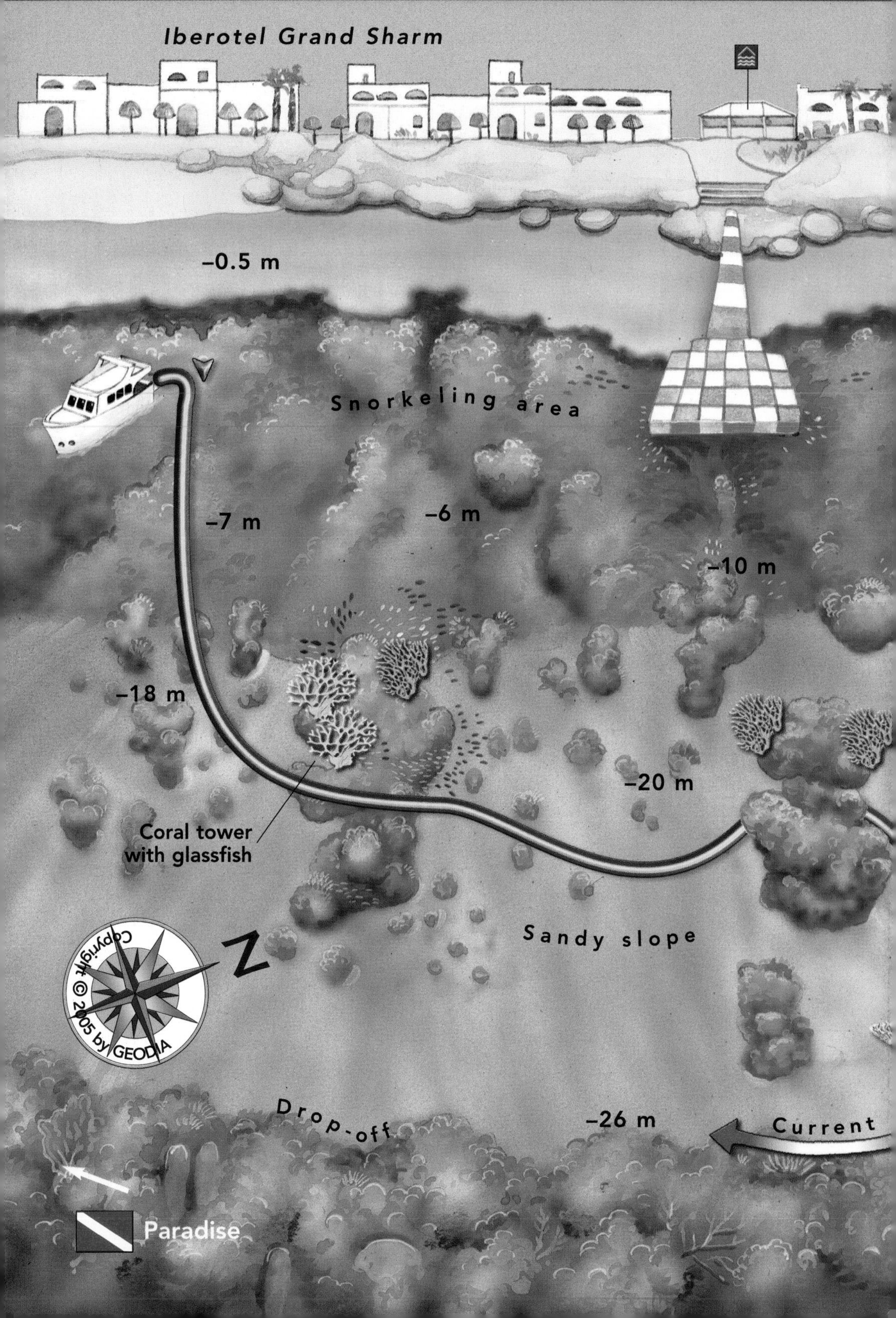

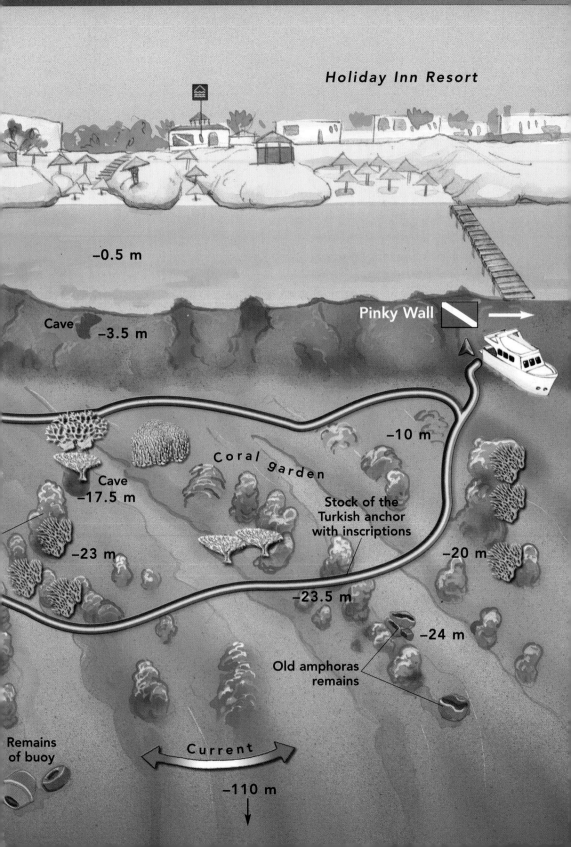

AMPHORAS 19

Holiday Inn Resort

−0.5 m

Cave −3.5 m

Pinky Wall

Cave −17.5 m

Coral garden

−10 m

Stock of the Turkish anchor with inscriptions

−23 m

−20 m

−23.5 m

−24 m

Old amphoras remains

Remains of buoy

Current

−110 m

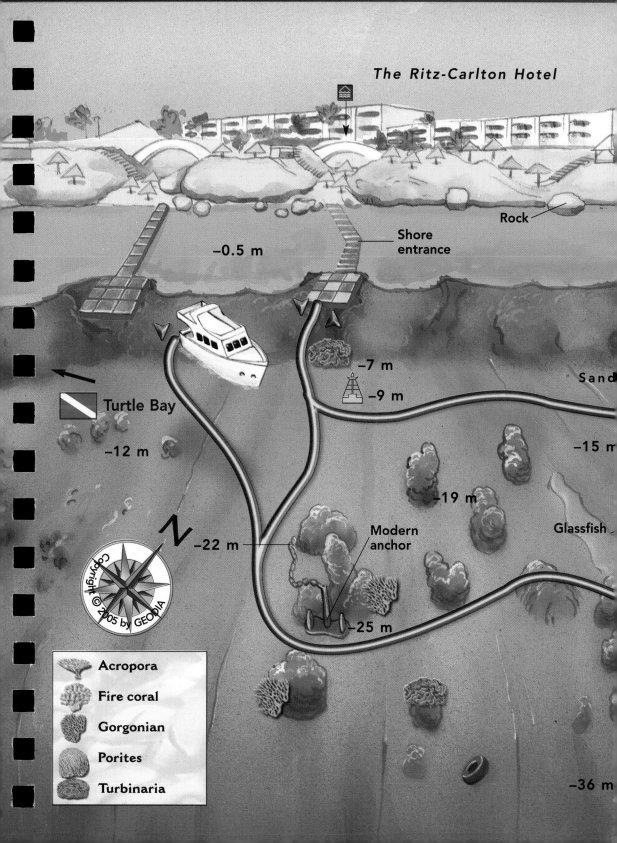

The Ritz-Carlton Hotel

Rock

−0.5 m

Shore
entrance

−7 m

−9 m

Turtle Bay

−12 m

Sand

−15 m

−19 m

Glassfish

Modern
anchor

−22 m

−25 m

−36 m

Acropora

Fire coral

Gorgonian

Porites

Turbinaria

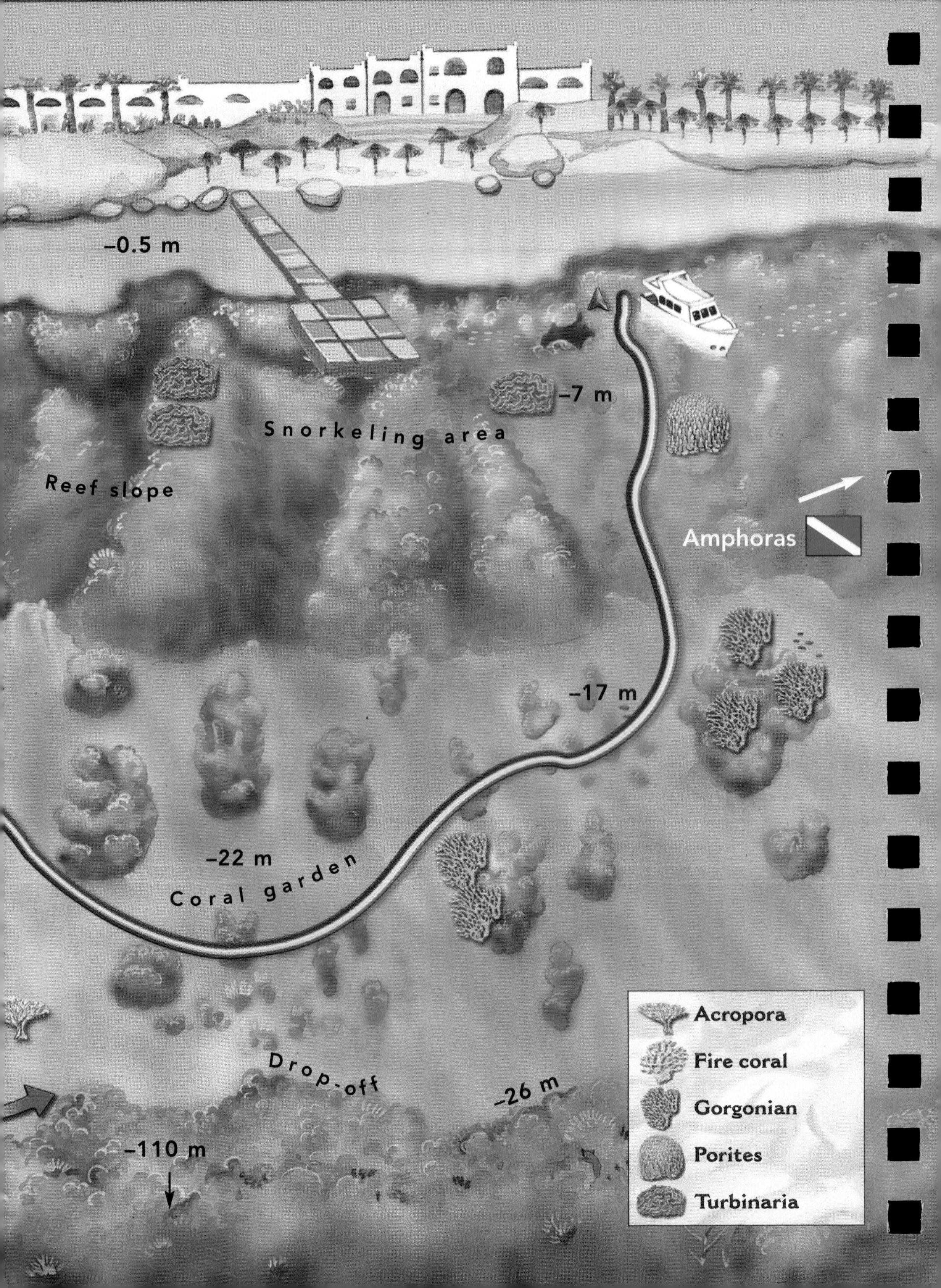

−0.5 m

−7 m

Snorkeling area

Reef slope

Amphoras

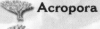

−17 m

−22 m

Coral garden

Drop-off

−26 m

−110 m

Acropora

Fire coral

Gorgonian

Porites

Turbinaria

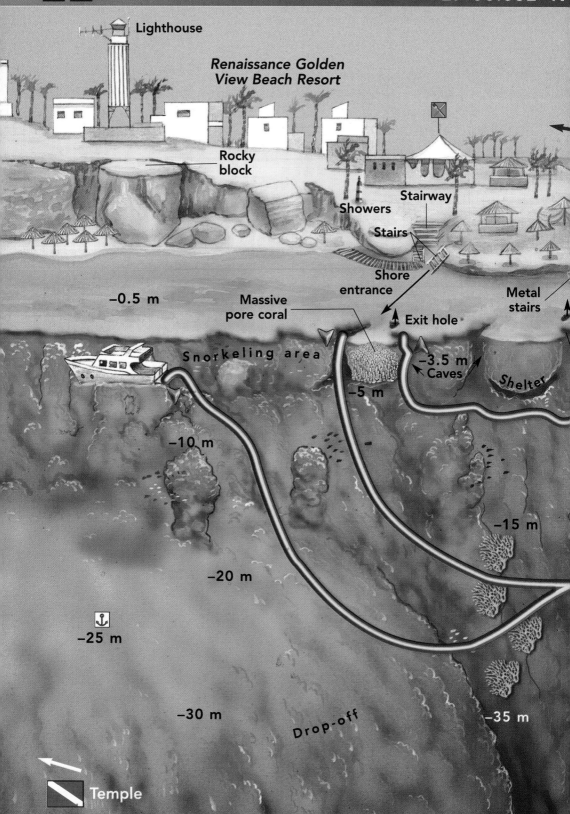

Lighthouse

Renaissance Golden View Beach Resort

Rocky block

Showers

Stairway

Stairs

Shore entrance

Metal stairs

−0.5 m

Massive pore coral

Exit hole

Snorkeling area

−3.5 m
Caves

−5 m

Shelter

−10 m

−15 m

−20 m

−25 m

−30 m

−35 m

Drop-off

Temple

Kiroseiz Three Corners Beach Club

−0.5 m

Floating pontoon

−7 m

Sand

Cave

Turtle Bay

st with gorgonians

Current

N

Copyright © 2005 by GEODIA

 Acropora

 Fire coral

 Gorgonian

 Porites

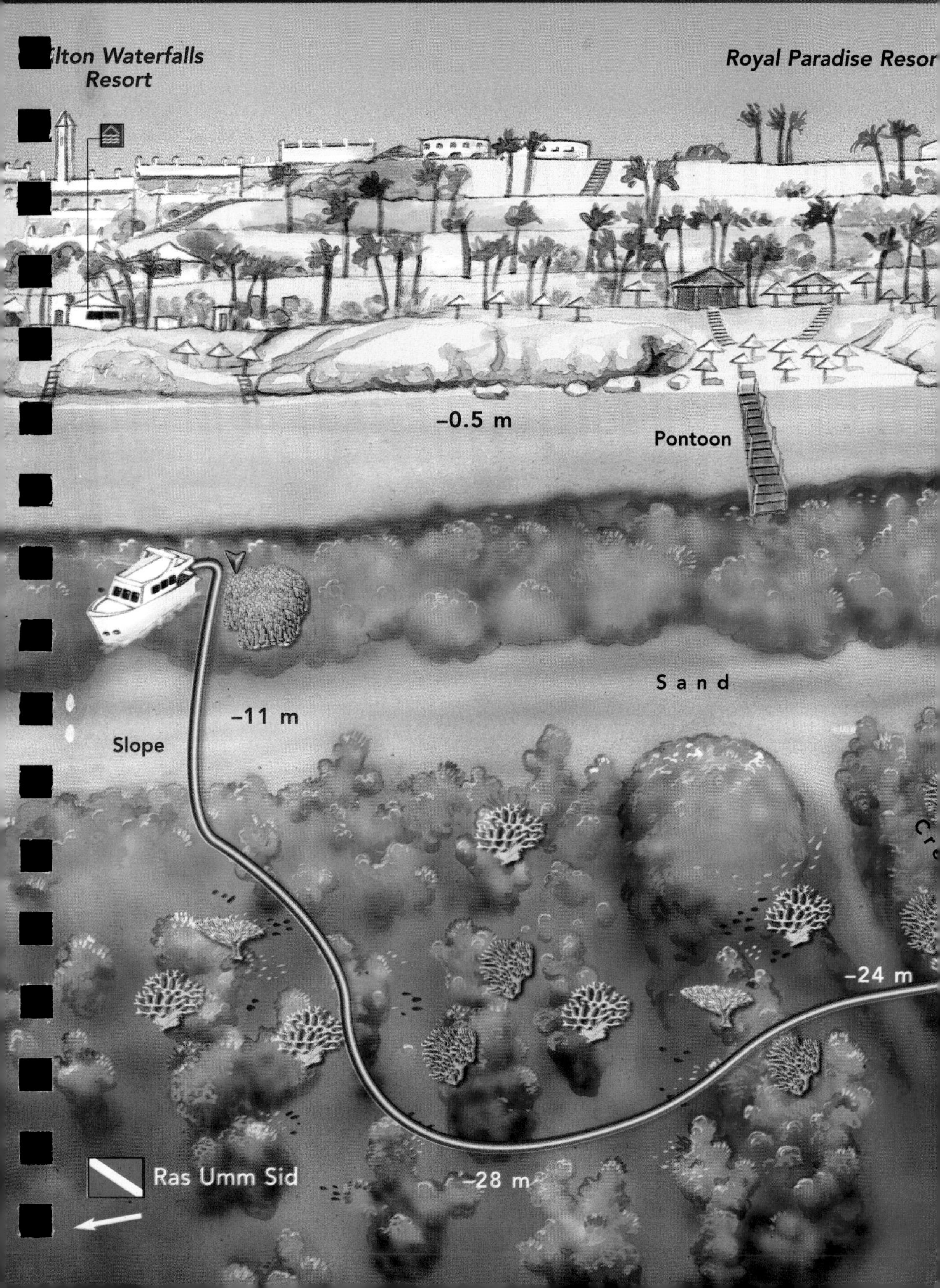

ilton Waterfalls
Resort

Royal Paradise Resor

−0.5 m

Pontoon

S a n d

−11 m

Slope

−24 m

−28 m

Ras Umm Sid

34°18.833' E

Paradise

Fiasco

N

Copyright © 2005 by GEO🗺

−0.5 m

Rock indicating the tide

White post

Cave

−3 m Cave with Cave sweepers

Plateau

Current

−14 m

−15 m

−20 m

−25 m

Drop-off

Shelter

−27 m

90°

Acropora

Gorgonian

Porites

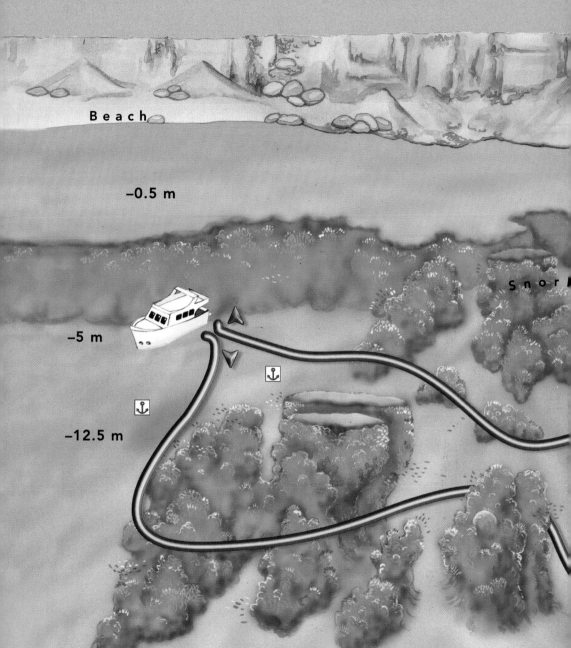

Beach

−0.5 m

−5 m

−12.5 m

−16 m

Snor

Drop-

Acropora

Gorgonian

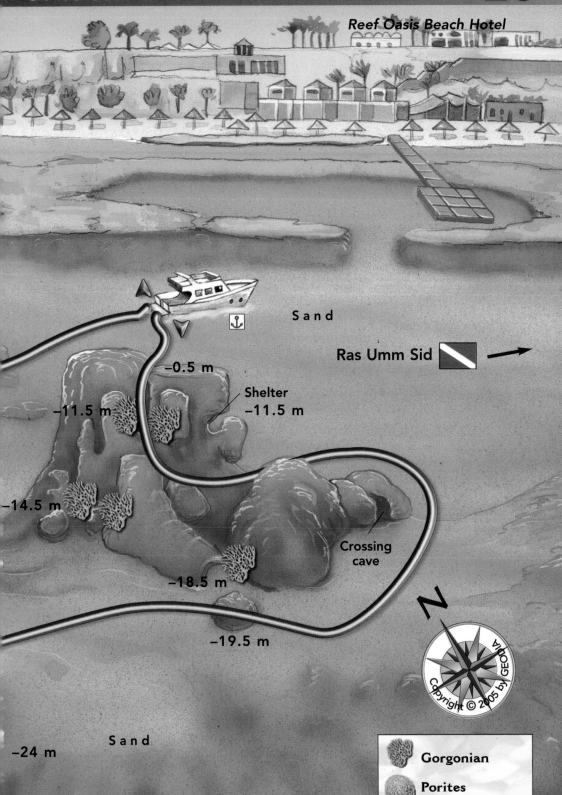

— 34°18.600' E

TEMPLE **23**

Reef Oasis Beach Hotel

Sand

−0.5 m

Shelter
−11.5 m

Ras Umm Sid

−11.5 m

−14.5 m

Crossing
cave

−18.5 m

−19.5 m

N

Copyright © 2005 by GEODIA

Sand
−24 m

Gorgonian

Porites

El-Farana King Snefru Hotel

−0.5 m

−0.5 m

Sand

−0.5 m   −6 m

−9/10 m

−7.5 m

Coral pillar
tilted during the
earthquake in 1995

−15 m

−13.5 m

Sand

Gorgonian
with glassfish

−30 m

Drop-off

Ras Katy

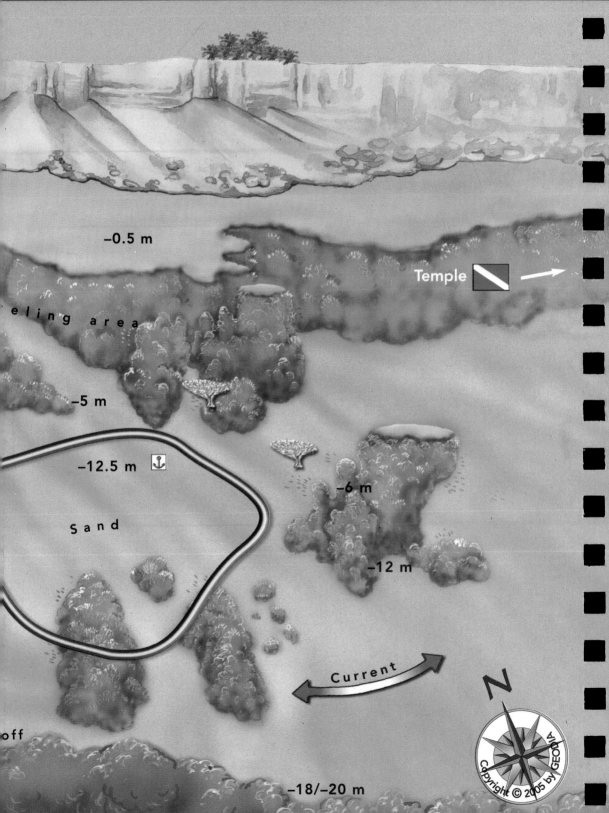

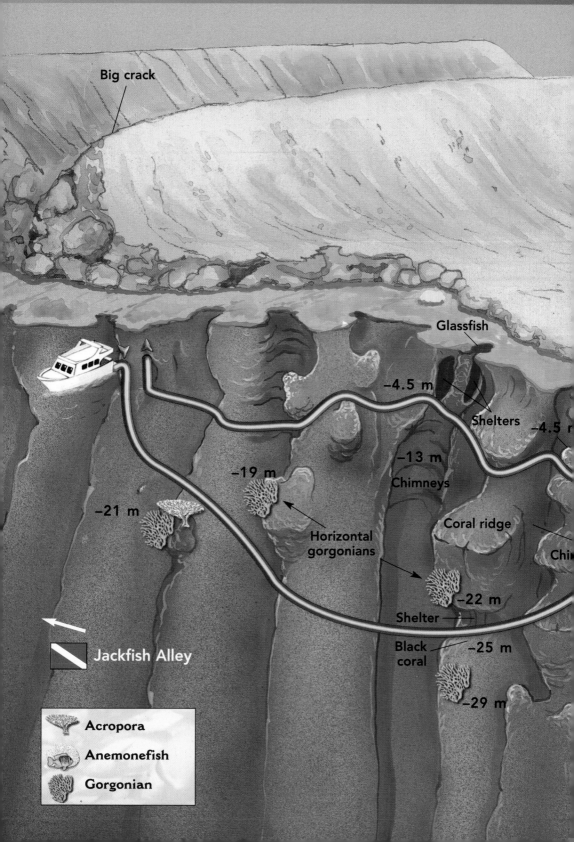

Big crack

Glassfish

−4.5 m

Shelters

−4.5 r

−13 m

Chimneys

−19 m

Coral ridge

−21 m

Horizontal
gorgonians

Chi

−22 m

Shelter

Black
coral

−25 m

−29 m

Jackfish Alley

Acropora

Anemonefish

Gorgonian

52' E

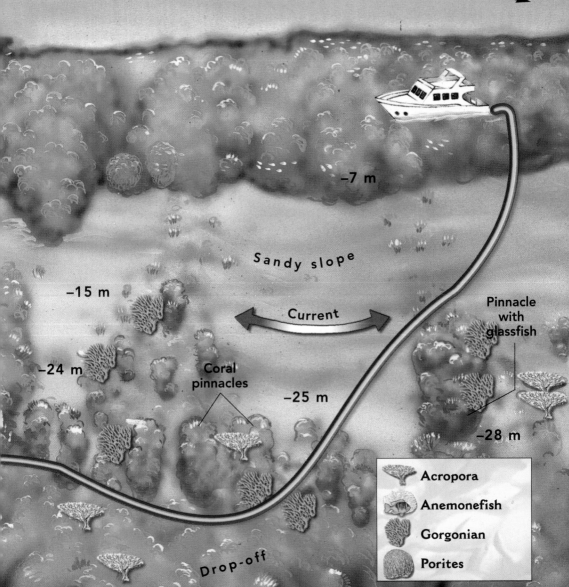

Marsa Ghozlani →

−7 m

Sandy slope

−15 m

Current

−24 m

Coral pinnacles

−25 m

Pinnacle with glassfish

−28 m

Drop-off

	Acropora
	Anemonefish
	Gorgonian
	Porites

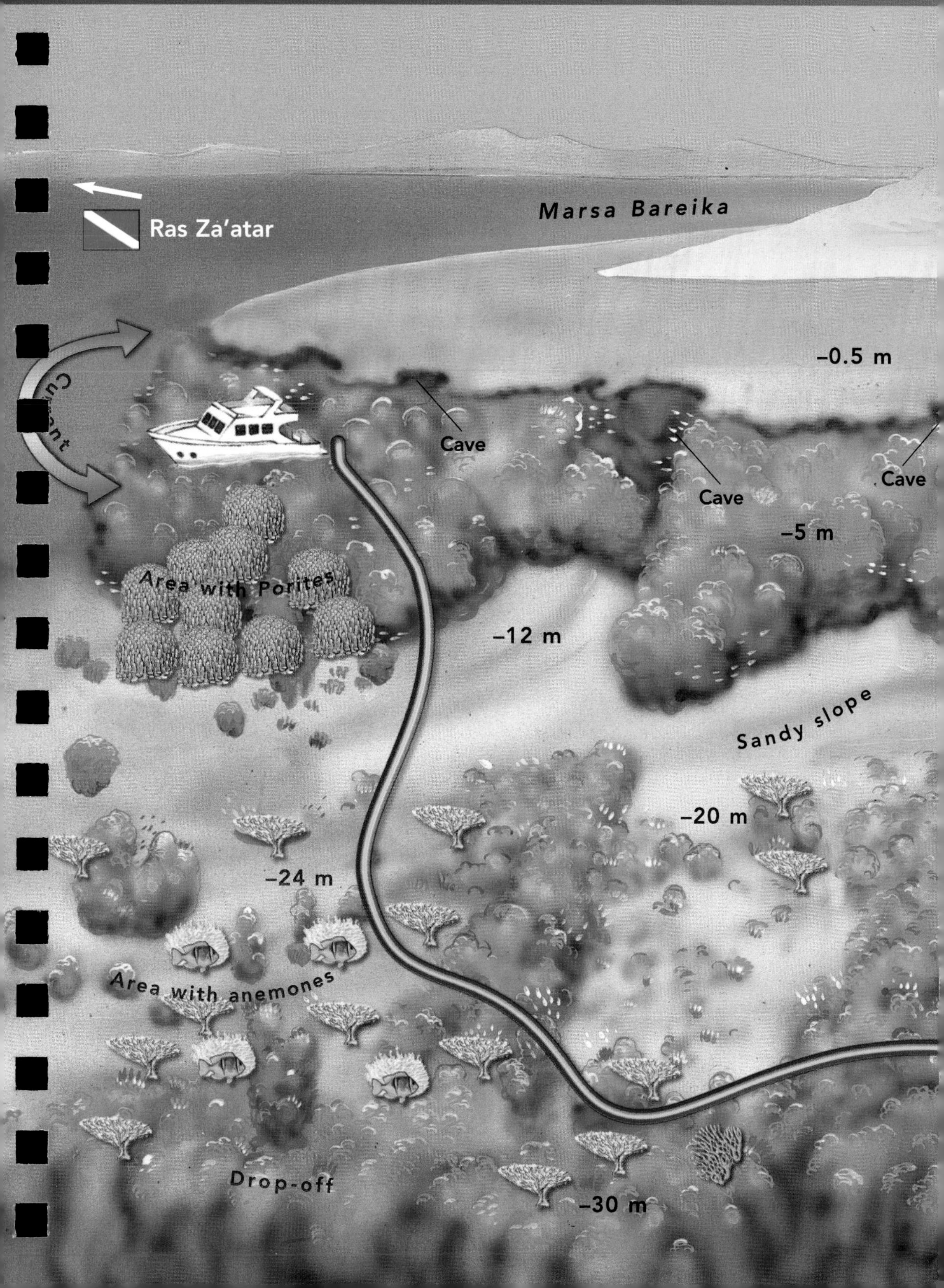

Ras Za'atar

Marsa Bareika

Current

Cave

Cave

Cave

−0.5 m

−5 m

Area with Porites

−12 m

Sandy slope

−20 m

−24 m

Area with anemones

Drop-off

−30 m

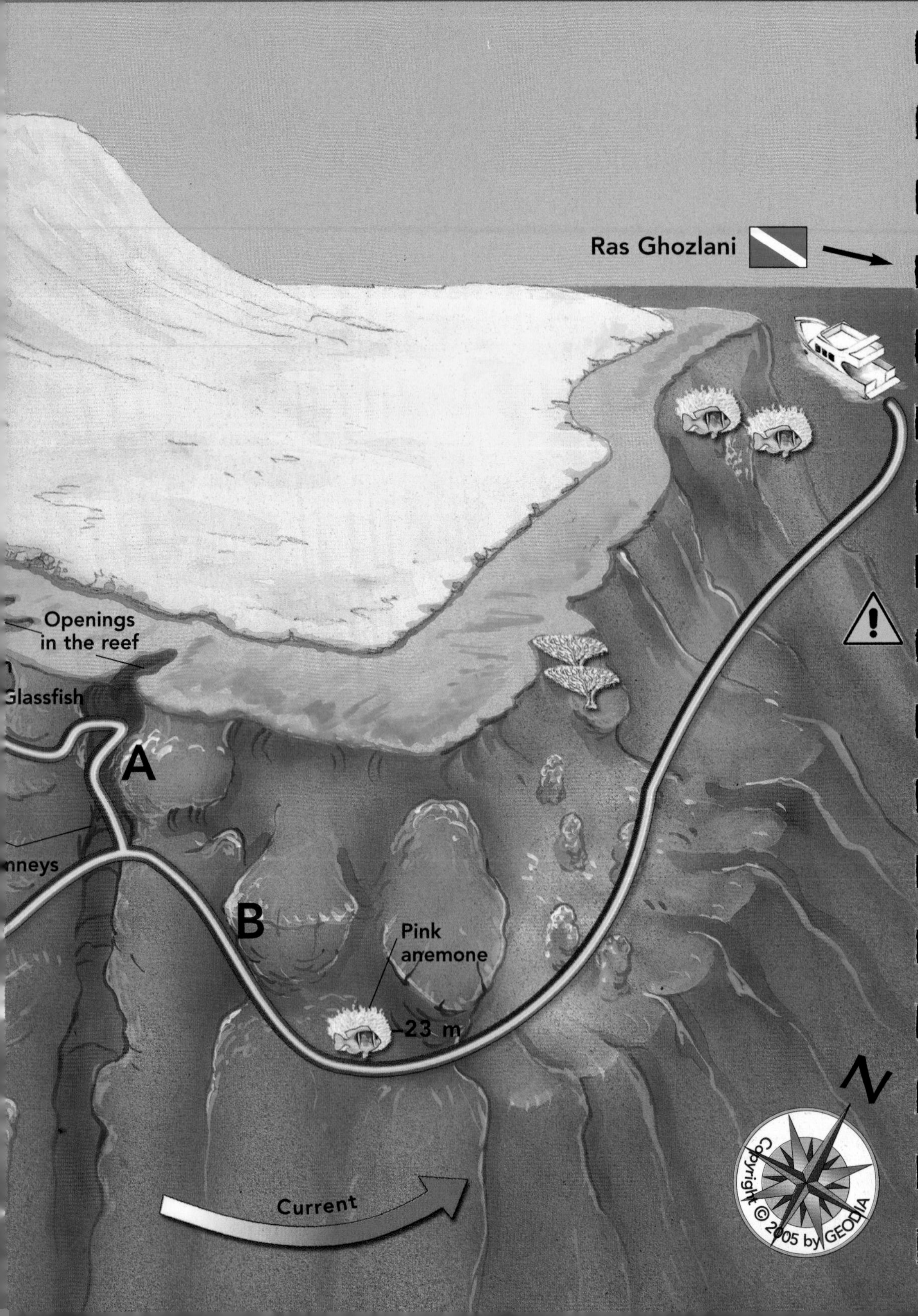

860' N — 34°15.364' E

Ras Ghozlani

Openings
in the reef

Glassfish

A

nneys

B

Pink
anemone

~23 m

Current

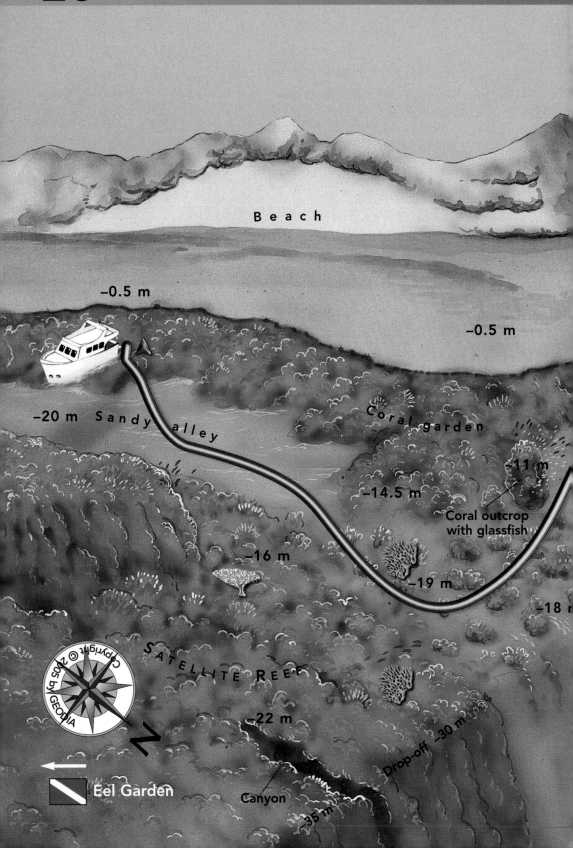

Beach

−0.5 m

−0.5 m

−20 m S a n d y a l l e y

C o r a l g a r d e n

−14.5 m

−11 m

Coral outcrop
with glassfish

−16 m

−19 m

−18 m

Copyright © 2005 by GEODIA

S A T E L L I T E R E E F

−22 m

N

Eel Garden

Canyon

Drop-off −30 m

−35 m

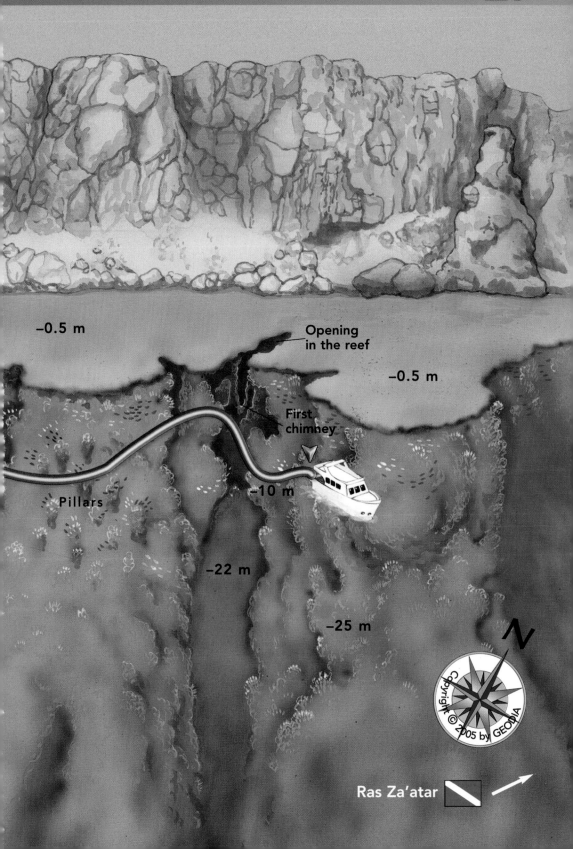

−0.5 m

Opening
in the reef

−0.5 m

First
chimney

Pillars

−10 m

−22 m

−25 m

N

Copyright © 2005 by GEODIA

Ras Za'atar

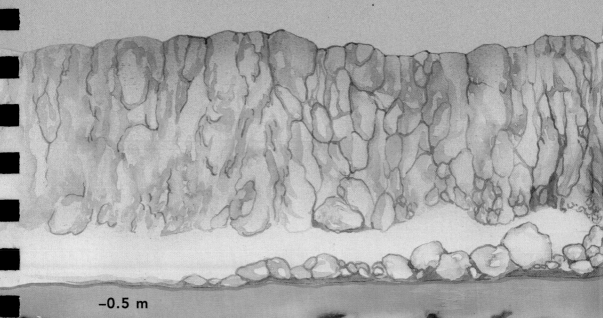

−0.5 m

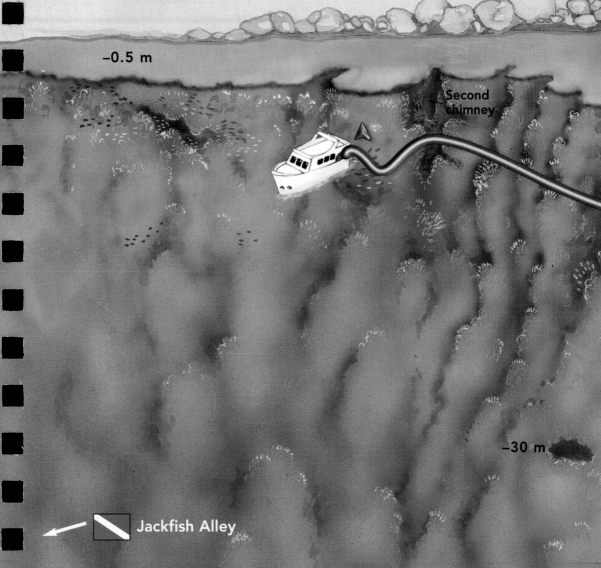

Second chimney

−30 m

Jackfish Alley

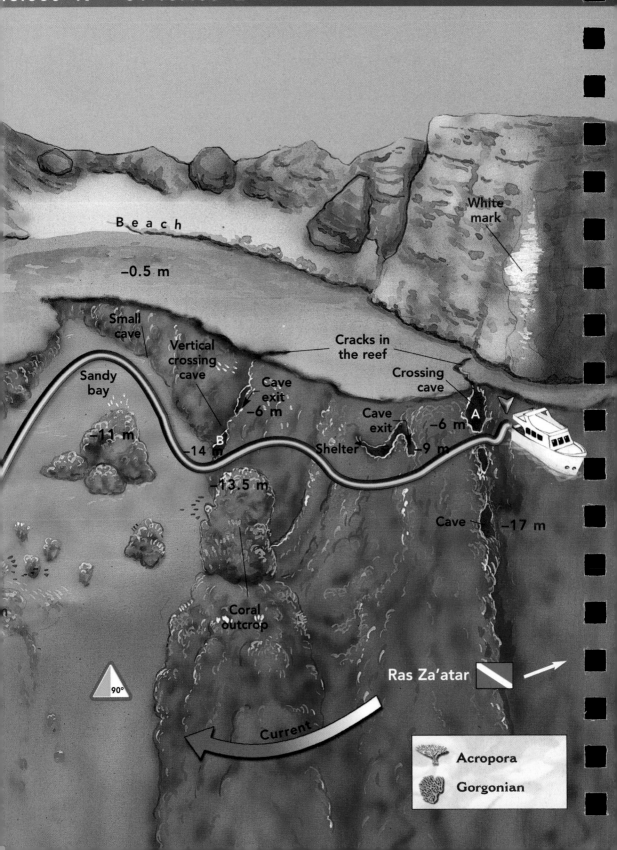

White mark

B e a c h

−0.5 m

Small cave

Vertical crossing cave

Sandy bay

Cracks in the reef

Crossing cave

Cave exit −6 m

−11 m

B

−14 m

Cave exit −6 m

−9 m

Shelter

−13.5 m

A

Cave −17 m

Coral outcrop

90°

Ras Za'atar

Current

Acropora

Gorgonian

30 Shark Observatory

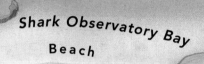

Shark Observatory Bay
Beach
–0.5 m
Opening
in the reef
Cave
Glassfis
–5 m
Sand
N
Copyright © 2005 by GEODIA
Shark Reef
Yolanda Reef

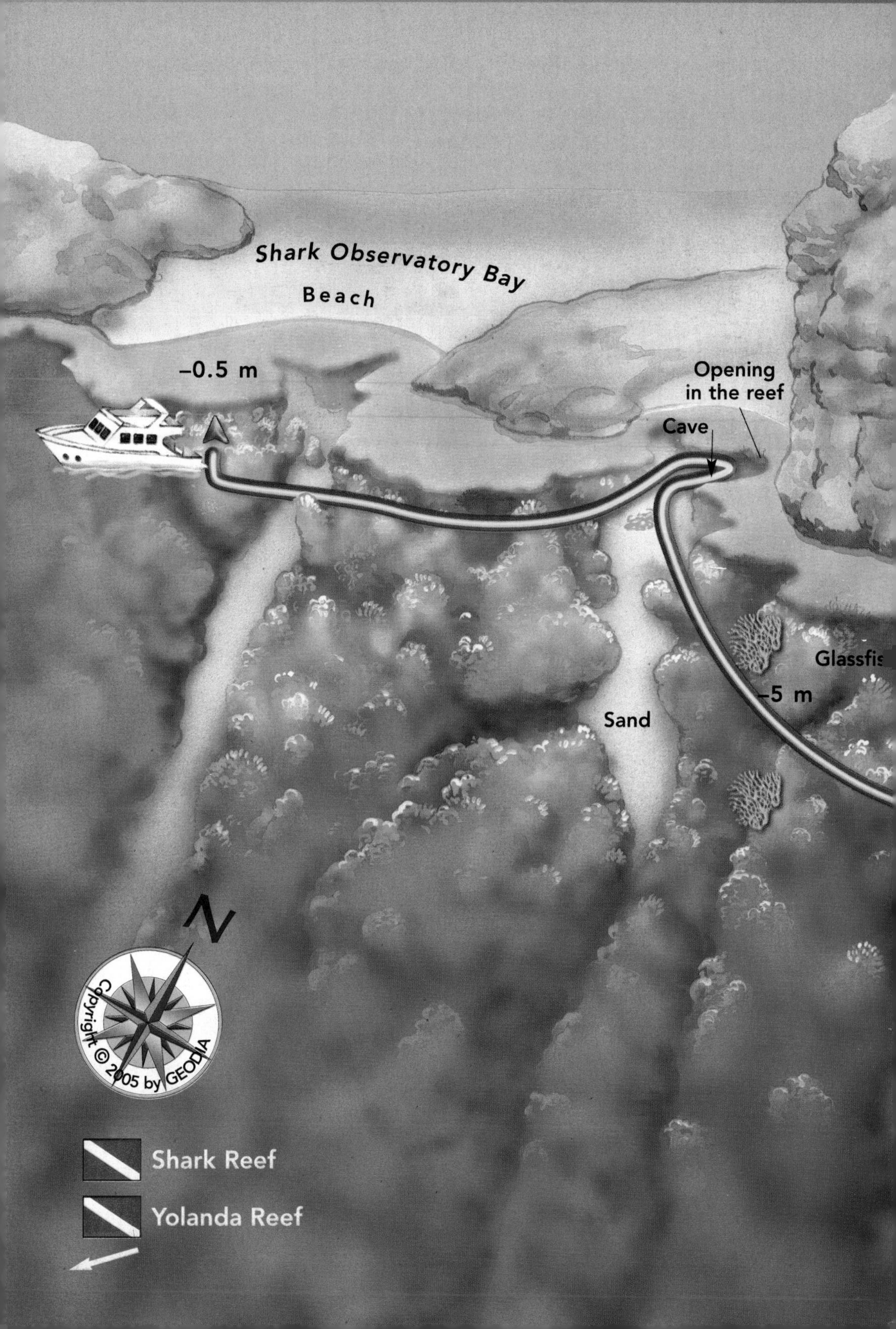

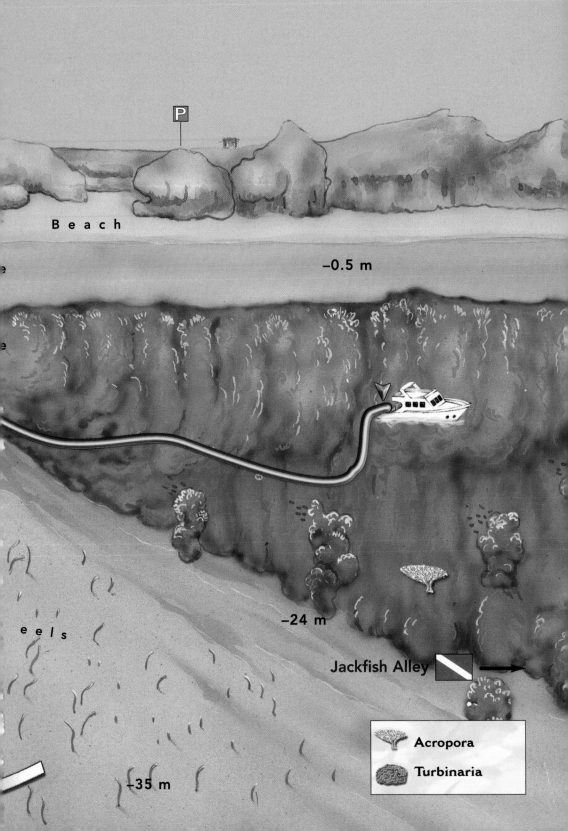

P

Beach

−0.5 m

−24 m

Jackfish Alley

−35 m

eels

Acropora

Turbinaria

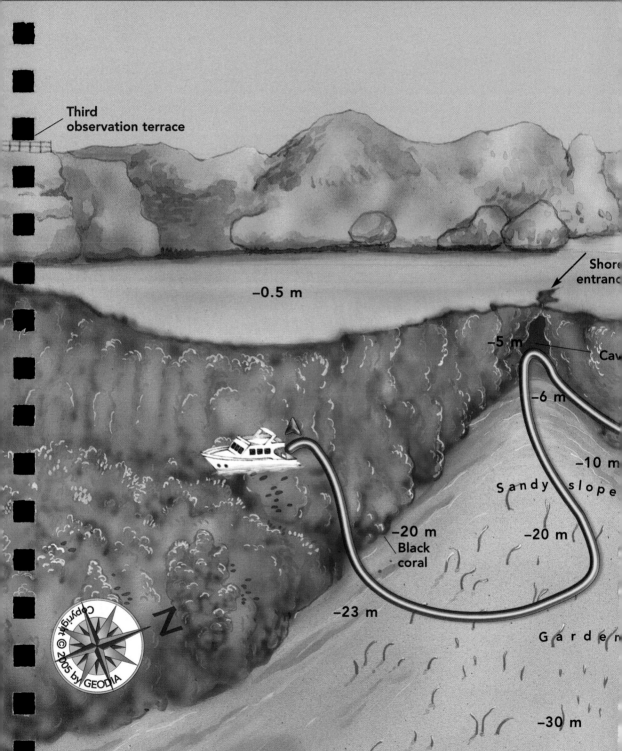

Third
observation terrace

Shore
entranc

−0.5 m

−5 m

Cav

−6 m

−10 m

Sandy slope

−20 m
Black
coral

−20 m

−23 m

Garden

−30 m

Copyright © 2005 by GEODIA

N

Shark Observatory

Current

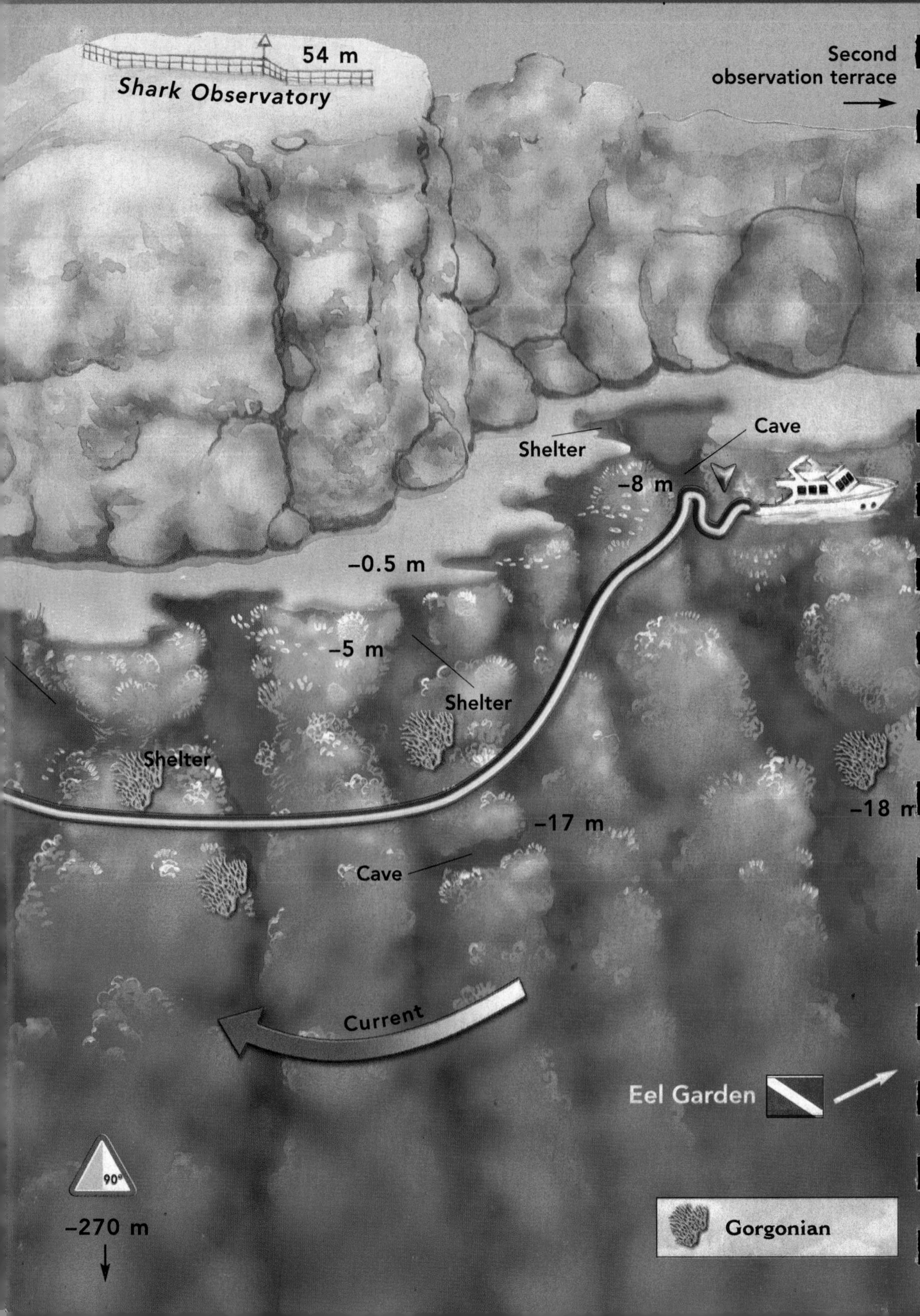

005' N — 34°15.605' E

Shark Observatory
54 m

Second
observation terrace

Shelter

Cave

−8 m

−0.5 m

−5 m

Shelter

Shelter

−18 m

−17 m

Cave

Current

Eel Garden

90°

−270 m

Gorgonian

Sha'ab el-Utath

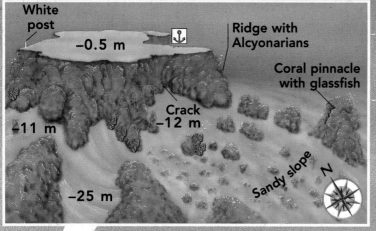

White post

−0.5 m

Ridge with Alcyonarians

Coral pinnacle with glassfish

Crack −12 m

−11 m

−25 m

Sandy slope

N

−10 m

Stingray Station

−0.5 m

Dunraven
Beacon Rock

3.48 miles

Gorg

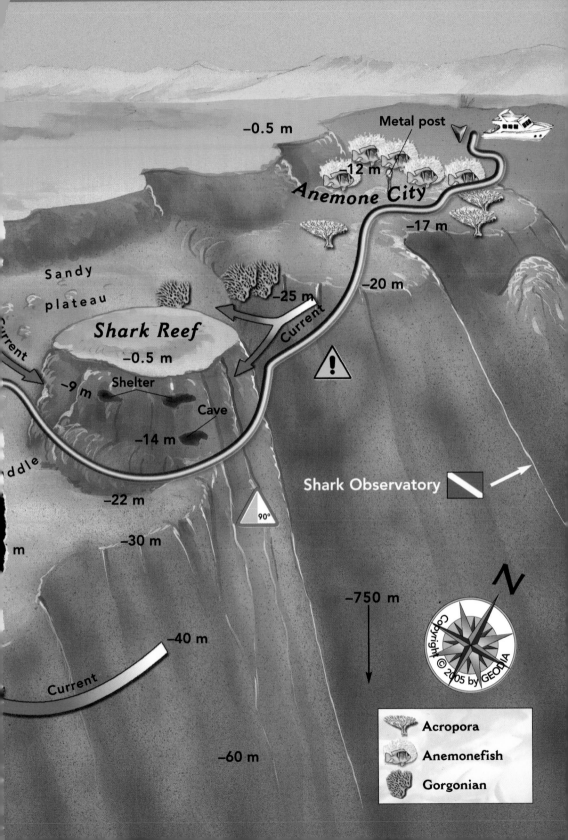

−0.5 m

Metal post

−12 m

Anemone City

−17 m

−20 m

Sandy

plateau

−25 m

Current

Shark Reef

Current

−0.5 m

−9 m

Shelter

Cave

ddle

−14 m

Shark Observatory

−22 m

90°

−30 m

m

−750 m

N

−40 m

Current

Copyright © 2005 by GEODIA

−60 m

Acropora

Anemonefish

Gorgonian

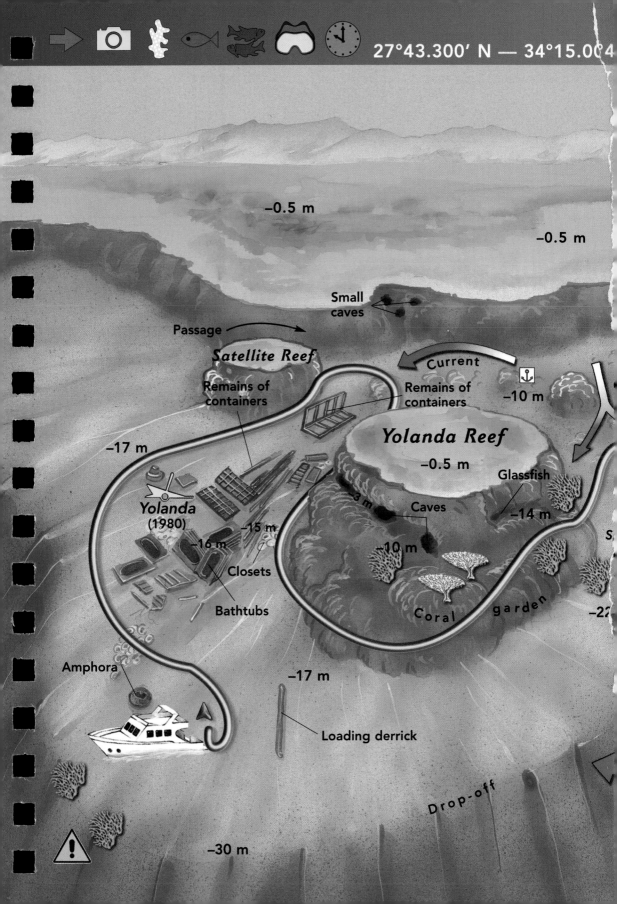

−0.5 m

−0.5 m

Small
caves

Passage

Satellite Reef

Current

Remains of
containers

Remains of
containers

−10 m

−17 m

Yolanda Reef

−0.5 m

Glassfish

Yolanda
(1980)

−3 m

Caves

−14 m

−15 m

−10 m

−16 m

Closets

Bathtubs

Coral   garden

−22

Amphora

−17 m

Loading derrick

Drop-off

−30 m

Ras Fanar

Ras Mohammed
2.70 miles

−8/−10 m

−25 m

Lagoon

−10 m ⚓

−0.5 m

−0.5 m

−12 m

0.6 miles

−0.5 m

−0.5 m ⚓

Cave

−10 m

−12 m

onian

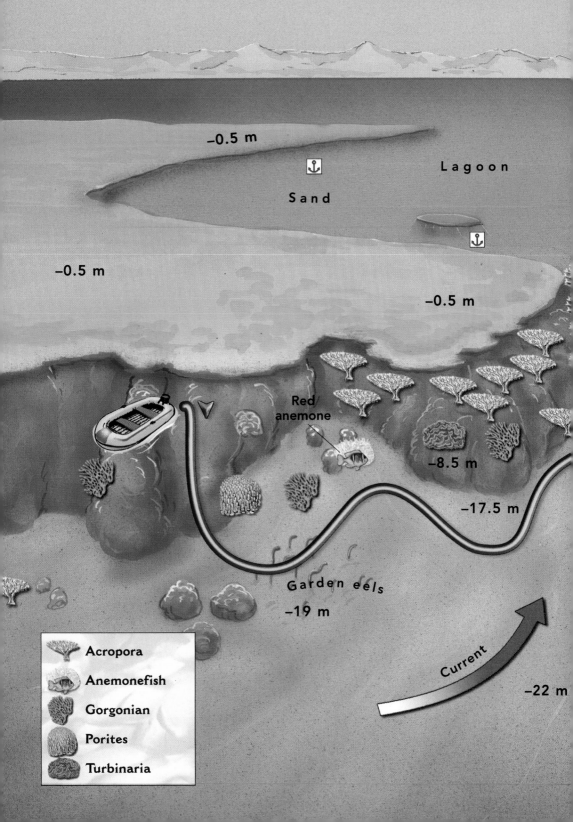

−0.5 m

Lagoon

Sand

−0.5 m

−0.5 m

Red anemone

−8.5 m

−17.5 m

Garden eels

−19 m

Current

−22 m

Acropora

Anemonefish

Gorgonian

Porites

Turbinaria

Beacon

Rock

Coral garden

Engine room
entrance

Propeller

−22 m

−24 m

STERN

−24 m

Remains
of the mast

Stern
entrance

−29.5 m

−28 m

−27.5 m

Porites

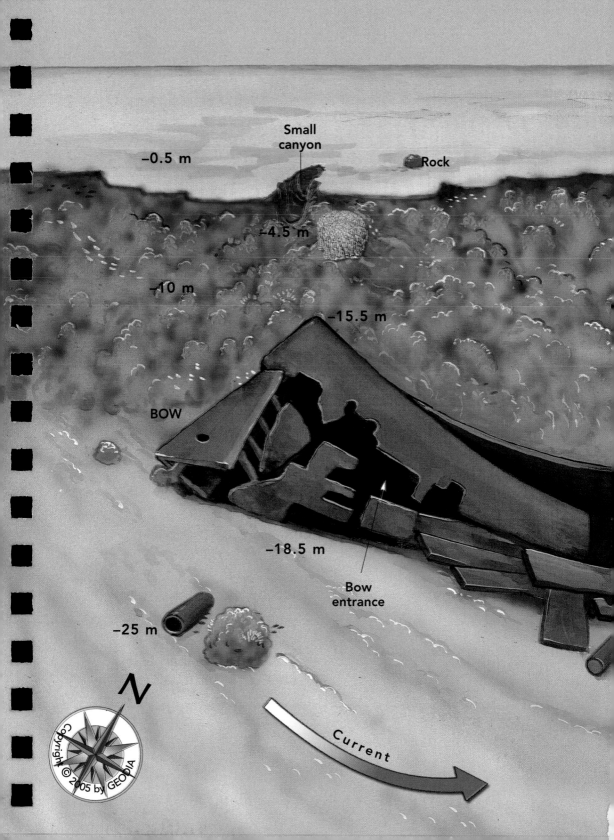

Ras Mohammed

Dunraven
Beacon Rock
2.4 miles

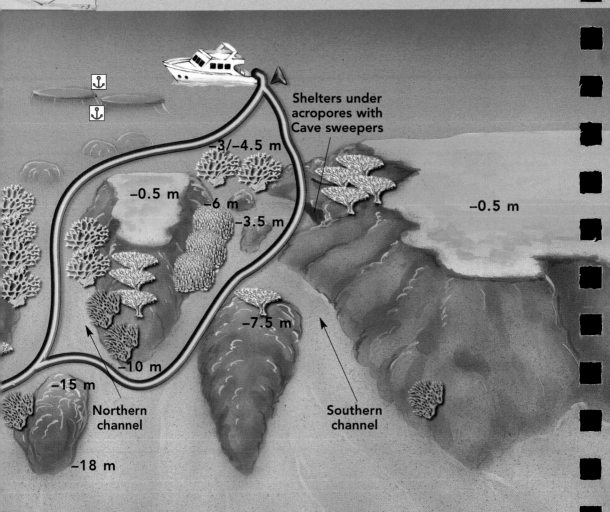

Shelters under
acropores with
Cave sweepers

−3/−4.5 m

−0.5 m

−6 m

−3.5 m

−0.5 m

−7.5 m

−10 m

−15 m

Northern
channel

Southern
channel

−18 m

S a n d

N

Copyright © 2005 by GEODIA

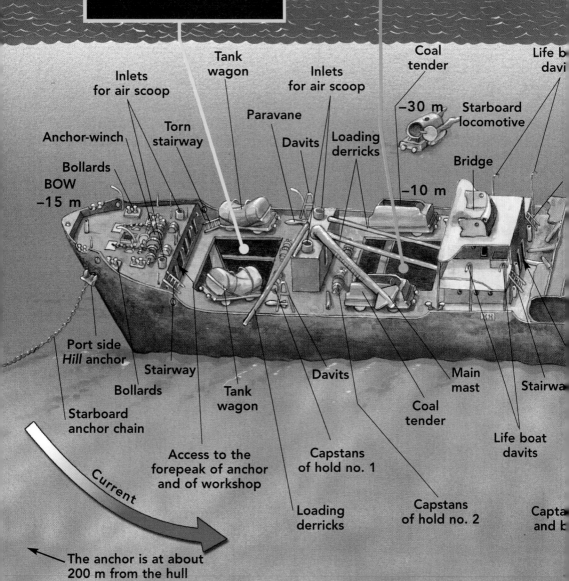

HOLD no. 1
On the upper level there are two empty trailers, motorcycles, cables, and electrical material; on the lower level, trucks, covers for radial airplane engines, crates of medicines, *Lee Enfield MK III* rifles, and portable electric generators.

HOLD no. 2
On the upper level there are *Ford* and *Bedford* trucks, *Morris* jeeps, and motorcycles; on the lower level, empty trailers, *Bedford* trucks carrying motorcycles, a *Tilling Stevens* truck, *Norton* motorcycles (some with sidecars), airplane spares, rubber boots, tires, and *Lee Enfield MK III* rifles.

Tank wagon

Inlets for air scoop

Inlets for air scoop

Coal tender

Life b davi

Paravane

−30 m

Starboard locomotive

Anchor-winch

Torn stairway

Davits

Loading derricks

Bollards
BOW
−15 m

Bridge

−10 m

Port side *Hill* anchor

Stairway

Davits

Main mast

Stairwa

Bollards

Tank wagon

Coal tender

Starboard anchor chain

Life boat davits

Access to the forepeak of anchor and of workshop

Capstans of hold no. 1

Current

Loading derricks

Capstans of hold no. 2

Capta and b

The anchor is at about 200 m from the hull

Beacon

−0.5 m

−4.5 m

−12.5 m

−10 m

−18 m

Propeller and mast pieces of a non identified wreck

−5 m

Mast

Current

N

Copyright © 2005 by GEODIA

Acropora

Gorgonian

Porites

27°43.884' N — 34°05.8°

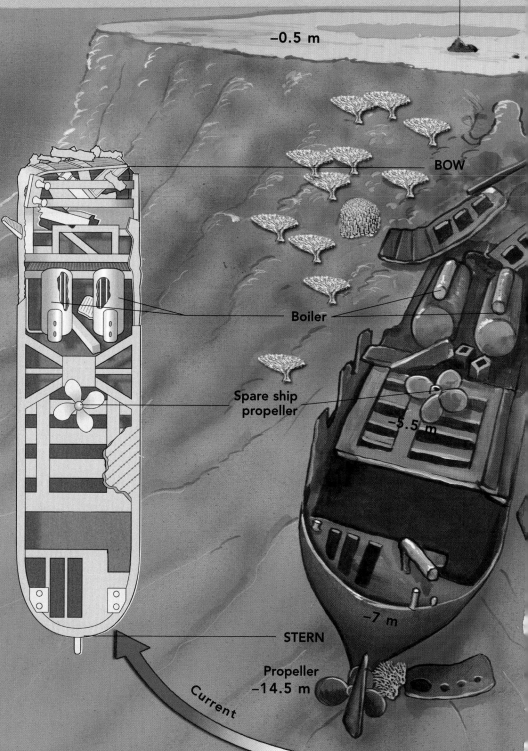

Bow of a
fishing boat

−0.5 m

BOW

Boiler

Spare ship
propeller

−5.5 m

−7 m

STERN

Propeller
−14.5 m

Current

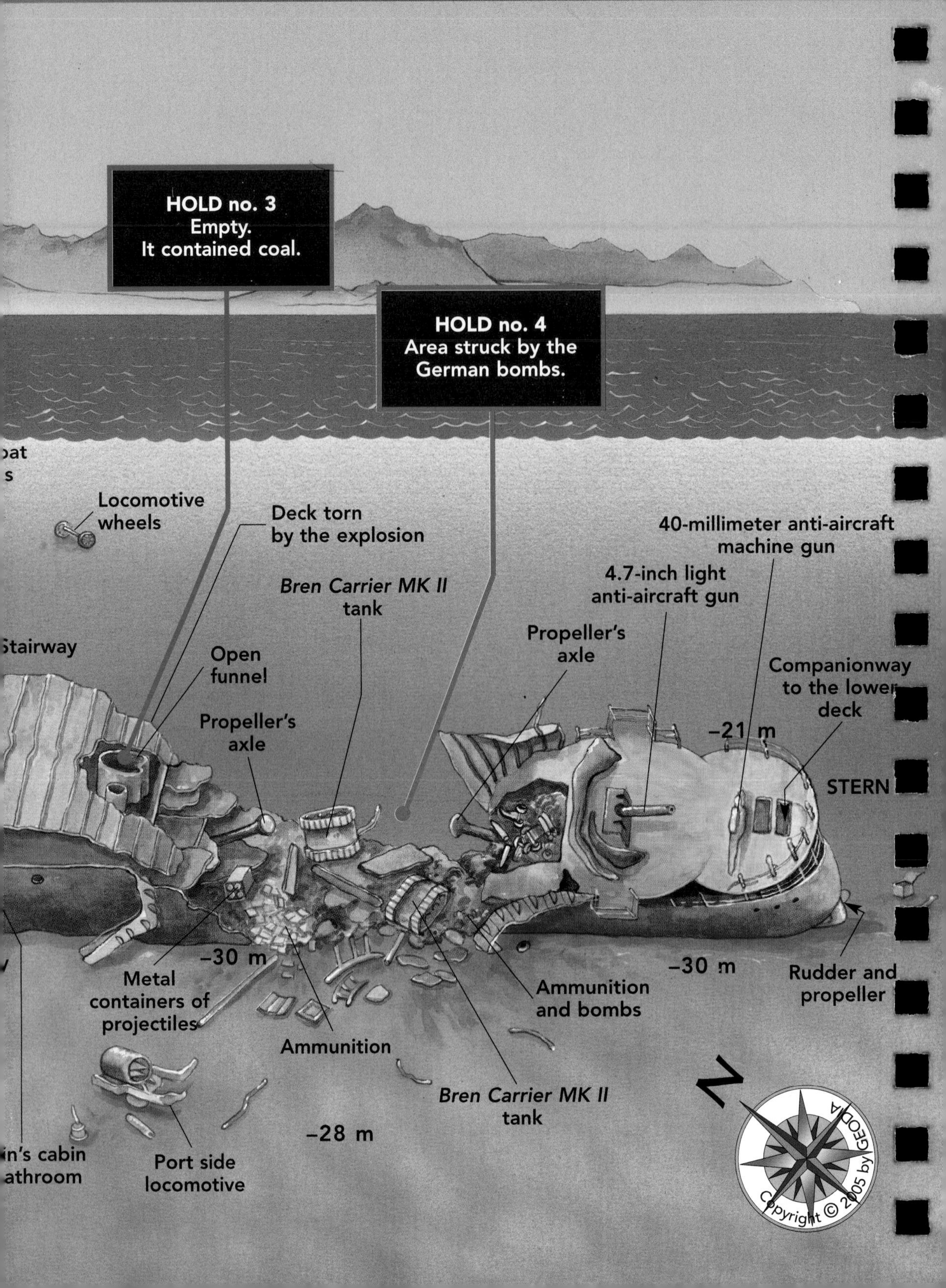

HOLD no. 3
Empty.
It contained coal.

HOLD no. 4
Area struck by the
German bombs.

oat
s

Locomotive
wheels

Deck torn
by the explosion

40-millimeter anti-aircraft
machine gun

4.7-inch light
anti-aircraft gun

Bren Carrier MK II
tank

Propeller's
axle

Stairway

Open
funnel

Companionway
to the lower
deck

−21 m

Propeller's
axle

STERN

−30 m

Metal
containers of
projectiles

Ammunition

Ammunition
and bombs

−30 m

Rudder and
propeller

Bren Carrier MK II
tank

−28 m

n's cabin
athroom

Port side
locomotive

N

Copyright © 2005 by GEODIA

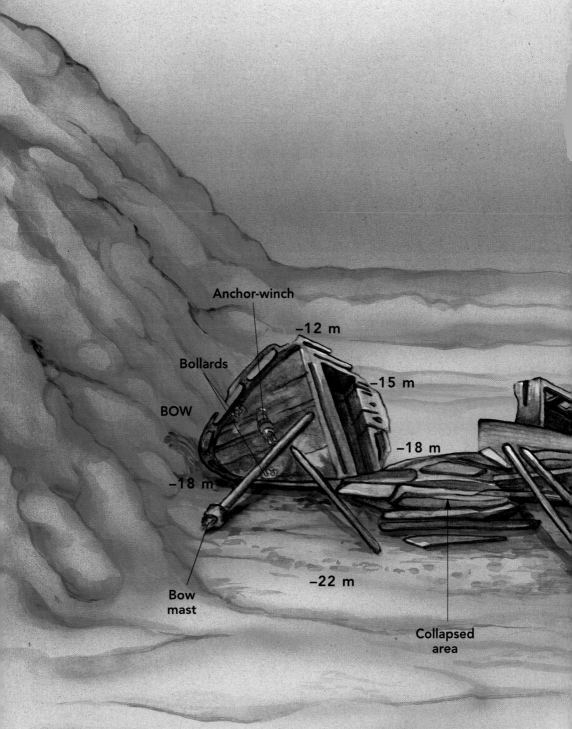

Anchor-winch

–12 m

Bollards

–15 m

BOW

–18 m

–18 m

–22 m

Bow mast

Collapsed area

Carnatic
(310 m)

BSA motorcycles

Sidecar

Bedford truck

Lee Enfield MK III rifles

HOLD no. 2

Tires

Tilling Stevens truck

Boots

Bren Carrier MK II tank

Empty trailers

Airplane wings

HOLD no. 3

HOLD no. 4

STERN

−30 m

Propeller

Anti-aircraft gun

nier 8 F locomotive

Bombs

Anti-aircraft machine gun

The stern

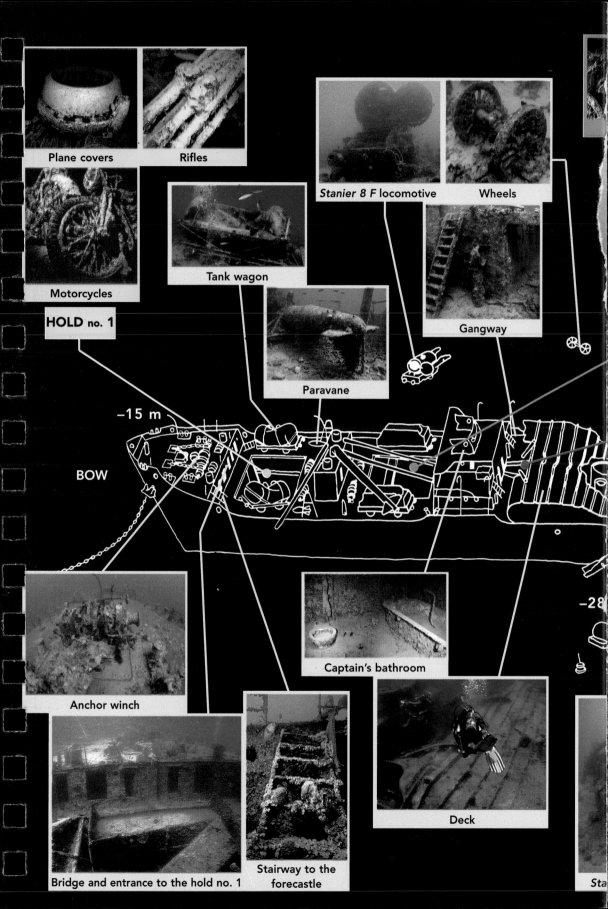

Plane covers

Rifles

Stanier 8 F locomotive

Wheels

Motorcycles

Tank wagon

Gangway

HOLD no. 1

Paravane

−15 m

BOW

Captain's bathroom

−28

Anchor winch

Deck

Bridge and entrance to the hold no. 1

Stairway to the forecastle

Sta

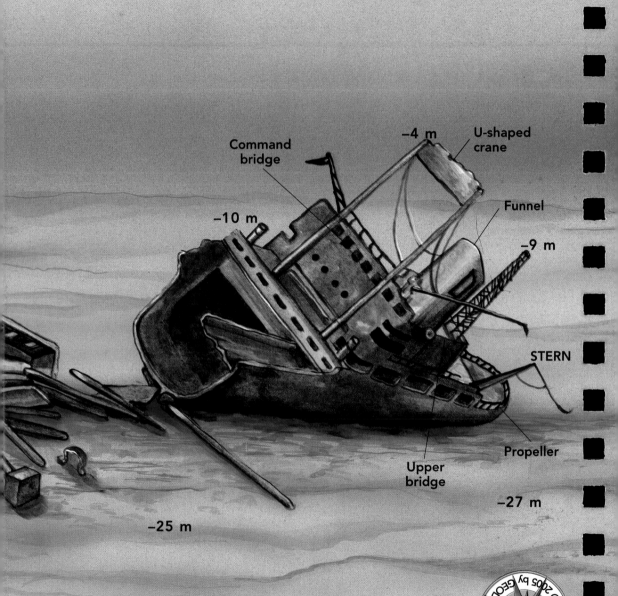

Command bridge

U-shaped crane

−4 m

Funnel

−10 m

−9 m

STERN

Upper bridge

Propeller

−27 m

−25 m

© 2005 by GEODO

Copyright

39 MARCUS

(WRECK OF THE TILES)

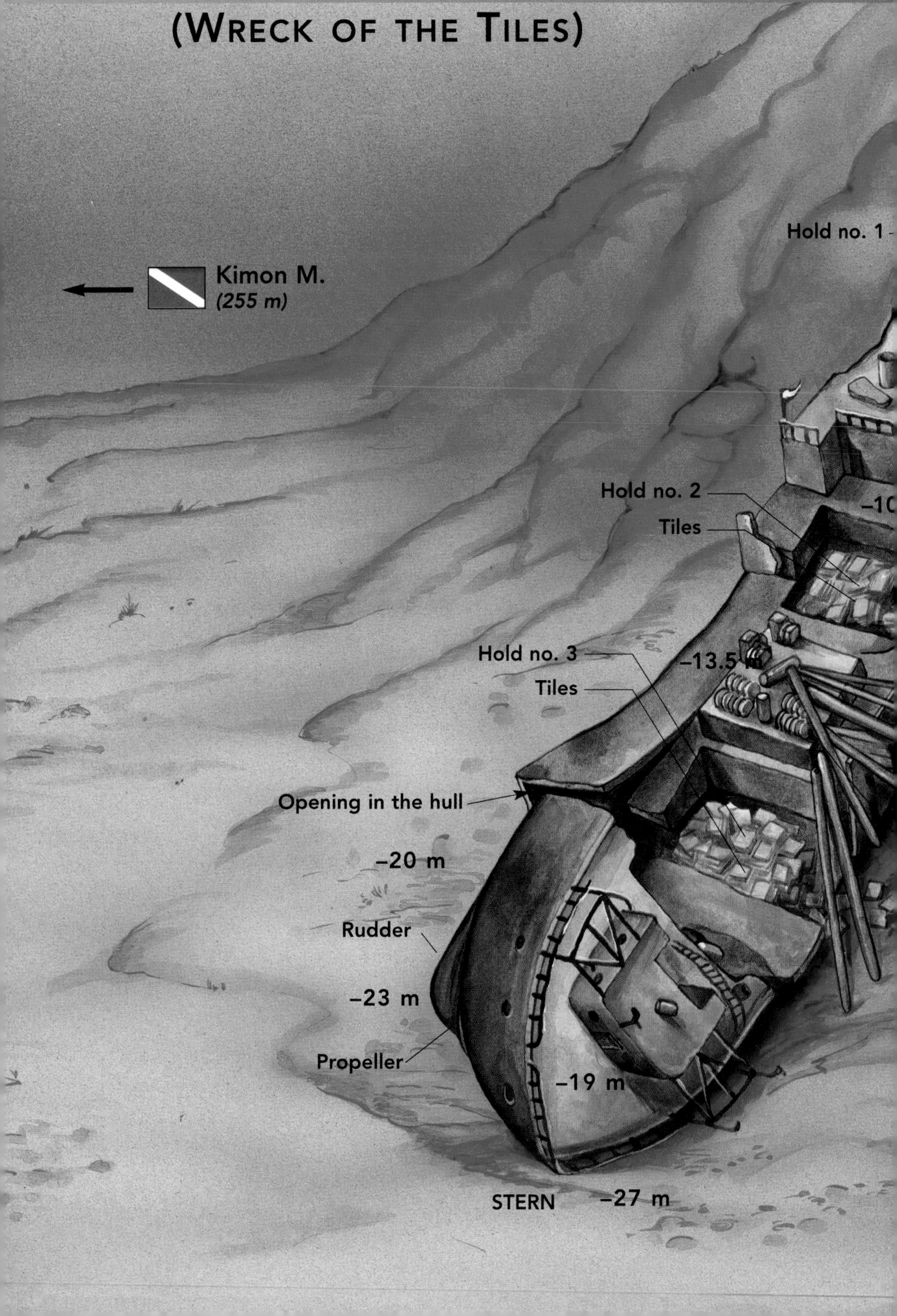
27°34.79
Hold no. 1
Kimon M.
(255 m)
Hold no. 2
Tiles
–10
Hold no. 3
–13.5 m
Tiles
Opening in the hull
–20 m
Rudder
–23 m
Propeller
–19 m
STERN
–27 m

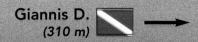
Giannis D.
(310 m)

Engine room

STERN

−27 m

Propeller

−24 m

−27 m

N

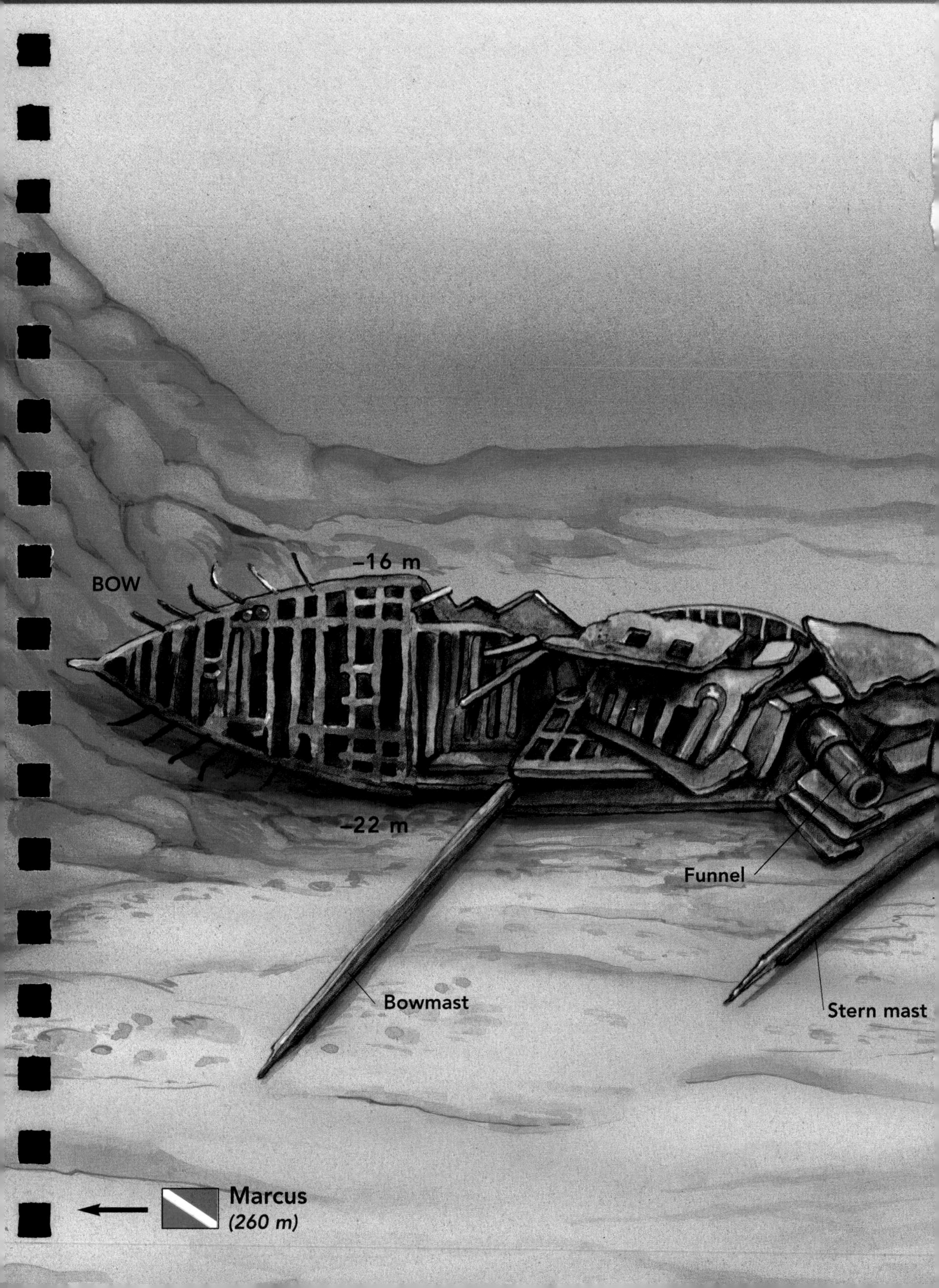

BOW

−16 m

−22 m

Bowmast

Funnel

Stern mast

Marcus
(260 m)

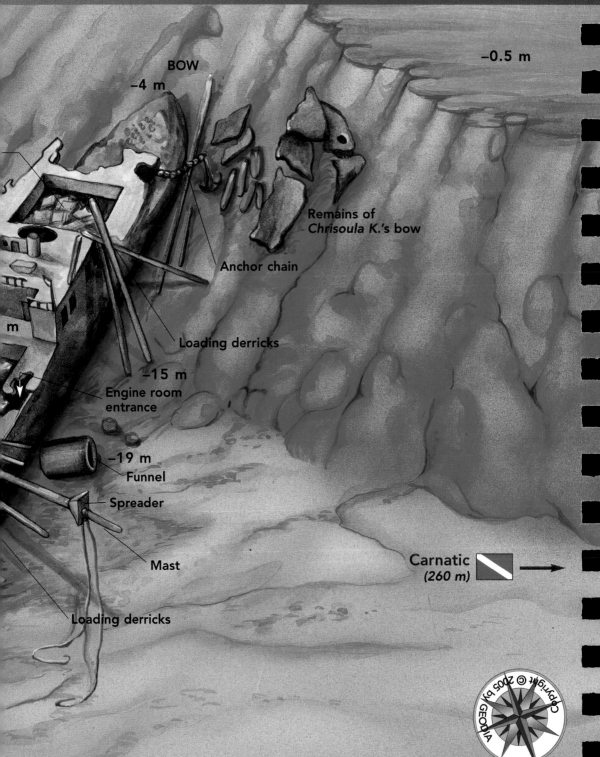

−0.5 m

BOW
−4 m

Remains of
Chrisoula K.'s bow

Anchor chain

Loading derricks

m

−15 m
Engine room
entrance

−19 m
Funnel

Spreader

Mast

Carnatic
(260 m)

Loading derricks

Copyright © 2005 by GEODIA

N

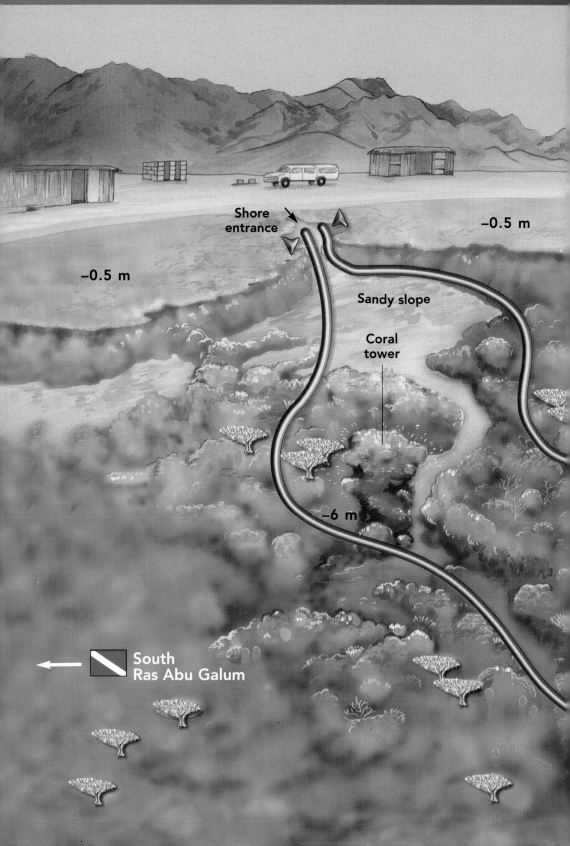

Shore entrance

−0.5 m

−0.5 m

Sandy slope

Coral tower

−6 m

South
Ras Abu Galum

(WRECK OF THE LENTILS)

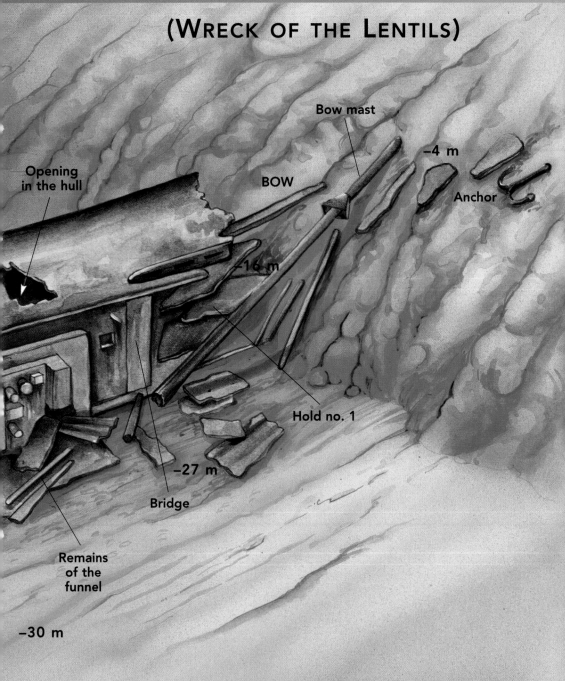

Bow mast

−4 m

BOW

Anchor

Opening
in the hull

−16 m

Hold no. 1

−27 m

Bridge

Remains
of the
funnel

−30 m

Marcus
(255 m)

Hold no. 2

Propeller

−27 m

Rudder

Winch

Winch

STERN

Mast

−32 m

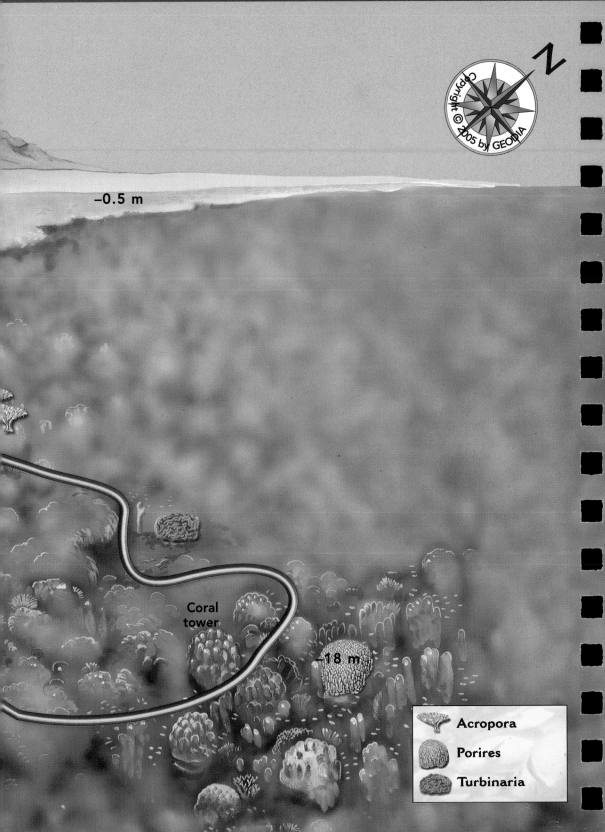

−0.5 m

Coral
tower

−18 m

Acropora

Porires

Turbinaria

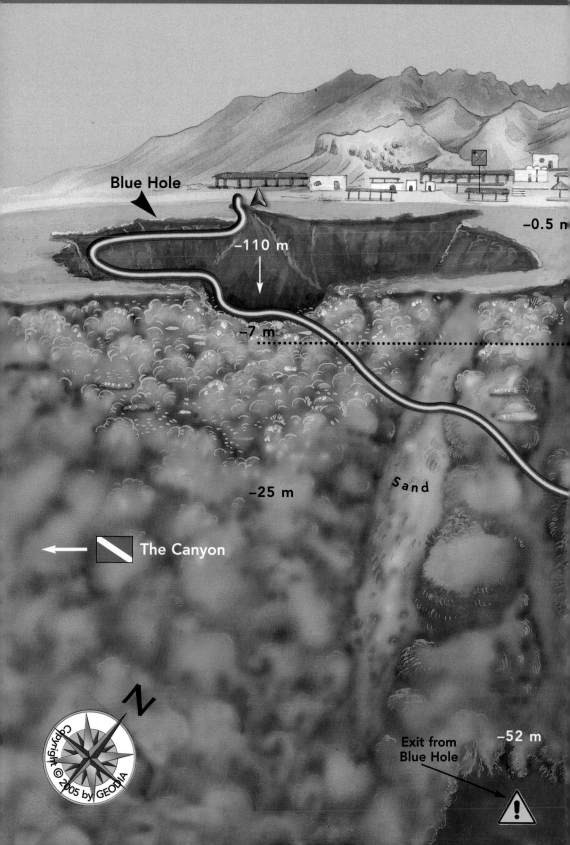

Blue Hole

−0.5 m

−110 m

−7 m

−25 m

Sand

The Canyon

Exit from
Blue Hole

−52 m

Copyright © 2005 by GEODIA

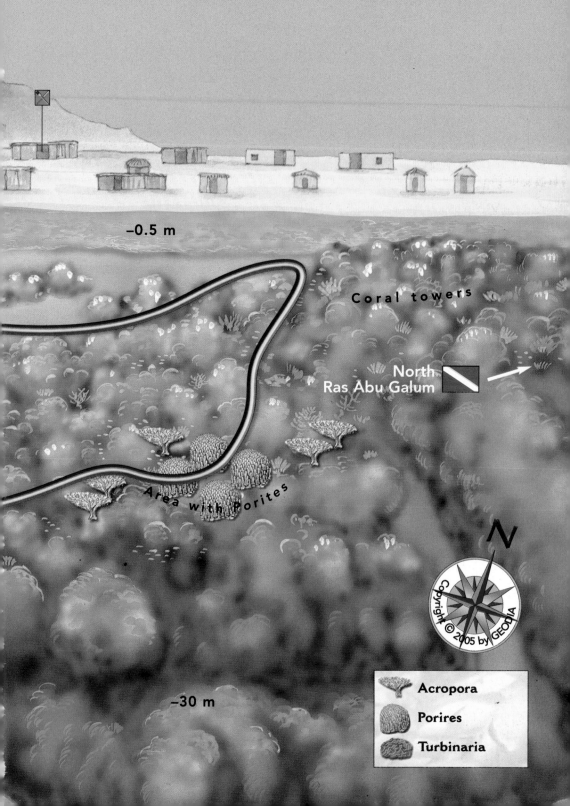

−0.5 m

Coral towers

North
Ras Abu Galum

Area with Porites

−30 m

N

Copyright © 2005 by GEODIA

Acropora

Porires

Turbinaria

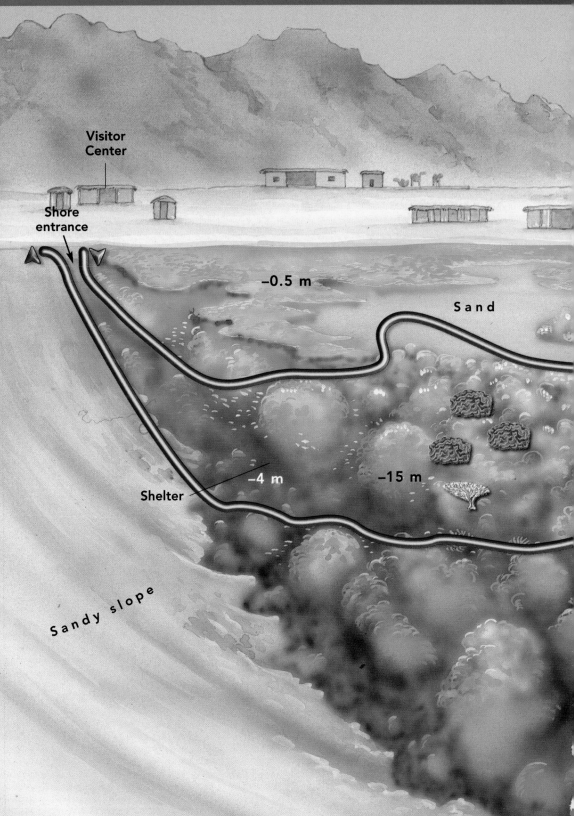

Visitor Center

Shore entrance

−0.5 m

Sand

Shelter

−4 m

−15 m

Sandy slope

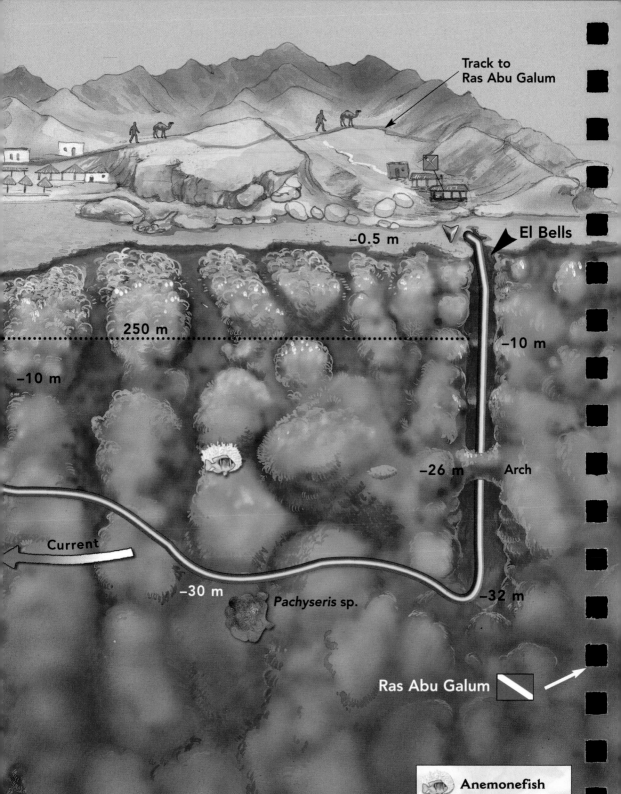

Track to
Ras Abu Galum

−0.5 m

El Bells

250 m

−10 m

−10 m

−26 m   Arch

Current

−30 m   *Pachyseris sp.*

−32 m

Ras Abu Galum

Anemonefish

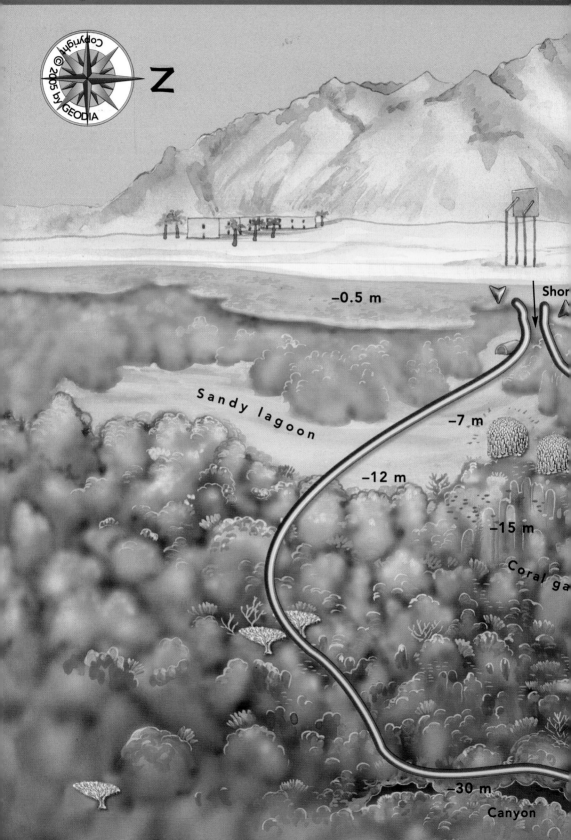

Z

Copyright © 2005 by GEODIA

−0.5 m

Shor

Sandy lagoon

−7 m

−12 m

−15 m

Coral ga

−30 m

Canyon

Blue Hole ➡

−0.5 m

Coral garden

Exit ↑   −14 m

,5 m

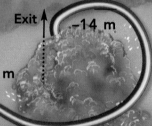

Garden eels

Hard coral
block

−20 m

Blue Hole – El Bells ➡

Entrance
↓

Current ⬅

N

Copyright © 2005 by GEODIA

Drop-off

 Acropora

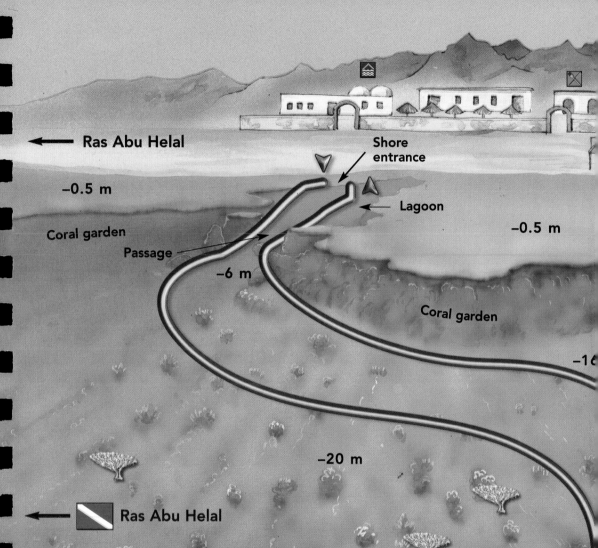

← Ras Abu Helal

−0.5 m

Coral garden

Passage

−6 m

Shore
entrance

Lagoon

−0.5 m

Coral garden

−16

−20 m

← Ras Abu Helal

−22 m

−54 m

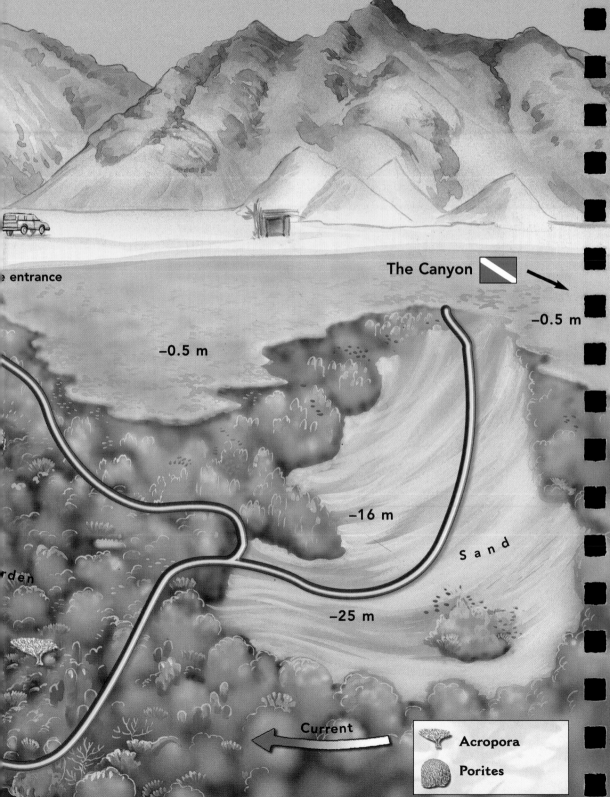

32.535' N — 34°30.977' E

e entrance

The Canyon

−0.5 m

−0.5 m

−16 m

Sand

−25 m

rden

Current

Acropora

Porites

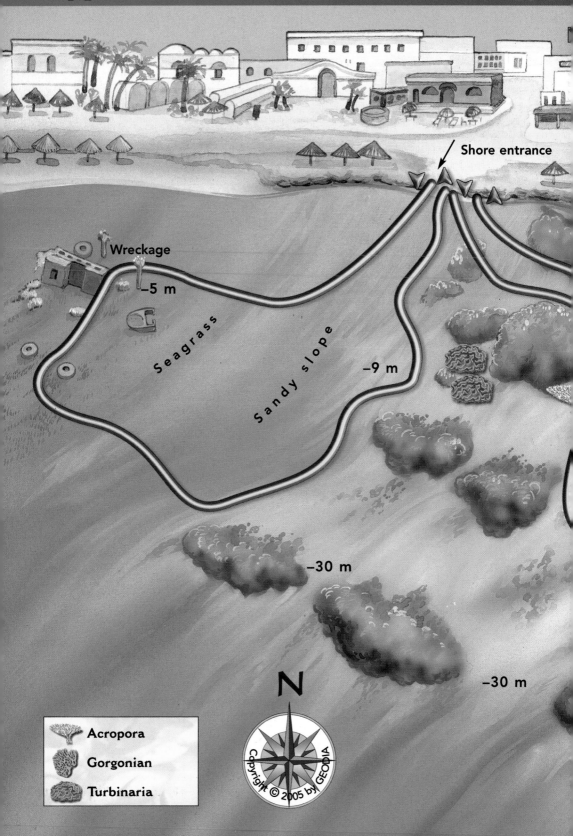

Shore entrance

Wreckage

−5 m

Seagrass

Sandy slope

−9 m

−30 m

−30 m

N

Acropora

Gorgonian

Turbinaria

Copyright © 2005 by GEODIA

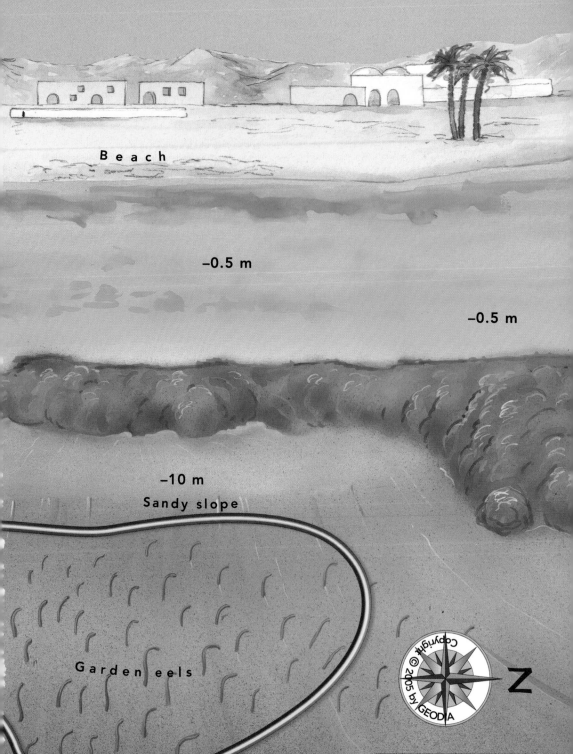

Beach

−0.5 m

−0.5 m

−10 m
Sandy slope

Garden eels

Porites

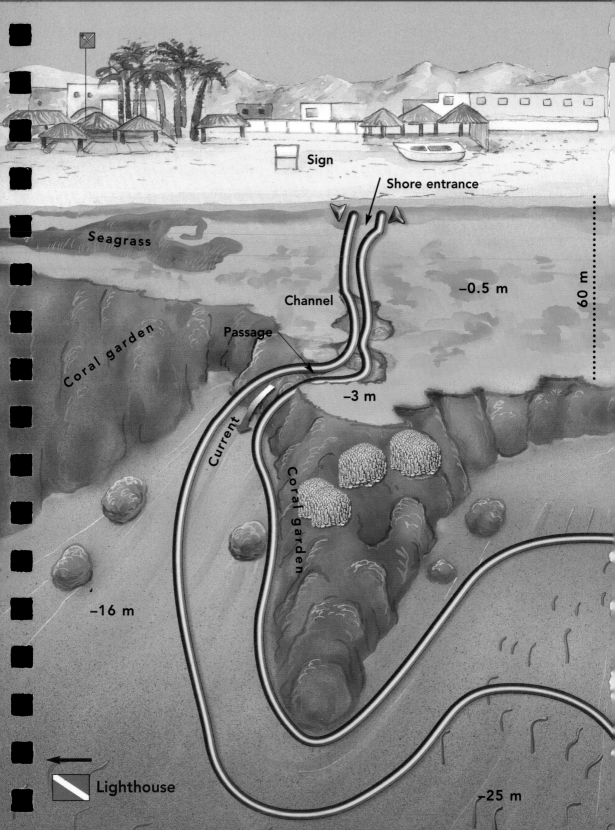

Sign

Shore entrance

Seagrass

Channel

Passage

−0.5 m

60 m

Coral garden

Current

−3 m

Coral garden

−16 m

Lighthouse

−25 m

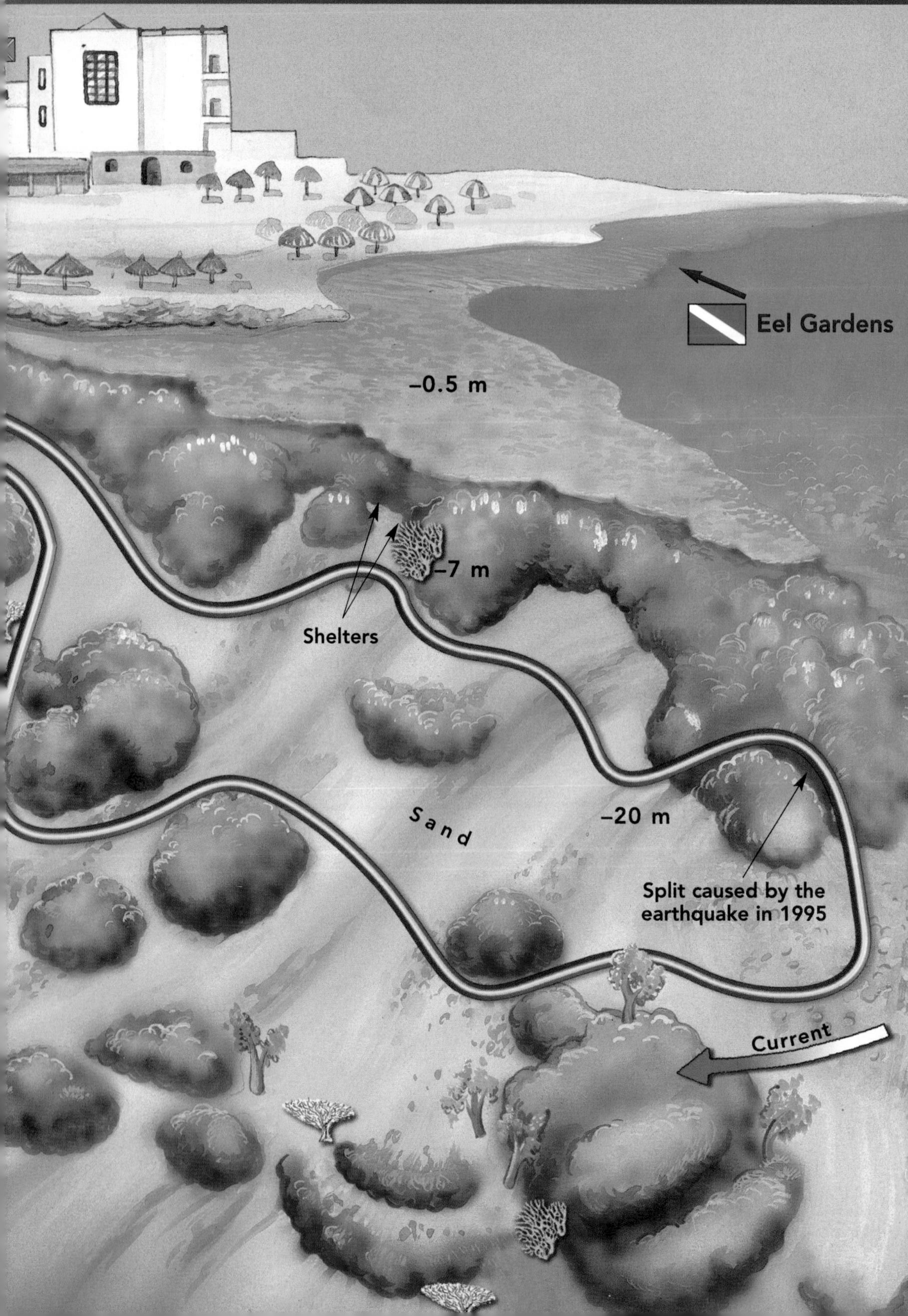

Eel Gardens

−0.5 m

−7 m

Shelters

Sand

−20 m

Split caused by the
earthquake in 1995

Current

DAHAB CITY

El-Qura Bay

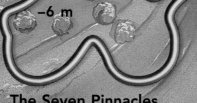

−6 m

−5 m

The Seven Pinnacles

−15 m

Sand

−30 m

Drop-off

Napoleon Reef

−15 m

−30 m

Acropora

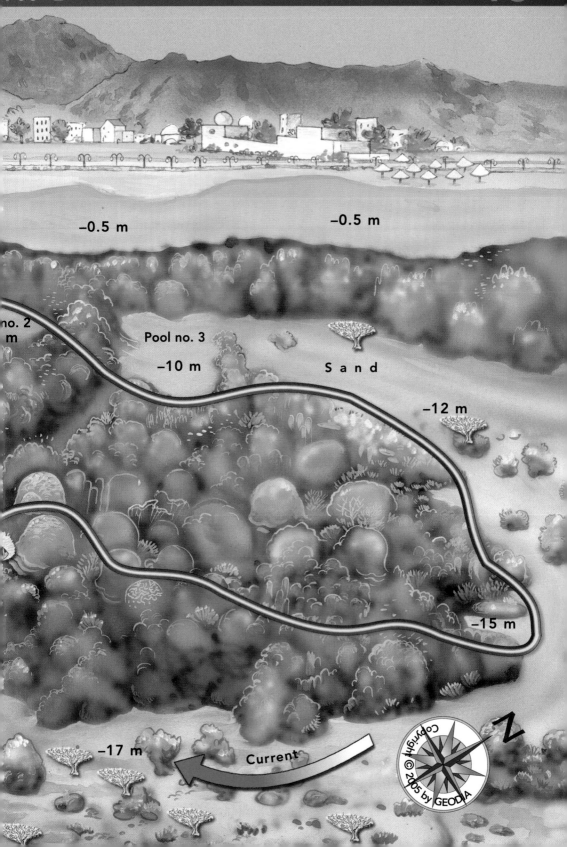

no. 2
m

Pool no. 3

−10 m

S a n d

−0.5 m

−0.5 m

−12 m

−15 m

−17 m

Current

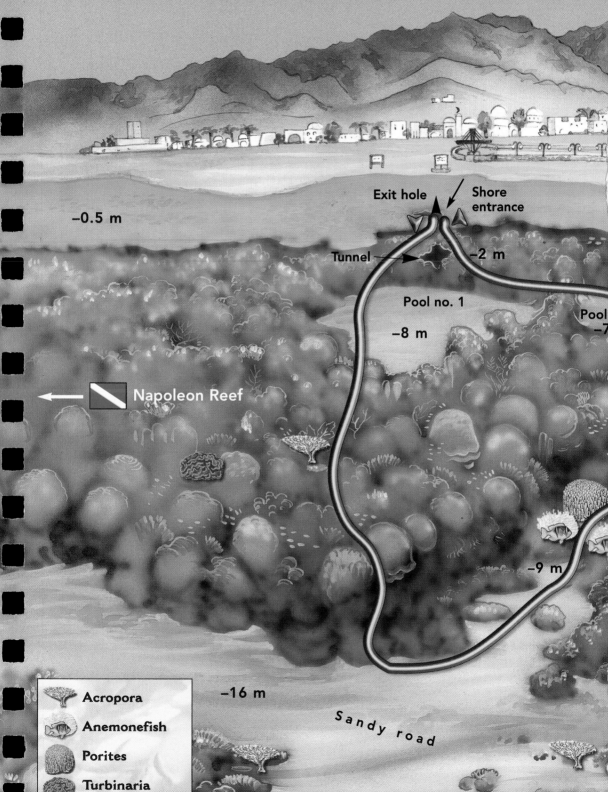

28°28.668' N — 34°30

−0.5 m

Exit hole

Shore entrance

Tunnel

−2 m

Pool no. 1

−8 m

Pool
−7

Napoleon Reef

−9 m

−16 m

Sandy road

Acropora

Anemonefish

Porites

Turbinaria

ASSALAH

Hotels

Salty Lake

Laguna

The Islands

Current

−0.5 m

−5 m

−15 m

−15 m

−20 m

Drop-off

−30 m

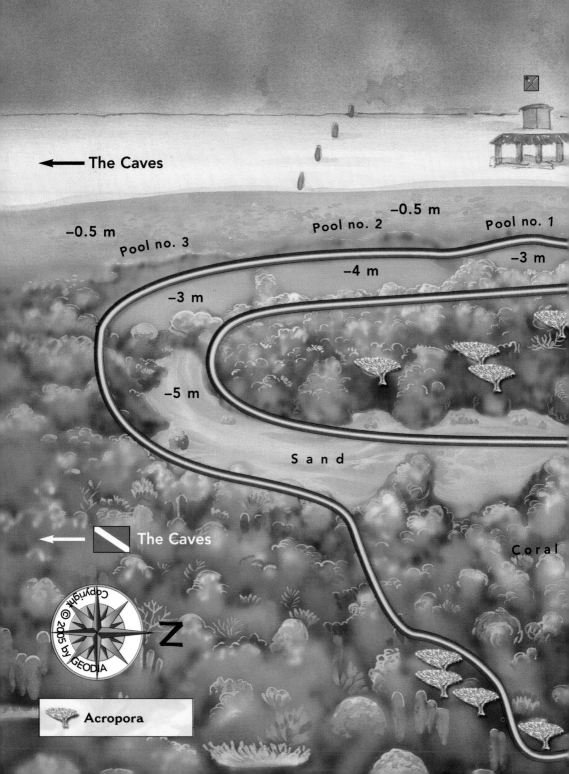

The Caves

−0.5 m
Pool no. 3

−0.5 m
Pool no. 2

−0.5 m
Pool no. 1

−3 m

−4 m

−3 m

−5 m

Sand

The Caves

Coral

N

Acropora

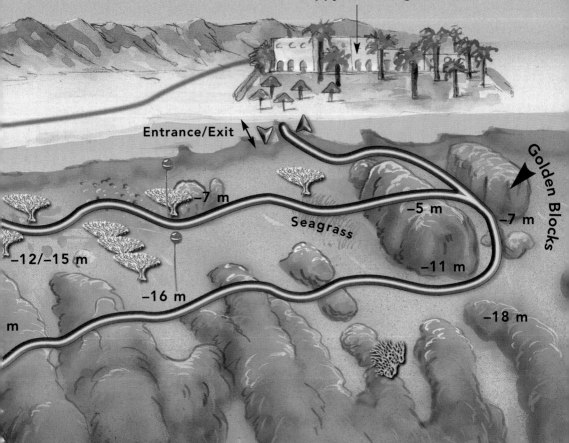

Happy Life Village

Entrance/Exit

Golden Blocks

−7 m

−5 m

Seagrass

−12/−15 m

−16 m

−11 m

−7 m

−18 m

m

m

n

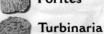

	Acropora
	Anemonefish
	Porites
	Turbinaria

Copyright © 2005 by GEODIA

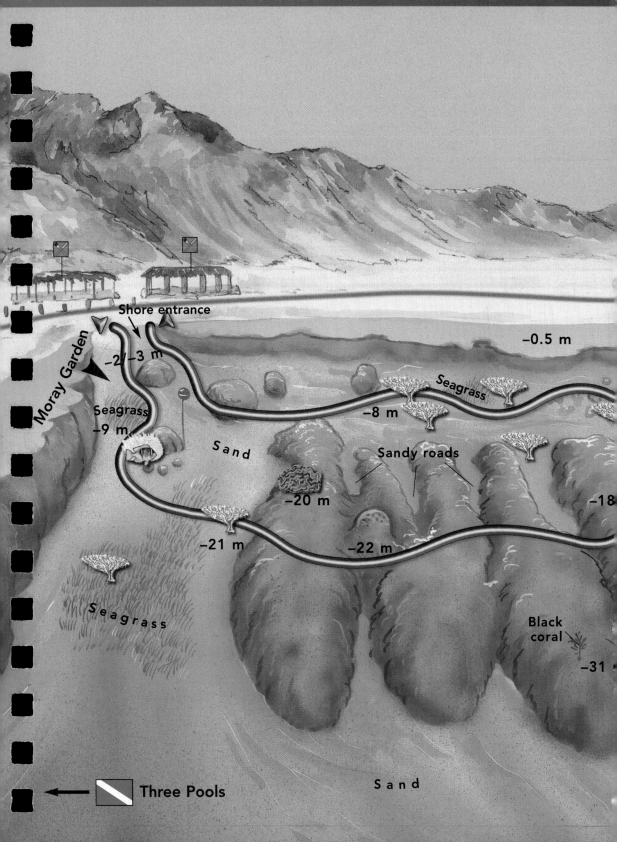

Shore entrance

−0.5 m

Moray Garden

−2 / −3 m

Seagrass

Seagrass
−9 m

Sand

−8 m

Sandy roads

−20 m

−18

−21 m

−22 m

Seagrass

Black
coral

−31

Three Pools

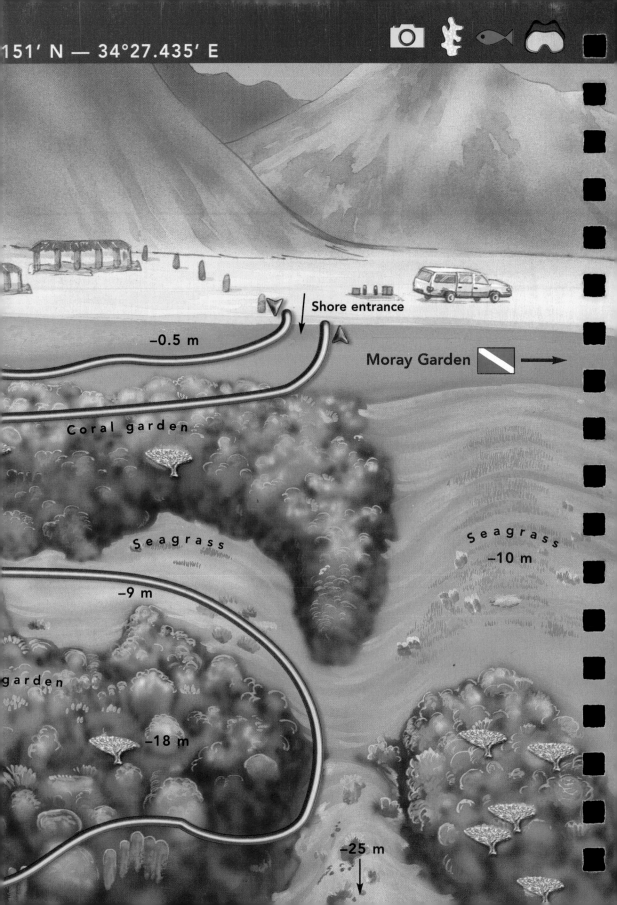

Shore entrance

−0.5 m

Moray Garden

Coral garden

Seagrass

Seagrass
−10 m

−9 m

garden

−18 m

−25 m

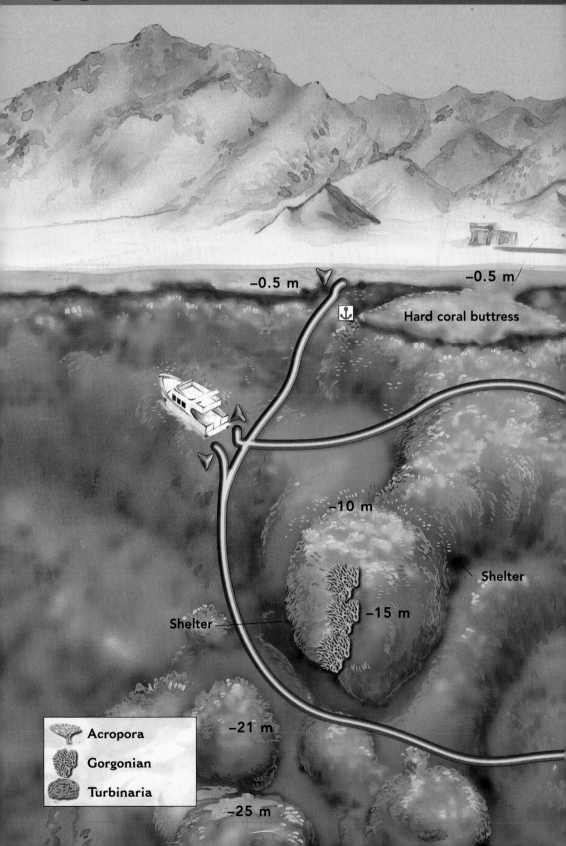

−0.5 m

−0.5 m

Hard coral buttress

−10 m

Shelter

−15 m

Shelter

−21 m

−25 m

Acropora

Gorgonian

Turbinaria

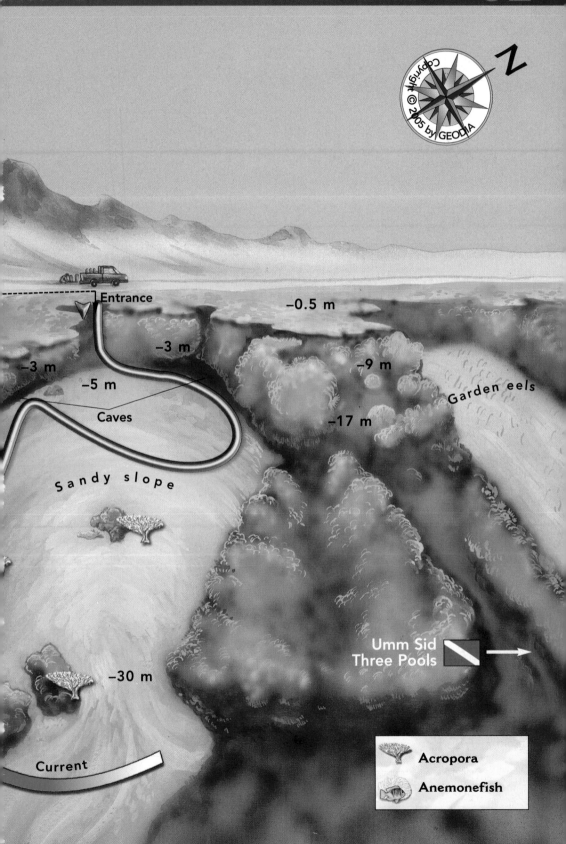

Entrance

−0.5 m

−3 m

−9 m

−3 m

Garden eels

−5 m

−17 m

Caves

Sandy slope

Umm Sid
Three Pools

−30 m

Acropora

Anemonefish

Current

28°25.000' N — 34°2

120 m

Exit

−0.5 m   −0.5 m

−13 m

Elephant
ear sponge

Sand
and gravel

Gabr el-Bint

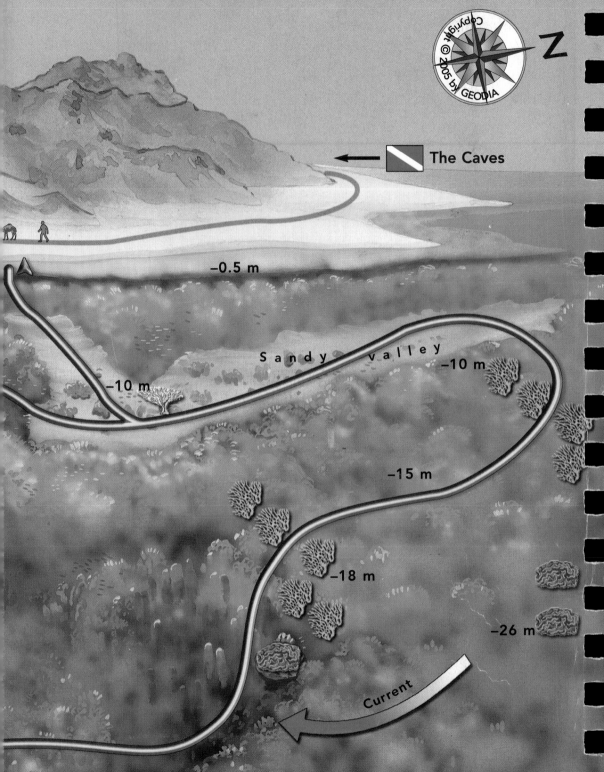

The Caves

Sandy valley

−0.5 m

−10 m

−10 m

−15 m

−18 m

−26 m

Current